P9-AZU-423

What Adolescents Deserve

A Commitment to Students' Literacy Learning

Editors

James A. Rycik
Ashland University
Ashland, Ohio, USA

Judith L. Irvin
Florida State University
Tallahassee, Florida, USA

INTERNATIONAL **Reading Association**

800 Barksdale Road, PO Box 8139
Newark, Delaware 19714-8139, USA
www.reading.org

Director of Publications Joan M. Irwin
Editorial Director, Books and Special Projects Matthew W. Baker
Special Projects Editor Tori Mello Bachman
Permissions Editor Janet S. Parrack
Associate Editor Jeanine K. McGann
Production Editor Shannon Benner
Editorial Assistant Tyanna Collins
Publications Manager Beth Doughty
Production Department Manager Iona Sauscermen
Art Director Boni Nash
Supervisor, Electronic Publishing Anette Schütz-Ruff
Senior Electronic Publishing Specialist Cheryl J. Strum
Electronic Publishing Specialist Lynn Harrison
Proofreader Charlene Nichols

Project Editor Matthew W. Baker

Photo Credits Cover, Image Productions

Library of Congress Cataloging-in-Publication Data
What adolescents deserve: a commitment to students' literacy learning/James A. Rycik, Judith L. Irvin, editors.
  p.   cm.
Includes bibliographical references and index.
  ISBN 0-87207-287-8
  1. Language arts (Secondary)—Social aspects—United States.   2. Literacy programs—United States.   3. Minority youth—Education (Secondary)—United States.   I. Rycik, James A.   II. Irvin, Judith L., 1947–
  LB1631.W375   2001
428'.0071'2—dc21   2001000845

Contents

Introduction

James A. Rycik and Judith L. Irvin

Now is an excellent time to focus renewed attention on adolescent literacy. For years many policy makers and educators have directed most of their energy, resources, research, and debate to the needs of primary-age children. This attention may have come at the expense of older students. Richard Vacca (1998), for instance, decries the "marginalization" of adolescent readers and offers the following observation:

> I am beginning to wonder whether there is a political mindset that literacy is critical only in early childhood. The faulty and misguided assumption, "If young children learn to read early on, they will read to learn throughout their lives," results in more harm than good. (p. 606)

Another reason to focus attention on adolescent literacy is the state of secondary reading as a field of study. For more than two decades, the topic of literacy for middle school and secondary school students has been limited in scope to the reading and writing that is done in school. The focus has been on how the instructional strategies of teachers can promote the thinking strategies of students. Although this has been important work, the time has come for a reexamination of the theories and practices that have been guiding teachers' work with adolescents. The term *adolescent literacy* itself signals a shift in thinking from previous terms such as *content area literacy* or *secondary reading* (Moje, Young, Readence, & Moore, 2000). New theories are raising questions, for instance, about the relation between the literacy activities students do in the classroom and those they do outside of school. At the same time, middle school and high school teachers are experimenting with new ways of helping students organize and direct their own learning. Approaches such as long-term collaborative projects and media productions emphasize creating effective contexts for student learning rather than designing individual lessons.

A final reason for renewed interest in adolescent literacy is a heightened awareness of the pace of change. A new millennium has brought an understanding that today's adolescents live in a world that differs significantly from the one in which their parents grew up. The first television generation is just beginning to consider what life will be like for the first Internet generation. Luke and Elkins (1998) reflect on the significance of these new times and conclude that the real challenge for literacy teachers is "coping with and understanding...how new technologies, workplaces, and institutions might place new demands on, create new opportunities for, and, for that matter exclude or discriminate against [our students]" (p. 4). New times call for reconceptualizing (Alvermann, Hinchman, Moore, Phelps, & Waff, 1998) or reimagining what it means to be literate.

The International Reading Association (IRA) has played a significant role in recognizing new opportunities for supporting the literacy growth of adolescents, especially through the Commission on Adolescent Literacy that was established in 1997. One of the main accomplishments of the Commission was the publication of *Adolescent Literacy: A Position Statement* (Moore, Bean, Birdyshaw, & Rycik, 1999), which was written to remind policy makers, educators, and the general public about the support adolescents need in order to achieve continuing literacy growth. This document is rooted in both a sense of changing times and a sense of renewed commitment to the largely forgotten group that was still living and learning beyond the fourth grade:

> Adolescents entering the adult world in the 21st century will read and write more than at any other time in human history. They will need advanced levels of literacy to perform their jobs, run their households, act as citizens, and conduct their personal lives. They will need literacy to cope with the flood of text they will find everywhere they turn. They will need literacy to feed their imaginations so they can create the world of the future. In a complex and sometimes even dangerous world, their ability to read will be crucial. Continual instruction beyond the early grades is needed. (p. 3)

The authors of the position statement identified seven principles for guiding the growth of adolescents into independent readers. These principles were intended to be broad enough to avoid endorsing any particular programs or strategies, but they also were meant to be specific enough to express a clear alternative to many prevailing practices.

1. **Adolescents deserve access to a wide variety of reading material that they can and want to read.** In contrast to this principle, many adolescents are currently restricted to a diet of textbook reading and assigned novels. The books in middle school and high school libraries are often outdated or too difficult for students to read without assistance.

2. **Adolescents deserve instruction that builds both the skill and desire to read increasingly complex materials.** Smith and Feathers (1983) found that students rarely read their textbook assignments because they knew their teachers would tell them what

was in the material. Unfortunately many classroom teachers have learned no alternatives to "assigning and telling" practices (Vacca & Vacca, 1999, p. 6). As a result, students may find themselves in a cycle of becoming less and less able to read their assignments as they continue to avoid reading (Brozo,1990).

3. **Adolescents deserve assessment that shows them their strengths as well as their needs and that guides their teachers to design instruction that will best help them grow as readers.** High-stakes tests are often designed to identify students and teachers as either "winners" or "losers." These tests are increasingly crowding out the use of performance tasks that are more frequent, more informative, and more closely connected to instructional goals.

4. **Adolescents deserve expert teachers who model and provide explicit instruction in reading comprehension and study strategies across the curriculum.** All students benefit from sustained and continuous instruction in reading, but untrained teachers who have taken only one course in reading are often justifiably uncomfortable with instructing students. Teacher education programs, induction year programs, and staff development often fall far short of preparing middle school and secondary teachers to act as learning "coaches."

5. **Adolescents deserve reading specialists who assist individual students having difficulty learning how to read.** Middle schools and high schools need a variety of professionals to meet the needs of all students. Recent years have seen a sharp increase in the number of students identified with learning disabilities or attention disorders. It is likely that an appropriate reading intervention program is the most pressing need for many of these students. Many schools, however, lack even one qualified reading specialist to work directly with students and to provide leadership and advice for other faculty members.

6. **Adolescents deserve teachers who understand the complexities of individual adolescent readers, respect their differences, and respond to their characteristics.** Legislators, reformers, or even well-intentioned teachers and administrators often seek a program that works for everyone. There is no program, however, that erases all differences among students, even if we wanted to do so. Appropriate instruction always starts with students—their

strengths and needs, and their interests, background knowledge, attitudes, and values. Rather than seeking to eliminate differences through tracking or testing, school policies should help teachers build on what students already know.

7. **Adolescents deserve homes, communities, and a nation that will support their efforts to achieve advanced levels of literacy and provide the support necessary for them to succeed.** Education is a powerful force, but schools alone cannot create adolescents who are fully literate. Literacy begins in the home and extends into the community and beyond. When communities have high expectations and high standards for students, they also need to provide necessary resources, recognition for achievement, and frequent opportunities for students to see the advantages of a literate life in the world beyond school.

Adolescent Literacy: A Position Statement already has proved useful to advocates for adolescents and their literacy growth. Kirk (2000), for instance, identifies perennial problems ranging from too little time for reading instruction to inadequate staff development and suggests that the statement helps make the case for rebuilding and maintaining adolescent literacy programs. She notes, "It not only states a position; it also puts the issues and recommendations in a context that makes them 'real' and confronts myths about adolescent literacy" (p. 574).

On the other hand, a publication as slim as the position statement, with so large an agenda and so wide an audience, is bound to have limitations. Elkins and Luke (1999) strongly endorse the statement but also advocate a much more comprehensive "redefining" of adolescent literacy:

> Literacy education has significant social and cultural outcomes, as well as cognitive and behavioral ones. And adolescent literacy education is the very forum where we shape identities and citizens, cultures and communities. This is not something we can do by default or as an afterthought. It is not something we can do simply by adding a program or specialist here or there. We need to rethink our strategies and approaches in line with a better, stronger understanding of youth cultures and adolescents' everyday lives. (p. 215)

Teachers, administrators, and staff developers have asked for more examples of practices that might renew and revitalize their efforts for middle school and high school students. This need has been addressed by the Commission on Adolescent Literacy through several years of preconvention institutes and symposia at the IRA Annual Convention as well as through a series of professional development forums sponsored by the Association. This volume represents a continuation of those efforts. It stands on its own, but also acts as a companion piece to *Adolescent Literacy: A Position Statement*. Our title echoes the insistence that "Adolescents deserve enhanced opportunities to grow into healthy, strong, and independent readers and writers." (Moore, Bean, Birdyshaw, & Rycik, 1999, p. 9), and reinforces a renewed commitment to making that goal a reality. We have selected articles from a variety of professional journals that will help teachers, administrators, and policy makers to reexamine current practices and to reimagine how they can work together and with parents and community members. We have grouped the articles around four commitments that we believe are critical to turning good intentions into good results for adolescent literacy learners.

Section One, "A Commitment to Literacy Access for All Students," includes articles advocating adequate human and material resources such as reading specialists, well-stocked libraries, and classrooms with a wide range of developmentally appropriate books and useful technology. The articles show how ESL students and struggling readers can be included in the literacy program rather than being labeled or marginalized, and how a literate community can help students find positive identities.

Section Two, "A Commitment to Challenging and Supportive Instruction," describes middle school and high school instruction that is based on sound principles of learning and teaching and shows how these principles meet the developmental needs of adolescents. The articles demonstrate a variety of tools and contexts ranging from traditional textbooks to literature units and technology. These classroom examples are used to illustrate key concepts of reflection, collaboration, coaching, and choice.

Section Three, "A Commitment to Comprehensive and Collaborative Programs," urges the development of literacy programs that broadly define literacy and are unified around a clear understanding of what proficient readers know and do. The articles also show how teachers can work together for their students' benefit, how school principals can lead meaningful collaboration, and how learning can be made more powerful when students use reading and writing activities to connect with their parents and community.

Section Four, "A Commitment to Reimagining Adolescent Literacy Learning," includes articles that challenge us to expand our notion of what it means to be literate for both today's adolescents and tomorrow's adults. They invite us to consider approaches to reading instruction that are still relatively rare, and they point out what we need to know in order to understand and meet the needs of our students.

IRA's Commission on Adolescent Literacy was charged to "reflect on the current state of affairs of adolescent literacy, revitalize professional interest in and commitment to the literacy needs of adolescents, and to make recommendations...concerning future directions for the field of adolescent literacy." These charges neatly summarize the purpose of this volume. The articles contained here were selected for the purpose of reenergizing anyone who works with adolescents or is in a position to advocate for increased attention to their literacy growth.

There *is* life and literacy after the fourth grade. Today's adolescents can have lives that are richer than any previous generation through the wide range of books, media, and digital texts that are readily available to them. They can share their lives with the world through the Internet, and they can use an unprecedented access to information and communication to make their community and their planet a better place for all. This vision of literacy is not a collection of skills that can be learned and tested in a few short years. It is a way of life that bridges home and school and requires a lifetime to learn.

REFERENCES

Alvermann, D.E., Hinchman, K.A., Moore, D.W., Phelps, S.F., & Waff, D.R. (Eds.). (1998). *Reconceptualizing the literacies in adolescents' lives*. Hillsdale, NJ: Erlbaum.

Brozo, W.G. (1990). Hiding out in secondary content classrooms: Coping strategies of unsuccessful readers. *Journal of Reading, 33*, 324–329.

Elkins, J., & Luke, A. (1999). Redefining adolescent literacies. *Journal of Adolescent & Adult Literacy, 43*, 212–215.

Kirk, C.A. (2000). A response to the Adolescent Literacy position statement. *Journal of Adolescent & Adult Literacy, 43*, 573–574.

Luke, A., & Elkins, J. (1998). Reinventing literacy in "New Times." *Journal of Adolescent & Adult Literacy, 42*, 4–7.

Moje, E.B., Young, J.P., Readence, J.E., & Moore, D.W. (2000). Reinventing adolescent literacy for new times: Perennial and millennial issues. *Journal of Adolescent & Adult Literacy, 43*, 400–410.

Moore D.W., Bean, T.W., Birdyshaw, D., & Rycik, J.A. (1999). *Adolescent literacy: A position statement*. Newark, DE: International Reading Association.

Smith, F.R., & Feathers, K.M. (1983). Teacher and student perceptions of content area reading. *Journal of Reading, 1*, 344–354.

Vacca, R.T. (1998). Let's not marginalize adolescent literacy. *Journal of Adolescent & Adult Literacy, 41*, 604–609.

Vacca, R.T., & Vacca, J.L. (1999). *Content area reading: Literacy and learning across the curriculum* (6th ed.). New York: Longman.

A Commitment to Literacy Access for All Students

Each adolescent in our schools should have easy and frequent access to rich and meaningful literacy opportunities. Many students, however, go day after day without reading anything that is appropriate for their interests and abilities. Having few opportunities to work with adults who know how to help, these students may simply withdraw from classroom literacy events. They remain outsiders, standing at the threshold of independent literacy but lacking the confidence or strength to open the door. What are the obstacles that keep some students outside the door? What can educators do to encourage them? To empower them? To welcome them?

Frank Smith's (1988) notion of the "literacy club" is a powerful metaphor for considering access to literacy. According to Smith, individuals who have the opportunity to see others using a wide range of texts with apparent ease and confidence will naturally want to "join the club." Given a warm welcome and appropriate mentorship by more experienced readers and writers, these new members will soon be engaging in activities similar (though not necessarily identical) to those pursued by their companions.

When all goes as it should, new members slip easily into the community and gradually widen and deepen their involvement in club activities. Think, for example, of an adolescent checking out a favorite performer on the World Wide Web. At first, the newcomer may mostly be an observer, reading information about the performer, clicking on pictures and video clips, and "lurking" silently in chat rooms absorbing the topics of discussion and the special abbreviations of more experienced fans (e.g., "LOL" for "laughing out loud"). Before long, however, the person may begin to explore related sites, download video and audio clips, and adopt an Internet identity for joining the constant stream of chat. In a relatively short time, this same fan may have gained enough confidence and knowledge to create a new Web site and invite the club to visit it.

This scenario is quite common, but it is not automatic. It does not happen if the teenager cannot get to a computer or is highly restricted in time online. If no one around is surfing the Web, potential literacy club members may not realize that these electronic fan clubs exist, or they may be unwilling to take the risk of trying to join. Additionally, if the online group is impatient with mistakes, indifferent or hostile to a newcomer's ideas, or exclusive in the kinds of people who can participate (e.g., discouraging younger fans), some "trial members" will drop away. Access requires time and resources. It also requires a community that models possibilities and encourages participation.

Adolescents' access to print literacy follows a similar pattern. To remain members of the literacy club, they need print material close at hand and the time to read it. They also need opportunities to see how others use reading and writing to pursue their needs and interests, not just to comply with school assignments. Adolescents need chances to read material they are ready to read, and they need chances to be awkward in using new text forms. Access is discouraged not only when time and materials are in short supply, but also when the individual feels unable to "measure up" to the club's standards. Members can be discouraged out of the club if the only reading that counts is from a narrow range of grade-level books, especially if no mentors are available to help them use the approved texts.

Finally, in order to remain in the literacy club, adolescents need to see that it welcomes diversity and encourages the development of identity. The literacy club that schools promote for today's adolescents needs to welcome both males and females from a wide variety of linguistic and cultural backgrounds and a wide range of actual and virtual experiences. Most important, access for all requires accepting and *expecting* differences in the literacy abilities of adolescent students. In classrooms where instruction is based on an assumption that all students will read the same material with the same degree of enjoyment and success, someone is certain to end up excluded from the club. Often these students are given labels such as "reading disabled" that explain their differences. Roller (1996) suggests an alternative notion of "variability not disability" that emphasizes what students *can* do and invites them to use those abilities.

When caring teachers have the resources and the knowledge to feel comfortable, they can bridge the gap between their students' needs, interests, and abilities and the assignments given in school. Three of the principles offered in *Adolescent Literacy: A Position Statement* (Moore, Bean, Birdyshaw, & Rycik,1999) relate particularly closely to literacy access: a wide range of reading materials, instruction that supports both the ability and the desire to read complex materials, and the need for skilled reading specialists to assist readers who are struggling. As the articles in this section show, those principles can go a long way toward making sure that no adolescent is left outside the club looking in.

Mary Roe describes how interventions based on involving and engaging struggling readers can help them at the middle school level, and Cynthia Fischer shows how concerned mentors can assist students who struggle at the high school level. In both articles, the combination of appropriate texts and knowledgeable guidance helps students overcome feelings of helplessness and frustration that alienate them from their classmates.

Cultural and linguistic differences also can have the effect of marginalizing or isolating students. Minority students are found in lower tracks much more often than other students, and students who speak English as a second language may find their previous cultural and linguistic knowledge ignored or unvalued. Alfred Tatum exposes how high standards may have the effect of excluding minority students by narrowing the curriculum, particularly when those standards are combined with tracking. Elizabeth Sturtevant outlines ways educators can welcome and support language minority students.

Adolescents' literacy development is certainly affected by gender issues (Brozo & Schmelzer, 1997), and gender roles complicate literacy teaching in middle school and high school classes. Marsha Sprague and Kara Keeling explore the complex relation between gender and reading. They point out ways in which literacy can help girls work through issues of gender and identity, and they highlight how gender-relevant books give girls better access to the literacy program.

REFERENCES

Brozo, W.G., & Schmelzer, R.V. (1997). Wildmen, warriors, and lovers: Reaching boys through archetypal literature. *Journal of Adolescent & Adult Literacy, 41*, 4–11.

Moore, D.W., Bean, T.W., Birdyshaw, D., & Rycik, J.A. (1999). *Adolescent literacy: A position statement.* Newark, DE: International Reading Association.

Roller, C.M. (1996). *Variability not disability: Struggling readers in a workshop classroom.* Newark, DE: International Reading Association.

Smith, F. (1988). *Joining the literacy club: Further essays into education.* Portsmouth, NH: Heinemann.

Combining Enablement and Engagement to Assist Students Who Do Not Read and Write Well

Mary F. Roe

On the first day of a new school year, Dale S. approaches his eighth-grade English teacher and loudly proclaims, "I hate you. I hate all teachers. The only teacher I've ever liked is Mrs. Schmidt." In another school in another region of the United States, a timid seventh-grade boy, Kevin J., sidles up to his seventh-grade reading teacher's desk and confesses to her, "I can't read." Elsewhere, Jill R., an eighth-grade student, reads and writes fairly well, but her involvement with drugs derails her possibilities for academic success. These students exhibit the range and complexity of the problems middle level colleagues across the nation face: meeting the demands of students like Dale, Kevin, and Jill who do not read and write well enough.

Some factors that complicate these and other middle level students' literacy development stem from community and home circumstances— deeper pockets of poverty, too much unsupervised time at home, increased exposures to physical and psychological violence, or the temptations of alcohol and drugs. These are not necessarily new problems, but their severity and pervasiveness are (Carnegie Council on Adolescent Development, 1995). Other challenges stem from a wide array of personalities exhibited by adolescents—a desire to please, to "fit in," to be an adult (Brown, 1990). Still other challenges stem from the wider range of students' physical and mental health needs that regular classroom teachers encounter. Overriding this cacophony of personal, home, and community challenges is the sobering fact, especially among adolescent populations, that the prestige of reading and writing has diminished radically. Other options, such as Nintendo, organized athletics, and "hanging out," tug on adolescents' time and willingness to invest themselves in reading and writing. The endless combinations of these realities portend Herculean challenges for a language arts teacher.

From the *Middle School Journal*, *28*(2), 35–41, January 1997. Reprinted with permission of the National Middle School Association.

In this article, I acknowledge the multiplicity of circumstances that individually and collectively impinge upon adolescents' literacy development and their potential impact on a teacher's efforts. However, the nature and quality of teachers' efforts can hasten or delay a students' literacy growth. Therefore, while the challenge is great, redesigning middle level literacy classrooms to expressly equip *all* adolescents for their future literacy needs is a high, but not utopian, aspiration. So, I focus directly on the classroom environment and a charge shared by middle level educators—creating helpful literacy environments for their students.

This focus on the classroom will embrace rather than discount the mitigating influences on students' literacy development. In fact, I take a strong position on the ecological attributes of literacy and its instruction (Roe & Kleinsasser, 1993)—outside events are linked with in-classroom occurrences. However, in this instance, I follow the lead of Taylor, Harris, Pearson, and Garcia (1995) who encourage teachers to avoid the labeling that is often used in attempts to explain failed efforts. Instead, I seek to strengthen the efforts of teachers who work unwaveringly to augment their students' literacy successes in light of (or in spite of) their students' circumstances.

To continue the dialogue about this important matter, I focus on two critical areas: (a) enabling students to read and write better, and (b) engaging them in literacy events. Combined, these two areas overlay our understandings of adolescents with recommendations from literacy theory, middle level educational theory, and research on instruction for students who have fallen behind in their literacy development. Some ideas contained in their explanation simply underscore the obvious, while others challenge the typical. Collectively, they represent my interpretive perspective on helping middle level students exhibit the reading and writing proficiencies we and the nation expect.

Why Emphasize Engagement and Enablement?

Some students read and write proficiently but fail to thrive in their language arts classrooms. Many students have the desire to read and write, and may even choose to do so, but the novice level of their literacy achievements impedes their desires. Still others are caught in a vicious cycle of "can't, don't, and won't." Those who teach the middle grades have daily encounters with these categories of students.

Confronting these students requires a consideration of skill and will (Paris, Lipson, & Wixson, 1983) in differing combinations and with different doses of each. This mixing of affect and cognition, engagement and enablement, for all students stands in stark contrast to the often-heard cries to return to the basics and work on skills (often defined as phonics for those who do not read well and grammar for those whose writing suffers) or simply to condemn those who can but will not. Considering enablement and engagement individually and in concert, however, optimizes real reading and writing growth. (See Spaulding, 1992, for a fuller discussion of these tensions.)

Point One: Engagement

Growth in reading and writing abilities demands a willingness to read and write. When thinking about student progress in reading and writing, I am often reminded of prominent sports figures who describe the hours they spend practicing. While preparing for tournament play, former Detroit Piston Isiah Thomas spent numerous evening hours shooting baskets from the three-point range, a shot that was not part of his arsenal. However, his commitment to developing this ability by practicing contributed to his personal and his team's success. Likewise, extending one's literacy necessitates this commitment to practice. Students must want to read and write so that they practice enough to become experts. They must engage in literacy. They must possess "will."

What can a teacher do? Several ideas come to mind. First, adolescents like control. We can offer this control as we allow them to select books to read and to select topics for their writing. They might need support in making these choices—a book related to their interest, another title by an author they enjoy, legitimization of a writing style (e.g., recognizing the poetry in rap or selecting dialect over standard English for the stories they write). In the end, however, their right to choose contributes to their engagement in literacy. Many models exist for inserting these choices into our middle level classrooms (e.g., Atwell, 1987; Krogness, 1995; Rief, 1992).

Second, by our own engagement in reading and writing, we can set a good example for students. Graves (1983) maintains that teachers of writing must be writers. The same is true for teachers of reading.

Third, the tasks we expect our unwilling students to complete must be authentic (real reading and writing) and possible. For example, a student participating in a Literature Circle (Peterson & Eeds, 1990) has opportunities to talk with others about a book. Real readers often do this. However, if the book is too difficult, the student can easily become discouraged, disengaged, surly, or disruptive. No book is so important that every middle school student must read it; and I might add, no topic is so important that every student must write about it. Instead, and this particularly true for those who need to read better, they need to exhibit the reading habit. A good activity can be undermined by the assignment of inappropriate materials.

If literacy materials matter, then their selection and use contribute to engagement. Several conditions increase this probability: (a) the availability of a wide array of materials, (b) the authenticity of related tasks, and (c) the expanded acknowledgment of students' need for status.

A diverse blend of materials increases the possibility of matching a reader with something to read. While I have changed many beliefs over the years, one remains intact: Students need to read texts that fit their instuctional reading level and their interest. While extreme interest in a text can sometimes make a difficult book readable, overall, students become frustrated when a text is too hard. Preteaching vocabulary and addressing prior knowledge can be important instructional interventions (Dole, Valencia, Greer, & Wadrop, 1991), but these and other prereading or during reading activities apply to a student reading an "instructional" text, not one that is simply too hard. In addition, teachers cannot always intervene with support when students read independently in self-selected materials.

This stance has important implications. Initially, a teacher must ascertain what a student can read independently and read with help. Then, the teacher must support the student's selection of a text or, if a common reading of a text seems advisable and appropriate, choose a text that will engage all students.

These teacher decisions require understanding the student and the text. Day-to-day observations provide important information about what and how students read and write. These observations become even more poignant when combined with information stemming from the administration of an informal reading inventory. Used for analyzing a text, readability formulas tell an incomplete story, but provide a starting point. Then, sources that offer book titles sorted by grade level (like those suggested by Taylor et al., 1995) can alert teachers to possible choices for their students.

This expectation to match a student with an appropriate text raises a question that many literacy teachers ponder: When is the assignment of a text to an entire class a good practice? The following scenario offers one example. Let us say that the least sophisticated reader in a class can (with instructional support) comprehend a fourth-grade text. Let us also say that the interdisciplinary team is exploring the concept of justice. *The Whipping Boy* (Fleischman, 1986), with its fourth-grade reading level and thematically relevant content, becomes a candidate for a class assignment in this instance. Of course, the teacher must maintain other opportunities for students to choose texts and have a solid explanation of why this book was selected for this class.

Middle level students also need variety, so what else might a teacher do? A colleague and I often discuss this question (Vukelich & Roe, 1995). Our prevailing concern that classroom literacy activities match what real readers do guides our response. Too often students with reading and writing needs engage in school activities that have little resemblance to what readers and writers actually do in real life. For example, when was the last time you could not wait to finish a book so you could answer a series of questions provided by a publisher or a computer program? How often have you been inspired to make a diorama? Instead, you may have talked with a friend about the book, reread favorite passage, had extended but private thoughts about the links between the book and your own life, or simply read another book by that author. What real readers do provides examples of active and enlivening engagements with a book. Too many middle level novices are asked to complete activities that strip the life from a book, sterilize literacy, and make reading and writing mere tasks to complete. I recently observed a classroom event that offered a brutal reminder of this possibility. Seventh-grade students, all classified as "disabled" were answering questions about *Missing May* (Rylant, 1992) posed orally by their teacher. They answered the questions correctly, but the intensity of the emotions Rylant's novel triggered in me and others who have read this book was absent. These students were not functioning as readers, but as workers. The "work" was to answer the question. As a student wrote to author Jerry Spinelli, "I like your book. It would have been better if I didn't have to do a worksheet on it" (Spinelli, 1996, p. 9). These "worksheets" can be written, oral, or on a computer screen. Changing these rote practices to engage our more novice readers and writers in real literacy activity is likely to snag their attention and positively influence their engagement in reading and writing.

Conversations about books is one example of a real literacy activity. In fact, the appropriate inclusion of "grand conversations" have the additional advantage of including peer interaction (Eeds, 1989). Therefore, guaranteeing that students receive this much-needed opportunity to interact with their peers can help match an appropriate literacy task to one characteristic of this age group. Ultimately, Literature Circles contribute to adolescents' attitude and subsequent willingness to engage in literacy events.

Finally, adolescents do not read and write in a vacuum. They are surrounded by their peers and others who may or may not support their engagement with literacy events. Consequently, merely carrying a book or a writing journal becomes an issue of acceptability and status. As

Orenstein (1994) discovered, female middle level students may disconnect from academic events to avoid stigmatization by their peers. Boys, perhaps, have an even more intensified focus on "posturing." Acknowledging these possibilities forces teachers to combine their concerns about literacy involvement with the students' concerns about image. Stated differently, teachers who listen to *all* the messages about literacy their students send rather than the ones more closely linked to teachers' literacy agendas increase the likelihood of affecting students' literacy engagement.

In summary, engaging students in literacy events requires shifts in the control teachers give to students, the models teachers provide, the tasks they assign and schedule, and the literacy materials they use. These shifts are simple to state but dramatically effortful to do. However, witnessing the impact these shifts portend for students' literacy engagement rewards the struggle.

Point Two: Enablement

Readers and writers need to be strategic (Paris et al., 1983). Accomplished readers and writers have a wide array of strategies available to them that they can tap as needed. Timely and explicit instruction can bridge gaps for readers and writers who encounter stumbling blocks and lack these strategies.

What are some implications of this stance? First, teachers must remain critical of their instructional choices. Distinguishing appropriate from inappropriate instruction is a first start, but the final determination of a topic's worth is its match with what a student needs to comprehend or compose better. So, strategy instruction, the building of skill, does not depend on finding the right program or imposing a predetermined sequence of lessons, but rather requires monitoring students as they read and write so that instructional needs can be detected and accommodated (Irvin, 1990). In fact, recent research (Dole, Brown, & Trathen, 1996) affirms the benefits of strategy instruction over story-specific and basal-directed interventions.

To reiterate, when student need drives instruction, a student's real reading or writing performances, rather than a performance on a standardized test of subskills or the ordering of "skills" in a teacher's manual, should unveil the strategies warranting instruction. In the preferred instance, the lesson links the student's need and the instruction (I find Paris, Cross, and Lipson's [1984] use of declarative, conditional, and procedural statements helpful for meeting this goal.) Practice, so crucial for those in need, is embedded in the subsequent acts of reading and writing—"real" reading and writing—rather than in the distribution of commercially prepared worksheets and tests.

This student focus leads to a consideration of the unique literacy development of individual students. If a student is already proficient in inferring meanings of unknown words or writing good leads, lessons designed to improve them become less important. Similarly, if a student's inability to grasp meaning from text stems from a limited sight vocabulary, even if he or she is the only student having this need, then a systematic series of lessons designed to provide this important information is crucial. So, at times a teacher will provide instructional support to the whole class, as students who read and write like novices or experts display comparable needs. At other times, small groups will be formed. These groups may be composed of students who need more assistance to grasp the focus of a large group lesson or those who have needs different from the remainder of experiences of their classmates. The experiences of Kevin J., Dale S., and Jill R. provide examples of how students can become enabled and engaged.

In each instance, their teachers allowed them to choose texts and writing topics. Dale's interest in sports directed his reading and writing. Jill was drawn to adolescent novels about young people with an array of problems. Kevin, the lowest achieving reader, selected from books provided by another teacher in the school—real books rather than those rewritten to fit a readability formula or labeled "high interest, low readability."

In considering skill and will, Jill needed more will; Kevin needed the most skill; Dale's deep-seeded emotional problems complicated his receptivity to the instruction he needed. To increase Jill's sense of responsibility to herself and others, her teacher and the school counselor arranged for Jill to become an aide for her seventh-grade English class. Kevin's teacher worked with him individually for 5 to 10 minutes of each period to provide the specific instruction he needed. In addition, he participated in large group lessons and activities. Overall, he remained an integral and connected member to his heterogeneously organized class. (See Roe, 1994, for a full account of Kevin and his teacher's experiences.) Dale remained a member of his regular class, but his severe rebelliousness and violent tendencies reduced the viability of interactions with classmates. Instead, his teacher worked at maintaining a forward progression of personal progress. Mrs. Schmidt, the teacher Dale liked, was unwilling to have Dale as a student for another year but became a valuable resource.

Kevin showed the most dramatic academic progress. He began the year unable to read the simplest of texts. By midyear, he was reading third-grade material. Dale's English class was one of the few in which he accomplished academic tasks. By midyear, he spent only half of his day in academic classes. English was one of them. Jill's literacy progress was never the real concern. Instead, the challenge was maintaining sight of literacy involvement while she struggled with a myriad of personal entanglements. Her troubled sense of self remained, as probably expected, unresolved. However, she attended school regularly; interacted with adolescent literature; and, as Murray (1985) acknowledged, used the books she read, discussed, and wrote about as a way to deal with her problems and to achieve a momentary distance from them.

Unfortunately, these teachers were unable to make connections between their literacy classes and the content classes their students took. This remains a challenge for all middle level educators as they encounter more Jills, Dales, and Kevins in the years to come.

In making the general and day-to-day determinations, decisions, and enactments, these teachers tapped an array of information. Without question, a deep understanding about the processes of reading and writing was paramount. This, then, requires personnel decisions to seek out beginning teachers who focus on middle level literacy in their undergraduate program, experienced teachers who willingly and enthusiastically deepen their understanding of literacy as inservice teachers, and others who use what they learn in advanced degree programs in middle level classrooms. Combining an ongoing commitment to deepening the understanding of literacy with knowledge of young adolescents and middle schools provides a powerful combination for engaging and enabling middle level readers and writers.

Unfortunately, the best of endeavors will not guarantee day-to-day success. As Barbieri (1995) discovered when she switched from an all girls school to a coeducational one, the days will more likely resemble a surfer's experiences—days of good waves to ride and other days when you feel staying home was the best bet. So, too, teachers must be willing to ride the waves and have the staying power to persevere rather than panic.

A circle of critical friends can provide valuable support. For too long teaching has been considered a solitary activity (Lortie, 1975). However, especially for teachers struggling to facilitate students' literacy engagement and enablement, collegial support is crucial. This circle of critical friends offers opportunities to share anecdotes, ponder choices, debrief, receive encouragement, vent, and rejoice. These opportunities replace a sense of isolation, of struggling alone, with a sense of community.

In Closing

Certainly, many of our students come to the middle grades reading and writing well, and for that we remain grateful. However, as the teachers of all students, we cannot afford a curriculum that offers reading and writing opportunities without empowering all students with equal participation in them. All students benefit from experiencing the role of texts (reading and writing them) as refuge from their daily circumstances and as vehicles for their expanded understanding of themselves and their world. All students should be able and willing to do so. As their teachers, we remain vehicles for this enabling and engagement.

Author Note

The author is indebted to Dr. Martha Waggoner, middle level language arts teacher, whose pointed comments on an earlier draft helped focus the ideas of this paper; to Dr. Carol Vukelich, associate professor at the University of Delaware, for her careful attention to its presentation; and Nancy McKay, educational specialist, for affirming that these points matter to practitioners.

REFERENCES

Allen, J. (1995). *It's never too late: Leading adolescents to lifelong literacy.* Portsmouth, NH: Heinemann.

Atwell, N. (1987). *In the middle: Writing, reading and learning with adolescents.* Portsmouth, NH: Heinemann.

Barbieri, M. (1995). *Sounds from the heart.* Portsmouth, NH: Heinemann.

Beane, J.A. (1993). *A middle school curriculum: From rhetoric to reality* (2nd ed.). Columbus, OH: National Middle School Association.

Brown, B.B. (1990). Peer groups and peer cultures. In S.S. Feldman & G.R. Elliott (Eds.), *At the threshold: The developing adolescent* (pp. 171–196). Cambridge, MA: Harvard University Press.

Carnegie Council on Adolescent Development. (1989). *Turning points: Preparing American youth for the 21st century.* New York: Carnegie Corporation.

Carnegie Council on Adolescent Development. (1995). *Great transitions: Preparing adolescents for a new century.* New York: Carnegie Corporation.

Dole, J.A., Brown, K.J., & Trathen, W. (1996). The effects of strategy instruction on the comprehension performance of at-risk students. *Reading Research Quarterly, 31,* 62–88.

Dole, J.A., Valencia, S., Greer, E., & Wardrop, J. (1991). The effects of prereading instruction on the comprehension of narrative and expository text. *Reading Research Quarterly, 26,* 142–159.

Eeds, M. (1989). Grand conversations: An exploration of meaning construction in study groups. *Research in the Teaching of English, 23,* 4–29.

Fleischman, S. (1986). *The whipping boy.* New York: Greenwillow.

George, P.S. (1988). *What's the truth about tracking and ability grouping really?* Gainesville, FL: Teacher Education Resources.

Graves, D.H. (1983). *Writing: Teachers and children at work.* Portsmouth, NH: Heinemann.

Hynds, S. (1990). Talking life and literature. In S. Hynds & D.L. Rubin (Eds.), *Perspectives on talk and learning* (pp. 163–178). Urbana, IL: National Council of Teachers of English.

Irvin, J. (1990). *Reading and the middle school student.* Boston: Allyn & Bacon.

Johnson, D.W., Johnson, R.T., Holubec, E.J., & Roy, P. (1984). *Cooperation in the classroom.* Alexandria, VA: Association for Supervision and Curriculum Development.

Krogness, M.M. (1995). *Just teach me, Mrs. K.* Portsmouth, NH: Heinemann.

Lortie, C.C. (1975). *Schoolteacher.* Chicago: University of Chicago Press.

Murray, D. (1985). *A writer teaches writing.* Portsmouth, NH: Heinemann.

Oakes, J. (1985). *Keeping track: How schools structure inequality.* New Haven, CT: Yale University Press.

Orenstein, P. (1994). *Schoolgirls.* New York: Doubleday.

Page, R.N. (1991). *Lower track classrooms.* New York: Teachers College Press.

Paris, S.G., Cross, D.R., & Lipson, M.Y. (1984). Informed strategies for learning: A program to improve children's reading awareness and comprehensions. *Journal of Educational Psychology, 26,* 1239–1252.

Paris, S.G., Lipson, M.Y., & Wixson, K.K. (1983). Becoming a strategic reader. *Contemporary Educational Psychology, 8,* 293–316.

Peterson, R., & Eeds, M. (1990). *Grand conversations: Literature groups in action.* New York: Scholastic.

Rief, L. (1992). *Seeking diversity.* Portsmouth, NH: Heinemann.

Roem, M.F. (1994). Kevin: A middle level literacy novice. *Tennessee Association of Middle Schools Journal, 21*(1), 17–24.

Roe, M.F., & Kleinsasser, R.C. (1993). Delicate balances: The ecology, culture and communication of reading teachers. *Reading Research and Instruction, 32*(2), 83–94.

Roe, M.F., & Radebaugh, M. (1993). One school's elimination of homogeneous grouping: A qualitative study. *Research in Middle Level Education, 17*(1), 47–62.

Rylant, C. (1992). *Missing May.* New York: Orchard Books.

Seligman, M.E.P. (1975). *Helplessness: On depression, development, and death.* San Francisco: Freeman.

Slavin, R.E. (1985). Cooperative learning: Applying contact theory in desegregated schools. *Journal of Social Issues, 41*(3), 45–62.

Smith, F. (1985). *Reading without nonsense.* New York: Teachers College Press.

Spaulding, C. (1992). The motivation to read and write. In J.W. Irwin & M.A. Doyle (Eds.), *Reading/writing connections: Learning from research* (pp. 177–201). Newark, DE: International Reading Association.

Spinelli, J. (1996). *A course in failure. Writing for children.* Chautauqua, NY: Highlights Foundation Writers Workshop.

Stevens, R., Madden, N., Slavin, R., & Farnish, A. (1987). Cooperative integrated reading and composition: Two field experiments. *Reading Research Quarterly, 22,* 433–454.

Taylor, B., Harris, L.A., Pearson, P.D., & Garcia, G. (1995). *Reading difficulties: Instruction and assessment.* New York: McGraw Hill.

Vukelich, C., & Roe, M.F. (1995). Imitations of life: Authenticity in classroom literacy events. *Contemporary Education, 66*(3), 179–182.

An Effective (and Affordable) Intervention Model for At-Risk High School Readers

Cynthia Fischer

I n an article titled "Catch Them Before They Fall," Torgesen (1998) made the case for early identification of and intervention with young children who have reading problems. This emphasis is logical given that in the United States "38% of our 4th graders are struggling to learn" basic reading skills (Riley, 1999). Nevertheless, many children are not caught early and continue into high school reading at low levels. Increasingly, these students are in danger of completing their education without the skills necessary to function in a technological society or of not completing their education at all. According to Vacca and Alvermann (1998), our complex society requires not just basic literacy, but "an unprecedented level of...literacy" (p. 6).

By the time students who are not reading well reach high school, the implications for those attempting intervention are grave. "The consequences of a slow start in reading become monumental as they accumulate exponentially over time" (Torgesen, 1998, p. 32). These consequences "do not diminish over time and continue to adulthood without appropriate intervention" (Grossen, 1997, p. 6).

There is an urgent need, then, for thoughtful and persistent interventions for those students who reach high school without necessary reading skills. But there are problems. Most high school teachers, including English teachers, are not trained to teach reading. Even those content area teachers who have taken preservice or inservice reading courses generally avoid incorporating literacy practices into their lessons (O'Brien & Stewart, 1992; Vacca & Vacca, 1996). Content area teachers who do try to use literary strategies are most often not able to provide help for a student who is reading on a very low level. Start-up time and running costs of programs for these students can be exorbitant (Office of Educational Research and Improvement, 1991).

Reprinted from the *Journal of Adolescent & Adult Literacy, 43*, 326–335, December 1999/January 2000.

This article describes an affordable program to catch those high school students who must raise their literacy levels if they are to become independent learners, successfully complete a secondary education, and function in today's society. The program is implemented in a public high school (grades 9 through 12) with an enrollment of approximately 975 students. However, the model can work in any setting by simply increasing the number of teachers facilitating it. Although the school has a rural setting in the foothills of the Blue Ridge Mountains in the eastern United States, it is located in a county (population 72,000) surrounding the city that is home to the University of Virginia and thus the area must be described as suburban. Approximately 80% of the graduates go on to higher education; 12.9% of the students are classified as gifted, 10% receive free or reduced-price lunch, and 13.4% require special education. The population is predominately white and English speaking. Not many students in the school have low reading scores, but all those who do are given an opportunity to improve their literacy competencies through this program.

Components of the Model

Three years ago I was asked to develop an intervention model for these students, most of whom are from working-class families. I was to be the only teacher facilitating the program. The budget for the year was US$500. Additional outlays were my salary and the cost of reproducing materials ranging from a newsletter to fliers that advertise the program in the community. (I already had some of the assessment and teaching materials.)

At that time as now, I found in the literature very little about establishing and implementing this type of program on the high school level. Of 18 exemplary reading programs listed in the Office of Educational Research and Improvement's publication *Educational Programs That Work: A Collection of Proven Exemplary Educational Programs and Practices* (1991), only 7 were secondary programs, and only 3 of the 7 specifically addressed the needs of remedial students. Journal articles and books described particular strategies that worked well with these students, but few gave concrete prescriptions for comprehensive programs. After reviewing the literature, I decided that such a program has to incorporate the following components if it is to succeed in raising reading levels and in providing other benefits to at-risk students:

- Students must be at least minimally motivated to improve their reading.
- Students should receive daily reading practice.
- Assignments should be tailor made for each student with an emphasis on direct, explicit instruction.

- Adult volunteers, peer tutors, and the teacher should provide as much one-to-one tutoring as possible.
- There should be opportunities for verbal sharing as well as writing and publishing.
- Students should read to younger children regularly.
- Materials should be at an appropriate level and hold students' interest.

Why These Components?

The research of Brophy (1988) and Leinhardt and Bickel (1987) underscores the interdependence of motivation and success in academic tasks. I require that the students express a desire, however minimal, to improve their literacy skills because I can serve only a limited number and want to benefit these students. Having been an English, reading, and special education teacher for over 20 years, I know that if students are able to meet me one or two steps of the way, their successful experiences can provide the momentum to increase motivation. Often one must acknowledge a problem before being able to solve it. By expressing interest in the course, the students are admitting that they need help with their literacy skills.

Allington (1977) cites an informal study that found that students in a remedial reading course did little reading. Because daily reading is vital, I built into the program consistent opportunities for the students to read to me, to volunteers, to each other, to elementary school children, and to themselves. The importance of daily reading practice was underscored by student responses to an exit evaluation at the end of the first year. One activity many of the students would have liked to do more of was Sustained Silent Reading (SSR).

I chose tailor-made programs and one-to-one tutoring because "instruction that fits the needs of the problem reader improves reading performance and promotes fluent reading with comprehension" (Walker, 1992, p. 1). The diversity of their problems means that these students cannot all be required to progress through the same materials at the same pace. Both tailor-made instruction and one-to-one tutoring are components of successful elementary programs (Clay, 1979/1985) and also work well in adult literacy programs such as that of the Literacy Volunteers of America. Slavin and Madden (1989) wrote that "given a skilled one-to-one tutor...every student without severe dyslexia or retardation...[can] attain an adequate level of basic skills" (p. 4). In addition, case studies of the use of tailor-made programs and one-to-one tutoring with a middle school student (Lee & Neal, 1992/1993) and a high school student (Ballash, 1994) indicated positive results.

Moreover, because high school students with reading problems are at high risk, these two components address this population's needs for direct, explicit instruction and customized reading material particularly well. When the tutors see problems, they or I can break down the processes and teach personalized strategies using concrete, hands-on types of instruction, as well as provide follow-up practice. Tutors can also help find materials related specifically to the interests of the student with whom they are working. They know quickly which content area course is giving the student problems, and they provide specific help in that area. Aside from the relevant, customized content and hands-on instruction available with a tutorial program, the interpersonal aspects also fulfill many emotional needs of at-risk learners, such as the need for individual rapport with a "teacher," personal connection with the school ("Can't be absent tomorrow—my tutor's coming"), a structured but not rigid environment, and immediate feedback and recognition (Hodge, 1991).

Because recognition is important for every student but especially for this population, several components of the program provide it. In addition to writing daily about their readings and being given opportunities to share these ideas verbally, students have a forum for publishing their writings so that they gain recognition from a larger group of people.

Requiring the students to read to elementary children regularly (Maheady, Mallette, Harper, Sacca, & Pomerantz, 1994) addresses their need for increased self-esteem, again provides recognition, and offers practice in fluency.

The last component, access to level- and interest-appropriate materials, is the dream of every literacy teacher. If the materials are interesting, the students usually have the motivation to continue and often also have at least some of the experiential background necessary to aid comprehension. Although students must be taught to understand content area textbooks, starting or enriching with self-selected materials of high interest can only increase the amount of time spent reading. Students in the program are aided in their selection of high-interest materials with an annotated bibliography of some of the books available in the reading classroom and school library. The reading levels of the books listed allow for success. We borrow the books the students read to the younger children.

I spend the major part of the budget for the program on high-interest trade books and magazines. Often books are purchased specifically to meet the interests of a particular student. The tutors sometimes contribute newspapers, books, and magazines they purchase to match the interests of their students, or they donate ones their own children have outgrown. In addition to materials purchased for the program, the students' own textbooks are used, when possible, to implement vocabulary development and teach comprehension and study strategies.

I also make many of the materials. For example, vocabulary (other than the specific vocabulary needed for content area subjects) is developed mainly through the study of Latin and Greek roots, prefixes, and suffixes. I write exercise sheets that explain and give practice in the use of homophones. Students make the pieces for their matching games from index cards. Sometimes I rewrite the information in a content area text so that it is on a student's level.

Recruitment and Assessment of Potential Students

Regular and special education teachers recommend most of the candidates for the program. Low standardized test scores and failure of state minimum competency tests also trigger scrutiny, and guidance counselor, administrator, and parental requests contribute to the pool. Ninth and tenth graders constitute the majority of students; however, the program is open to all. In the spring, recommendations are solicited from eighth-grade teachers regarding incoming students.

After recommendation, I interview each candidate. These interviews, which take approximately 40 minutes each, help me formulate diagnostic hypotheses. A combination of formal and informal measures is used. The reading subtest of the Kaufman Test of Educational Achievement (KTEA), Brief Form, gives a broad picture of decoding, fluency, and comprehension skills. After the formal testing is completed, I return to some of the test's tasks to assess miscues (Cohn & D'Alessandro, 1978) and vocabulary knowledge. In addition, silent reading passages are sometimes included in the session using the think-aloud format and diagnostic questions suggested by Walker (1992). Throughout, I observe the strategies and cues the student uses to extract meaning. I also discuss with the students their concerns about and assessments of their reading performances.

At this point, if a student needs literacy intervention and seems to be a good candidate, I explain the procedural aspects of the program (i.e., the classes meet for one block per day as all other classes do, successful completion earns one credit toward graduation, the course is taken in addition to English, each student has a tailor-made program, students can expect at least 15 minutes of homework each night, a student may have a tutor). Next, I ask a most important question: "Do you think a program like this could help you, and [if so] would you like to be in it?" I accept students only if they express at least a minimal desire to participate.

Students may enter the program at any time during the school year, as space permits. Space depends on the number of tutors and the needs of the students as a group. At present, the program is able to serve up to about 30 students per year.

Tailor-Made Assignments

The model allows the teacher to use any strategies she or he feels will help the student to be successful. It does not dictate one type of lesson plan for all students. However, it does require (a) that instruction be provided through interaction with authentic, meaningful texts and (b) that students be given direct, explicit instruction in the use of skills and strategies. Such instruction may include prediction through Directed Reading-Thinking Activities, Self-Monitoring Approach to Reading and Thinking, Know–Want to Know –Learned Plus, Guided Reading Procedure, Question-Answer Relationships, story mapping, the use of other types of graphic organizers, Survey-Question-Read-Recite-Review, decoding and word attack, structured note-taking, summary and restate practice, and using text structure frames. These skills are, when possible, taught using content and subject area materials because at-risk students need to feel that what they are learning relates immediately to their lives.

With the two ground rules in mind, I formulate an initial program using instructional techniques chosen on the basis of the diagnostic hypothesis for each student as derived from the interview, school records, and consultations with teachers. This initial program is flexible; I expect it to change as the needs of the student change. Assessment of needs and performance is informal, personal, and ongoing.

A look at the information gathered about a student we will call Sally indicates that she was referred by her middle school guidance counselor. She had been dropped from special education services because recent testing found that the discrepancy between her aptitude and achievement scores was no longer great enough for her to be eligible. Her counselor knew she would need extra help with reading if she were to have a chance of success in high school. He added that she had good relationships with peers and adults, was hard-working, and would seek assistance when she needed it.

The interview session revealed that Sally had excellent verbal fluency and the ability to attend to and recall details. She had low decoding skills and no real decoding system that worked. If she did not know a word, she often just looked at the initial letters and guessed. This behavior was noted with words both in and out of context. This lack of decoding skills severely hampered her fluency. Her literal comprehension was not strong, and summarizing seemed to be very difficult. Further, she often did not demand that her reading make sense. Checking school records added the information that she had poor receptive language skills and could benefit from repetition of new concepts and lots of practice with the skills being learned. Her standardized test scores were below average in all areas, and she had had to take the state minimum competency test in reading three times before she passed it.

Sally's initial program, then, included a phonogram approach to decoding, repeated readings for fluency, and reciprocal teaching using content area texts (if possible because of her low reading level). Figure 1 is a sample week's schedule for Sally.

Tutors

Literacy volunteers are recruited from the community through a media campaign I conduct during the opening weeks of school. Newspapers, TV, and radio stations carry free announcements that the school is looking for volunteers. I post fliers in shops. In addition, during those first weeks, the school distributes to parents interest and availability questionnaires covering many types of volunteer activities. Sometimes older students are tutors. Frequently, tutors from previous years volunteer again. Next year I will have as tutors some "graduates" of the program who volunteered to tutor the new students. (What better way to practice and reinforce the skills they have learned?)

I meet with each volunteer in order to explain the program and get to know with what type of student the tutor would work best. I try to elicit and intuit as much information as I can, including the extent of the person's experience with teenagers, amount and type of education, warmth, patience, ability to take rejection, reliability, and availability. I then try to match the students' literacy and personality needs with the tutors' characteristics. After tutor and student are paired, I discuss the student's tailor-made assignments with the tutor, who has been given a manual I developed containing instructions on how to perform every activity used in the lessons. This not only provides explanations of strategies but also contains information about how to be an effective tutor (Herrmann, 1994) in the sections on getting to know the students and interacting with them. I explain the first specific lesson plans I have written, which include rapport-building activities and interest inventories as well as reading materials and suggested strategies, and I give the volunteer practice in using the techniques if necessary.

The lesson plans are on forms that have much space for a dialogue between the volunteer tutor and the teacher. Through this dialogue, the tutor can signal when a strategy is not working, when an activity worked well, or if the student's needs have changed. I can then offer strategies

FIGURE 1
A student's sample schedule

Sally				September	8–12
Monday	Tuesday	Wednesday	Thursday	Friday	
1. Large-group homophones	With tutor	1. Work with Kaneesha	With tutor	Read to elementary children	
2. Large-group SQ3R	1. Decoding clusters, review 18 & 19 new 20 & 21 *Follow Through* book, pp. 20 & 21	Review clusters 4 & 5 new 6 *Follow Through* book, p. 6	1. Decoding clusters, review 20 & 21 new 22 & 23 *Follow Through* book, pp. 22 & 23		
Start to use SQ3R with volcanos article	2. Fluency readings	2. Finish SQ3R with article if not finished	2. Practice reading two or three children's books with expression and make up questions		
	3. Check SQ3R work she did Monday	3. SSR	3. Continue summary and restate practice with earth science text		
	4. Summary and restate practice with earth science text				

that fit these situations. This process sounds terribly time-consuming for the teacher, and in the beginning it is. However, soon the tutors become confident and comfortable enough to write their own lesson plans. The rapport they establish helps them find materials that interest the students, such as magazine and newspaper articles.

A few times each year the tutors get together for program-sponsored pizza socials, where they can meet and share experiences. At the end of the year they are honored with a luncheon and given a framed certificate attesting to their selfless help.

Sometimes the students serve as tutors, which is especially helpful if volunteers are scarce. For example, with some older students who have decoding problems, it is beneficial to use a phonogram approach that introduces phonic principles by using sound clusters within whole words (Glass, 1973). Once students have mastered the method and a specific cluster, they can teach the cluster to another student, thus reinforcing their own learning and boosting their self-esteem. This procedure also frees the teacher to work individually with other students on days when the tutors are not present.

Whole-Group Activities

Because tutors usually volunteer for a period per day, 2 days a week, at times the class must function as a whole, or at least I must work with groups of three or four students at a time. Most of the fun we have in the classes occurs during these times. For example, we play a version of the word game Blurt! in which I substitute their vocabulary words for the words included on the game cards. Or they use flashcards with vocabulary words, homophones, or content area facts to play a matching game; in the process they learn that this technique is a good study method.

Often, some time is spent introducing and practicing various sound clusters. Most of these students have been in the same classes for years and are used to giving one another the correct pronunciation of a word. At the beginning of the year I tell them that I think they are all wonderful for trying to help, but that I would like them to let me help in a special way so that the person will be able to read the word when alone. I tell them that unless they are prepared to marry the person they are helping and always be there when a word is not known, it is better not to help. This leads to much laughter when various pairs of students forget to be quiet. While we are practicing the clusters and reading aloud, I maintain a list, for each student, of personal pronunciation demons. Usually they groan when another word is added to this list. I tell them I could not sleep at night if I thought they would go through life not knowing that word. Recently, I was amazed when Terrell, very seriously, reminded me to put a word on his list because, he said, he knew I would not want him to not know that word for his whole life

These whole-group times offer opportunities for other activities including book shares, opportunities for writing, and explanations of strategies everyone in the class can benefit from, such as Survey-Question-Read-Recite-Review, mnemonic devices, and notetaking. Recently we were doing a Know–Want to Know–Learned Plus (Carr & Ogle, 1986) activity with a lesson in their earth science book about volcanoes. After we had completed the K-W-L part and the graphic organizer, the students proposed that they draw figures on the graphic organizer to help them "see" the list on the organizer better (see Figure 2). Now we use this suggestion every time it is possible with the graphic organizers we are working on.

A lesson the students have enjoyed is one in which they read "The Sniper" by Liam O'Flaherty. We start by discussing how a civil war is different from other wars, filling in a Venn diagram with civil war on one side and other wars on the other. Luckily, most of the students are somewhat familiar with the U.S. Civil War. I thought they would not know what a sniper is but most of them do. After reading the boldfaced introduction in the textbook to them and discussing it, I write the following question on the chalkboard to establish a purpose for their reading: "How does the writer want us to feel about war and what it does to people?" I then give them copies of the story on which, at various points, I have written a *P* and told them to work in pairs. I pair stronger readers with weaker ones and have them read together. Every time a *P* appears in the story, they stop reading and write a prediction about what will happen next. At the end of reading the next section, they discuss their predictions, place a plus sign if they are accurate or a minus sign if they are not, and make their next predictions.

When they finish reading the story I ask five true-false questions to assess how well they have understood it. Finally, I use the following writing prompt: "The author does not tell us what happens to the sniper after he discovers he has killed his brother. Write what you imagine happened." My knowledge of their interests, their prior knowledge, a visual cue about how civil wars are similar to and different from other wars, prediction questions to facilitate attention and comprehension, and paired reading to ensure that each person can experience the story provide a whole-group reading activity we all thoroughly enjoy.

I also use these periods to present minilessons, such as explaining sets of homophones that are frequently used incorrectly. In addition, when the

FIGURE 2
K-W-L Plus with additional figures

Know	Want to Know	Learned

Kill them
destroy land and people
kill wildlife
 	
pollution
Mt. St. Helens
Kilauea
	name of other
	– active volcanoes
	– where location
	– how hot they are
	– how often they erupt
	– where is lava going
	– how much do the
	  H islands grow every
	  15 years
		Pinatubo-Philippines
		nearly 900 people killed
		
		Unzen—Japan
		1991 + 1993
		41 people killed
		
		Kilauea—world's
		most active—Hawaii
		– 1990 no one hurt—
		  slow flow of lava
		
		Mt. St. Helens—
		Washington state
		1980
		– hot enough to melt
		  snow from last peaks
		  and caused flooding
		  63 people killed

destroy

people

air quality

property

wildlife

volcanoes

Name of volcanoes

| Pinatubo
Philippines | Unzen
Japan
1991 & 1993
sulfur
41 killed | Kilauea
Most active
volcano
no one
was
killed | Mt. St.
Helens
Washington
State
1980
63 killed |

tutors are not there, students may work independently on implementing the strategies they have been taught, tutor one another, or do SSR.

Another whole-group activity the students enjoy immensely is reading to kindergarten students every Friday at the elementary school that is within walking distance of the high school. To prepare, in the beginning of the year they all receive direct instruction in how to read to children. Pace and expression are modeled. Especially important, they are taught how to question the students to whom they read ("What do you think will happen next?" "How do you think the kitten felt when that happened?") in order to ensure attention and comprehension. Often, at some time during the week they practice (with tutor, teacher, or classmate) the books they will read on Friday.

With the help of a volunteer, the class also publishes newsletters, which contain mostly book reviews and other end-of-the-book activities. Pictures of and interviews with tutors, snapshots of each student reading to an elementary child, annotated suggestions for summer reading, and ideas for how parents can encourage reading at home have also appeared. These publications—distributed to the volunteers, administrators, and all students in the program and their parents—offer many opportunities for the students to raise their self-esteem and receive positive recognition while sharing with a larger group than just their classmates. The recognition from tutors, administrators, parents, siblings, and classmates is a very positive aspect of the program. As one administrator, who made it a point to compliment the students on their writing, wrote, "It is so good to see these kids, who at times don't make good decisions, being productive and doing well" (E. Browder, personal communication, December 19, 1996).

Homework

All students are required to read from a book of their choice for 10 to 15 minutes every night and to write a few sentences about their reading. After recording the number of pages read, they can summarize what they read or give their reactions or both. ("Bob is looking in Jenny's windows at night, and she doesn't know it. She'd better watch out.") In addition to keeping this action/reaction log, the students record in their notebooks the book's genre, author's name, title, setting, characters, conflict(s), resolution(s), and ending. They fill in the relevant notebook sections as they encounter the information in their readings. For example, characters' names are listed with large spaces after them. The student adds new information about a character piece by piece until a character sketch emerges. I call this procedure "keeping GAT SCCORE"—genre, author, title, setting, characters, conflict(s), order of key events (the action/reaction part), resolution(s), and ending. Using this format immediately provides students with a connection to their English classes in that they are improving their literacy skills at the same time as they are learning and using literary terms. Obviously, this format does not lend itself to nonfiction. With this type of book the students are required to make longer notations about the main ideas and important details in their action/reaction homework.

Grading

Because students receive credit toward graduation when they pass the course, grading must be considered. The major portion of the grade is based on completion of the short homework assignments. Each night's readings and log entry are carefully tracked and recorded. End-of-the-book activities such as book reviews and book talks also are part of the grade. Primarily because of the tailor-made assignments and the fact that students help each other through peer tutoring, there is a noncompetitive atmosphere in the classes. This is another important factor when dealing with at-risk students (Hodge, 1991).

Evaluation of the Model

Until early interventions are successfully used everywhere, there will be a need for last-ditch interventions at the high school level. The model illustrates that a program need not be expensive or require much staffing to be effective. During the 3 years of the program's existence, pre- and postintervention scores on the KTEA Brief Form have shown skills growing at an average rate of 2.2 years (and students gaining an average of 14 national percentage points) over the 9 months of instruction. This measure may not be the most sensitive for detecting specific results of many of the interventions used. However, it does indicate the overall effectiveness of the model, as does the fact that to date only 1.4% of the students who have finished the course have not continued with or completed their schooling. The overall dropout rate for the high school is approximately 5%.

Significant changes in the students also take place in the affective domain. Feedback from teachers includes stories of students volunteering to read aloud and generally participating more in class. Recently a student complained to me, "You know, Nat and Terrell [students in the program] would never read aloud in earth science, and now they won't let anyone else have a chance. You've got to talk to that teacher." Students actively seek books by favorite authors, and they often share opinions of books in their informal conversations. Students become elated when a study strategy enables them to pass a test in another course. Students do not want to be absent on the day their tutor comes or on Fridays when we read to the younger children. Parents comment on the gains the children have made in reading and self-confidence.

Because there is a lot of camaraderie associated with having a reading problem and overcoming it, these students form close, healthy bonds with one another and with me. They read to "the little ones who need your help because no one at home reads to them," and they become more willing to help others. For example, when school started this year, I had a room to myself for the first time. It badly needed painting, and I was told that I was on the list and it would be done in a few weeks. Two former students, knowing how excited I was to have a room, obtained the paint through the assistant principal and painted the room for me in two of their free periods.

A parent whose son was in the program last year shared this story with me. During their annual beach vacation, 14-year-old A.J. met his first girlfriend. At the end of the vacation they decided to write to each other. When the first letter arrived, the mother, who usually had to help her son with reading, asked whether he wanted her help or, because of the personal nature of the letter, that of his older sister. He informed her that he could now read it by himself. Later in the summer he told her that he would be taking 2 semesters of the program this year instead of the single semester he had originally intended to take. He is one of the boys who volunteered to tutor next year. Last year he entered the program reading at the 1st percentile (grade equivalent 2.8) and ended the year at the 21st percentile (7.3 grade equivalent level).

Future Benefit

Parts of the program positively touch each student each day. However, the aspect that I believe has the most promise for the students' future, even if they do not complete their education, is their reading to elementary children. Although many students are initially fearful or resistant, every one of them—from the school "tough" to the painfully withdrawn student reading on a second-grade level—has come to enjoy, to be effective at, and to realize the importance of reading to young children. If this program did nothing more than give them the skills to read to their own children, and a realization of how necessary that activity is, maybe the cycle of functional illiteracy in these students' families would be broken. Until we get to the point where we catch all youngsters before they fall, this type of program is a last opportunity to catch them at all.

REFERENCES

Allington, R.L. (1977). If they don't read much, how can they ever get good? *Journal of Reading, 21*, 57–61.

Ballash, K.M. (1994). Remedial high school readers can recover, too! *Journal of Reading, 37*, 686–687.

Brophy, J. (1988). Research linking teacher behavior to student achievement: Potential implications for instruction of Chapter 1 students. *Educational Psychologist, 23*(3), 235–286.

Carr, E., & Ogle, D. (1987). A strategy for comprehension and summarization. *Journal of Reading, 31*, 626–631.

Clay, M.M. (1979/1985). *The early detection of reading difficulties*. Auckland, New Zealand: Heinemann.

Cohn, M., & D'Alessandro, C. (1978). When is a decoding error not a decoding error? *The Reading Teacher, 32*, 341–344.

Glass, G. (1973). *Teaching decoding as separate from reading*. Garden City, NY: Adelphi University Press.

Grossen, B. (1997). *30 years of research: What we know about how children learn to read*. Santa Cruz, CA: Center for the Future of Teaching and Learning. (ERIC Document Reproduction Service No. 415 492)

Herrmann, B.A. (1994). *The volunteer tutor's toolbox*. Newark, DE: International Reading Association.

Hodge, E.A. (1991). *Intervention for at-risk students at the secondary level*. Montgomery, AL: Alabama State University. (ERIC Document Reproduction Service No. ED 339 764)

Lee, N.G., & Neal, J.C. (1992/1993). Reading rescue: Intervention for a student "at promise." *Journal of Reading, 36*, 276–282.

Leinhardt, G., & Bickel, W. (1987). Instruction's the thing wherein to catch the mind that falls behind. *Educational Psychologist, 22*(2), 177–207.

Maheady, L., Mallette, B., Harper, G.F., Sacca, K.C., & Pomerantz, D. (1994). Peer-mediated instruction for high-risk students. In K.D. Wood & B. Algozzine (Eds.), *Teaching reading to high-risk learners* (pp. 269–290). Needham Heights, MA: Allyn & Bacon.

O'Brien, D., & Stewart, R. (1992). Resistance to content area reading: Dimensions and solutions. In E. Dishner, T. Bean, J. Readence, & D. Moore (Eds.), *Reading in the content areas: Improving classroom instruction* (3rd ed., pp. 30–40). Dubuque, IA: Kendall/Hunt.

Office of Educational Research and Improvement. (1991). *Educational programs that work. A collection of proven exemplary educational programs and practices* (17th ed.). Washington, DC: National Diffusion Network. (ERIC Document Reproduction Service No. ED 338 618)

Riley, R. (1999, February 16). Sixth annual state of American education address, given at California State University at Long Beach.

Slavin, R.E., & Madden, N.A. (1989). What works for students at risk: A research synthesis. *Educational Leadership, 46*, 4–12.

Torgesen, J. (1998). Catch them before they fall. *American Educator, 22*, 32–39.

Vacca, R.T., & Alvermann, D.E. (1998). The crisis in adolescent literacy: Is it real or imagined? *NASSP Bulletin, 82*, 4–9.

Vacca, R.T., & Vacca, J.L. (1996). *Content area reading* (5th ed.). New York: HarperCollins.

Walker, B.J. (1992). *Diagnostic teaching of reading: Techniques for instruction and assessment*. New York: Macmillan.

Against Marginalization and Criminal Reading Curriculum Standards for African American Adolescents in Low-Level Tracks: A Retrospective of Baldwin's Essay

Alfred W. Tatum

For the past 7 years, I have sought ways to empower and accelerate the reading achievement of African American adolescents assigned to low-level reading tracks. Late one evening while I was reading a compilation of James Baldwin's works, his essay "A Talk to Teachers" (1963), resonated with me as I thought about the current momentum toward minimum standards and high-stakes testing and their effects upon this population. The essay remains a brilliant statement of the challenge facing teachers of African American students. Baldwin invoked teachers to reconceptualize the role of teaching; a re-conceptualization that is just as pressing now as it was more than 30 years ago.

Baldwin called for a type of teaching that connects the social, the economic, and the political to the educational. He understood that "the whole process of education occurs within a social framework and is designed to perpetuate the aims of society" (p. 679). He highlighted the paradox: As one begins to become conscious, one begins to examine the society in which he or she is being educated. If the society is one that oppresses, then those being oppressed must be taught how to overcome their oppression, or forever remain oppressed.

Baldwin's essay is a call to strike against the current trends occurring in the reading education of poor, urban African American adolescent students who are marginalized by the political exclusion, economic disenfranchisement, and social isolation of their families and by poor, inadequate instruction. The education of these students needs to go far beyond curriculum dictates satisfied by test-driven instruction that prevent more comprehensive approaches for teaching reading, thwart critical compe-

Reprinted from the *Journal of Adolescent & Adult Literacy, 43*, 570–576, March 2000.

tencies, and unfairly consign this group to the bottom of the economic, social, and political ladder. The essay helps us understand the need to strike against a functional orientation for teaching reading that is gaining momentum in some large urban school districts in the United States.

Tests Widen the Gap

Now that there is a nationwide thrust toward minimum standards on high-stakes standardized tests for promotion to the next grade level, many teachers are being forced to adopt, or opt for, a skills-based approach to reading instruction for adolescent students struggling with reading. Standardized tests should be used only with other forms of assessments such as observations, classroom work, tests administered throughout the year, and teacher evaluations to make decisions of promotion and retention. High-stakes testing concerns educators who do not align student achievement with test scores.

As a research intern at the Rainbow/PUSH Coalition, a civil rights organization headquartered in Chicago, Illinois, I received a plethora of test-related complaints from parents, teachers, community representatives, and local school councils. Increased standards, the elimination of social promotion, and established grade-level equivalent scores for grade promotion and retention have been implemented as part of a reform initiative in Chicago. This initiative has received national attention as a model for reform. Concerns about test abuse and an unfair licensure of failure for African American students were expressed. "Kids are being unfairly abused by a system with an adopted quick-fix approach of standards to a problem that is leading to increased placement in alternative schools that serve as warehouses for the underachieving students of color," said one teacher. The misuse of assessments and misinterpretation of increased standards are harmful.

The emphasis on meeting a competency measure is leading to a widening gap between a more comprehensive approach to literacy teaching and the widespread practices of classroom teachers of struggling African American adolescent readers. We must carefully reconsider the role of minimum standards and high-stakes testing if we are serious about addressing the needs of African American adolescents in low-level reading tracks. "Focusing on minimum standards goes against the grain of pushing these students toward their 'maximum competency level' " (Hillard, 1995, p. 108).

The approach to teaching in a system that focuses on test-driven instruction lacks the vitality to strengthen human potential. The promise to provide training so that students master a basic skills curriculum is not enough. With so much attention being given to a curriculum of basic skills, other critical competencies are being abandoned. Students must develop social consciousness through which they challenge the current social order. The effort for developing such competence and consciousness is being thwarted on a massive scale by those who identify academic success along the lines of minimum standards.

Providing Possibilities

Pedagogical approaches and curriculum must give students the opportunity to critically examine the society in which they are born. Freire (1970) stated that for him conscientization is a process in which people are encouraged to analyze their reality, to become aware of the constraints of their lives, and to take action to transform their situation. Dealing with students honestly helps them understand that the U.S. mainstream has been afflicted by cultural hegemonic practices that have caused fixed economic, political, and social stratifications. With this in mind, teachers must realize that it is their immediate pedagogical practices that broaden the prospects and range of possibilities for students, increasing chances for full economic, social, and political participation in society. "We can again let our students know they can resist a system that seeks to limit them to the bottom rung of the social and economic ladder" (Delpit, 1992, p. 301).

The crux of Baldwin's essay suggests ways for teachers to help their students understand that the U.S. suffers from a sense of its own identity, an identity structured by the creation of race as an issue by some of the nation's earlier cultural shapers. Students should be provided with the possibility to understand who they are in ways that are different from identities formed by the dominant culture. Differences should be discussed, and these differences should be organized within combinations of inequitable existing race and class relations. The identification of oppressive and unjust relations within which there are limitations placed on human action, feeling, and thought are integral parts of restructuring literacy practices.

Opportunities must be created for repeated and meaningful applications of reading skills. A curriculum that treats reality as something to be questioned and analyzed should be developed. Opportunities for developing strategies and hope for overcoming barriers to economic success in the mainstream should be contrived. Freire (1970) advanced the idea that opportunities to experience social structures as impermanent and changeable should be sought and highlighted. Students must develop a broader sociopolitical consciousness that allows them to critique the cultural norms, values, mores, and institutions that produce and maintain social inequities (Ladson-Billings, 1992). To allow for students to do this is very difficult under circumstances where minimum standards are emphasized over academic excellence and cultural competence. Changes in society call for different dictates that are more comprehensive than aligning curriculum with formal testing.

Test-driven reading instruction narrows the curriculum. There must be a thrust toward comprehensive reading instruction that encompasses explicit strategy instruction and authentic opportunities to read culturally relevant materials. Materials that challenge students to think about the historical context of the African American struggle and ways of overcoming these struggles should be selected. Themes of the readings should include changes in the history of the African American struggle; substantiating existence/identity formation; and political, economic, and cultural critiques. Attempts should be made to connect the historical to the contemporary so that the students view the reading curriculum as meaningful and relevant. Examining historical and social constructs would help students understand how images of African Americans were constructed to exploit labor, define class distinctions, and create the hegemonic distinctions present today. Test-driven reading instruction is depoliticized and does not allow for this to happen. As a result, there is a reproduction of racism and classism, and the maintenance of the economic and political status quo.

A Changing Vision

"One of the paradoxes of education was that at precisely the point you begin to develop a conscience, you must find yourself at war with your society. It is your responsibility to change society if you think of yourself as an educated person" (p. 685), was Baldwin's concluding remark to teachers in his essay. He suggested a way to think about teaching that can be currently applied to strike at the systematic silencing of African American adolescents across generations.

Reading education must presuppose a changing political, economic, and cultural vision for the future. If fear or curriculum constraints curtail a teacher's passion for creating this change, large groups of African American adolescents will have their possibilities limited. This is criminal. Reading educators must embrace a reading pedagogy to reverse the trend of marginalizing generation after generation of African American adolescents in low-level reading tracks.

REFERENCES

Baldwin, J. (1963). A talk to teachers. In T. Morrison (Ed.), *Baldwin-Collected essays* (pp. 678–686). New York: Library of America.

Delpit, L. (1992). Acquisition of a literate discourse: Bowing before the master? *Theory Into Practice, 31*, 266–271.

Freire, P. (1970). *The pedagogy of the oppressed.* New York: Seabury.

Hillard, A. (1995). *The maroon within us: Selected essays on African American community socialization.* Baltimore, MD: Black Classic Press.

Ladson-Billings, G. (1995). But that's just good teaching! The case for culturally relevant pedagogy. *Theory Into Practice, 34*, 159–165.

What Middle and High School Educators Need to Know About Language Minority Students

Elizabeth G. Sturtevant

I n the past two decades, extensive research in both second language acquisition and literacy education has provided important clues to ways schools can work effectively with their language minority learners. Following is a brief overview of some key ideas educators can use to support their decision making about program development for these students.

Understanding Language Minority Learners

1. Language minority learners are diverse.

Language minority adolescents are a highly diverse population with diverse needs. Like all adolescents, they are different from one another and individuals and are in a time of personal growth and change. They are diverse in personal history; some have spent their whole lives in the United States; some arrived during childhood; others arrived or will arrive during their secondary school years.

Language minority students' past school experiences also vary greatly. Young people entering the United States from areas experiencing political unrest may have had interrupted schooling or may never have attended school at all (Gabor, 1996). Other students, such as migrant children and others affected by poverty, may have changed schools repeatedly either in their home country or in the United States. A third group of language minority students has had a stable school experience either in the United States or their home country.

By adolescence, language minority students in the United States also will have achieved greatly varying levels of competence in English. While some are fully bilingual, others will have developed only partial or very limited fluency and literacy in English. Although many students with low English proficiency are recent arrivals, others have attended

From the *NASSP Bulletin, 82*(600), 73–77, October 1998. Reprinted with permission of the National Association of Secondary School Principals.

schools in the United States for many years and have struggled with academic learning and literacy throughout their school careers.

2. While learning English is important, it takes a long time.

Whatever students' background, success in most U.S. secondary schools requires strong English language proficiency, including literacy. This poses a serious dilemma for students who either have not been in U.S. schools long enough to develop English language proficiency or who have developed proficiency more slowly than has been expected.

It is essential for educators to understand that differences in the speed of English language acquisition are normal, and that second language acquisition is complex and often takes much longer than anticipated. Thus, while students may seem to be "failing" to acquire English at an appropriate pace, it may actually be the school's expectations that are faulty (Cummins, 1994).

It is also important for educators to understand the different types of language acquisition, with one taking much longer than the other. Linguists who have studied second language development report two "faces" of language: conversational and academic (Cummins, 1994). While conversational proficiency may develop fairly quickly (approximately 2 to 5 years to "catch up" with native English speakers), on-grade-level academic proficiency in content-related English for school takes much longer, from 5 to 10 years (Collier, 1995).

Individual students' length of language learning varies according to their number of years of schooling in the first language, type of school program in the United States, and other factors such as home and community influences. Those who arrive in the United States with little or no schooling in their first language have been found to acquire a second language more slowly than those who received at least 2–3 years of schooling in their home language (Gabor, 1996).

3. Literacy and concept development in the first language can support literacy and concept development in the second language.

Another important issue is whether students should be taught in their home language or in English. These decisions are frequently affected by political and practical concerns as well as instructional issues. Research has found repeatedly that it is very important for cognitive development of the first language to continue while the second language is developing. For adolescents entering U.S. schools who have never been to school at all, for example, precious time is wasted when concept development in academic subjects is delayed until the students learn English. In addition, young people who have already developed literacy in their first language have been found to develop literacy in English more easily than those who do not have this background in their first language (Gabor, 1996).

Key Concepts for Program Planning

1. Many instructional practices are appropriate for both fluent English speakers and those who are still developing their English.

A wide variety of instructional practices have been recommended as appropriate for both language minority and native English speakers. For these learners, academic development, cognitive development, and language development are interrelated (Au, 1993; Luz Reyes & Molner, 1991; Vacca & Vacca, 1996).

In her extensive review of research related to the instruction of language minority students, Collier (1995) reported the following common characteristics of the most effective programs: "Thematic, interdisciplinary instruction"; "multicultural, global perspectives…[with] lessons connect[ed] to past experiences"; "collaborative, interactive learning"; "challenging students cognitively"; and "teaching reading and writing…[as]…an integral part of any academic course…" (pp. 36–38). Secondary school teachers across disciplines will recognize these program recommendations as similar or identical to those of professional national standards documents written in the past decade (e.g., IRA/NCTE, 1996; NCTM, 1989).

While effective programs can be constructed in a variety of ways, Collier's (1995) longitudinal study found that two-way bilingual programs that included both native English speakers and second language learners had the most long-term benefits. These programs worked toward bilingual language proficiency, cognitive growth, and academic development for all students.

2. Administrators should facilitate collaboration between educators who work with language minority students.

A language minority adolescent may be served by a wide variety of school and district-based educators. These may include content area teachers in different disciplines, ESL (English as a Second Language) or bilingual educators, reading specialists, or other personnel. Coordination among these professionals is essential for a coherent, effective program.

3. Students' families should be included in planning.

Families of language minority adolescents are sometimes left out of the educational process. Barriers between home-school communication can include language differences, parents' work schedules, or the attitudes of educators. In addition, adolescents of every background seek independence and sometimes discourage their teachers and families from interacting. Despite these difficulties, schools that develop strong family connections reap many positive benefits. Important elements of effective programs include the availability of translators (professional or volunteer) and a positive atmosphere that values each family's contributions.

4. Steps should be taken to increase understanding of cultural diversity and language minority issues throughout the school community.

To succeed in their secondary schools, language minority students must feel they are accepted by both peers and adults as a valued part of the school community. Curriculum goals across disciplines should include global awareness and teaching all students to value diversity. In addition, particular efforts should be made to provide all students with adult role models from a wide variety of ethnic, racial, and language backgrounds.

Conclusion

While adolescent language minority students have specific needs, they also contribute a richness to the school environment. Many are resilient risk takers dedicated to improving their lives and the lives of their families. Positive steps taken by district and school-based educators can greatly assist these students and, at the same time, improve the global understanding of their entire school community.

REFERENCES

Au, K.H. (1993). *Literacy instruction in multicultural settings.* Fort Worth, TX: Harcourt Brace Jovanovich.

Collier, V.P. (1995). *Promoting academic success for ESL students: Understanding second language acquisition in school.* Elizabeth, NJ: New Jersey Teachers of English to Speakers of Other Languages.

Cummins, J. (1994). The acquisition of English as a second language. In K. Spangenberg-Urbschat & R. Pritchard (Eds.), *Kids come in all languages: Reading instruction for ESL students* (pp. 36–62). Newark, DE: International Reading Association.

Gabor, F. (1996). *Effective programs for low first language literacy limit English proficient middle and high school students* (Unpublished manuscript). Fairfax, VA: George Mason University.

International Reading Association & National Council of Teachers of English. (1996). *Standards for the English language arts.* Newark, DE: Authors.

Lara, J. (1994). Demographic overview: Changes in student enrollment in American schools. In K. Spangenberg-Urbschat & R. Pritchard (Eds.), *Kids come in all languages: Reading instruction for ESL students* (pp. 9–21). Newark, DE: International Reading Association.

Luz Reyes, M., & Molner, L.A. (1991). Instructional strategies for second-language learners in the content areas. *Journal of Reading, 35*(2), 96–103.

National Council of Teachers of Mathematics. (1989). *Curriculum and evaluation standards for teaching mathematics.* Reston, VA: Author.

Vacca, R.T., & Vacca, J.L. (1996). *Content area reading* (5th ed.). New York: HarperCollins.

A Library for Ophelia

Marsha M. Sprague and Kara K. Keeling

I n 1994 Mary Pipher galvanized educators and society at large with her best-selling book *Reviving Ophelia: Saving the Selves of Adolescent Girls*. The book describes, through a series of case studies, the traumatic experience of many girls in the United States during their passage through adolescence.

Certainly Pipher was not the first to sound the alarm. Gilligan, Lyons, Hammer, and others describe the anguished "relational world" of adolescent girls in *Making Connections: The Relational Worlds of Adolescents Girls at Emma Ward School*, published in 1990. In 1992 the American Association of University Women (AAUW) commissioned a report that synthesized research on adolescent girls in schools. This report, *How Schools Shortchange Girls* (1993), summarizes the devastating findings on the loss of self-esteem and decline of academic achievement experienced by adolescent females. This report was followed by *Hostile Hallways* (1994), which details the sexual harassment endured by adolescent girls in schools.

In the same year that Pipher published *Reviving Ophelia*, Peggy Orenstein wrote *SchoolGirls: Young Women, Self-Esteem and the Confidence Gap* (1994). Unlike Pipher's descriptions of individual adolescent females gleaned from counseling sessions, Orenstein's book examines three middle schools from the perspectives of the girls who inhabited them. However, both books came to the same frightening conclusions: In the United States, girls are at risk of academic failure, substance abuse, pregnancy, sexual disease, and suicide to a degree unimaginable to most parents and teachers. The statistics are frightening. Compared with boys, adolescent girls experience greater stress, are twice as likely to be depressed, and are four times as likely to commit suicide (Rothenberg, 1997). In the United States, girls under 15 are five times more likely to give birth than those in other industrialized nations (Brumberg, 1997). Sadly, problems also exist in the cases of high-ability girls. Despite some closing of the gender gap in mathematics and science achievement, current estimates are that high-ability boys outperform

Reprinted from the *Journal of Adolescent & Adult Literacy, 43*, 640–647, April 2000.

high-ability girls by about two to one in mathematics achievement and seven to one in science for students who score in the top 5% of national distributions (Hedges & Nowell, 1995, as cited in Meece & Jones, 1996).

As Pipher so eloquently argues, American popular culture is responsible for most of the problems. Media saturation of confusing sexual messages, wide exposure to a variety of addictive substances, and uncontrolled access to information formerly reserved for adults has given dangerous fuel to normal adolescent rebellion. The fact that most of this change has taken place in the last 10 to 15 years prevents current mothers and female teachers from relating to, much less understanding, the experiences of their daughters and students.

The current focus of much research is on how to address the problems so clearly defined. An example is the AAUW publication *Girls in the Middle: Working to Succeed in School* (Reseach for Action, Inc., 1996). This publication describes programs and strategies that seem effective in helping girls navigate adolescence. The report concludes with a number of desired outcomes for schools:

1. Expand the range of acceptable behaviors for girls, particularly "nonconforming" behaviors such as argumentative and assertive actions.

2. Create a mentor program for girls and support the mentors.

3. Build identity development into the school curriculum. Have opportunities for girls and boys to explore and discuss gender issues.

4. Foster opportunities for girls to assume leadership positions within the school and the classroom setting.

5. Examine the current practices of handling gender issues.

6. Make gender equity a school priority.

7. Create public forums to address the issue of gender equity.

8. Conduct research on gender issues.

It is the third outcome that holds the most interest to us as English educators. It addresses specific ways in which teachers can contribute to students' development of skills that strengthen identity and prevent undermining of female potential. One recommendation from the report is that teachers stress "active, real-world learning [to] help youngsters struggle with developmentally critical issues of autonomy, role playing and responsibility." Also, the report recommended that teachers should "open dialogue on gender issues in the classroom. Discuss gender as an aspect of students' lives, curricular materials, and classroom dynamics" (p. 88).

Nowhere is the opportunity for dialogue and real-world learning more accessible than in the study of literature. A number of novels that have been written in the past 10 to 15 years directly address the issues of girls' development through various plot devices. Adler and Clark (1991) advocate the use of novels in addressing the development of adolescent girls. While recognizing the limitations of literature to solve psychological problems, they quote Spache (1978, as cited in Adler & Clark): "It is through facilitated discussion that readers recognize that they are not the first to meet and solve problems, become aware of previously unrecognized problems, and find solutions without experiencing feelings of inferiority, guilt, fear or shame" (p. 758). Even when the discussions result in the realization that there are no simple solutions for problems, they may assist girls in developing a more authentic sense of who they are in the context of their culture.

An AAUW study conducted in 1990 (Sadker & Sadker, 1994) compared the self-esteem of girls in elementary school versus those in high school. In elementary school, 60% of girls said "I'm happy the way I am." By high school, only 29% responded positively to that statement. Brown and Gilligan (1992) exposed the differences in the ways 10-year-old girls talk about their world versus 12- to 13-year-olds. The older girls tend to hide their strong feelings, to repress anger and outrage, so that they will receive approval from peers and adults. They become unable to articulate who they are and what they value.

It is our feeling that girls can and should be exposed to discussions about what causes that slide in self-esteem, the loss of confidence and voice. In the following pages we will review books that are particularly helpful in generating this kind of discussion and consider ways to teach these books in the classroom.

Criteria for Selection

Adler and Clark (1991) analyzed Newbery Medal winners and honor books from 1984 to 1989, but found only two with female protagonists. In selecting the books for our list, we used several excellent resources to begin our search. Odean's *Great Books for Girls* (1997) proved especially helpful. We looked at books that were suitable for girls ages 10 to 14. We also included books that are taught in our university program in the Adolescent Literature course.

For our first criterion, we looked at the central issue that we believed must be addressed in order for the discussions to be helpful to girls. We targeted books in which the central character is an adolescent female who struggles to articulate her true voice. Second, we wanted a book that demonstrated real and typical restrictions of females. However, we did not eliminate books of fantasy as long as they contained situations analogous to real-life challenges. Third, we insisted on a heroine who had to negotiate society, including males. This caused us to reject such appealing books as Scott O'Dell's *Island of the Blue Dolphins* and Jean Craighead George's *Julie of the Wolves* on the basis that the "girl against nature" theme, while inspiring, did not reflect the most acute struggle of girls today, which is that of negotiating the society around them. Fourth, we demanded that the books be gripping; that they capture the attention of any reader and not just those with a particular interest. This caused us to eliminate some excellent books with a sports or music focus (such as Virginia Euwer Wolff's *The Mozart Season*). Finally, we demanded that the books not inadvertently reinforce the stereotypic role of the woman in fiction, that she is somehow rescued by a handsome male and lives happily ever after. These latter "texts of desire," as they are termed by Christian-Smith (1993), are the predominant source of girls' fictional reading in and out of school. Applying these criteria reduced our potential hundreds of books to around 40.

As we refined our search, we conceived of a central theme: expression versus suppression. The main theme of the book must focus on a girl who is struggling to express herself against forces (cultural, familial, personal) that seek to suppress her true voice. The central character must be this female. This caused us to eliminate several excellent books that include strong female characters (e.g., Madeline L'Engle's *A Wrinkle in Time*, Sharon Creech's *Walk Two Moons*) but that do not, in our opinion, deal with expression versus repression as the central issue. We also reluctantly omitted books in which historical context overshadowed the struggle of the central female (as in James Duffy's *Radical Red* and Ruth Park's *Playing Beattie Bow*). This helped narrow the number of books even further.

Selected Books

Using the criteria above, we selected 20 books that have potential for engaging girls in dialogue around central issues. In analyzing the books, we conceived a schema that would serve as a basis for discussion and reflection. As outlined in the Figure, here are the central questions: Who is the main female? What is she trying to express? What is keeping her from expressing this? Specifically (these are the satellite issues), how does the culture assist her or suppress her? What about the role of parents and other adult figures? Peers, both male and female? What particular strengths does the main character bring to this struggle? What

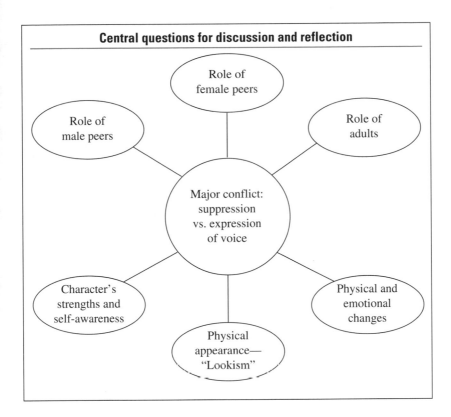

Central questions for discussion and reflection

- Role of female peers
- Role of male peers
- Role of adults
- Major conflict: suppression vs. expression of voice
- Character's strengths and self-awareness
- Physical and emotional changes
- Physical appearance— "Lookism"

awareness does she have of these strengths? How does "lookism" enter into the equation? What physical and emotional changes is the character experiencing due to adolescence, and how do those help or hinder her?

Although there is not space to describe all 20 books here, we summarize 10 and give the complete list in the sidebar.

Avi. *The True Confessions of Charlotte Doyle*. Avon, 1990. 232 pp.

The year is 1832. Thirteen-year-old Charlotte is returning from boarding school in England to rejoin her family in Boston. Unfortunately, her chaperones fail to arrive on the ship, and Charlotte finds herself crossing the Atlantic while caught up in a crew's mutiny. Realizing that the captain is cruel, Charlotte forsakes her station in life and aligns herself with the crew, dressing as a boy and learning to handle the ship. When the ship finally arrives in Boston, Charlotte finds herself fundamentally changed. The book offers excellent opportunities to discuss society's approved roles and options for girls in the past and in the present. Historical fiction.

Cushman, Karen. *Catherine, Called Birdy.* Harper Trophy, 1994. 212 pp.

In 1490, 14-year-old Catherine, nicknamed Birdy, keeps a diary of her daily life at her father's manor in England. Disliking her daily "lady lessons" in sewing and deportment that restrict her behavior, Birdy rebels against the narrowness of the role she has been born to in medieval society. Now old enough for marriage, she subverts her father's attempts to marry her for his own financial gain, using her wits to chase off each of her suitors, especially the crude, disgusting old knight to whom her father "betrays and betroths" her. In the end, Birdy finds a way to balance the social demands of her rank within society with her own sense of self. The diary form of this novel lets Birdy's distinctive, buoyant, and humorous voice shine through, as well as her intense curiosity as she reports the world around her. Though in some respects Birdy's mind-set may be more 20th century than medieval, she deals cleverly with issues of society's expectations. Historical fiction.

Levine, Gail Carson. *Ella Enchanted.* HarperCollins, 1997. 232 pp.

When Ella is born, a fairy gives her a gift that becomes the curse of her life: the gift of obedience. How can Ella ever be her true self when the curse compels her to do whatever anyone orders her to do, no matter how careless or unintentional the command? Rather than becoming truly obedient, she turns into a rebel, always resisting the orders she is given by finding ways around them, obeying the letter but not the spirit of the law. Feisty and intelligent, Ella finds within herself the means of solving her problem. In the end, she saves not only herself but her prince as well in this adaptation of the Cinderella story. Fantasy.

Levy, Marilyn. *Run for Your Life.* Houghton Mifflin, 1996. 217 pp.

Kisha lives in an inner-city neighborhood; she sees poverty, drug dealing, and broken families around her daily. Her life changes when Darren, the director of a nearby community center, starts a track team for the girls of the neighborhood. In addition to the daily practices, Darren demands that the girls get decent grades, remain drug free, and abstain from sex to participate on the team. Despite initial difficulties and temptations to quit, Kisha and her friends flower under the bonding they experience as they train. Students can discuss how the self-discipline the girls learn benefits them in more than one aspect of their lives, and how their achievements become a justifiable source of pride in themselves, despite difficulties. Realistic fiction.

McCaffrey, Anne. *Dragonsong*. Bantam, 1976. 176 pp.

Musically gifted Menolly lives in a remote fishing village on the world of Pern. Her parents forbid her to play music, for traditionally only men become Harpers. They beat her when she disobeys and even allow an accidental wound to heal awry so that she will no longer be able to play instruments. Lonely, frustrated, and miserable because no one understands her, Menolly runs away from the village to live on her own in a cave on the coast. There she finds and adopts nine "fire lizards," semi-intelligent miniature dragons who enjoy her music and even accompany her. Caught outside during Threadfall (a fiery rain that plagues Pern), Menolly is rescued by a dragonrider and taken to a Weyr. The people there appreciate her talents, including the Masterharper of Pern, who invites her to study at Harper Hall as an apprentice Harper. Discussion issues include the connection between self-image and social pressures, and the necessity of following one's gifts. Fantasy.

Paterson, Katherine. *Lyddie*. Puffin, 1991. 182 pp.

In 1840s Vermont, 13-year-old Lyddie struggles to provide for her family after her parents desert them. Working as a factory girl gives her a chance to earn enough money to pay the debt on the family farm and bring her younger brother and sister back to live there. Lyddie faces the rough working conditions of the factory—the noise, heat, long hours, injuries, lung diseases, and sexual harassment from the overseer—with courage matched by desperation. Asked to join the labor movement, she must weigh the consequences of the exploitative laboring conditions on herself and her friends with her own need for money for her family. When a neighbor's son offers her marriage, a safe and easy solution to her problems, Lyddie chooses instead to seek a college education for herself. This novel presents abundant issues for discussion, especially the meaning of independence, education, and the values that underlie Lyddie's choices. Historical fiction.

Staples, Suzanne Fisher. *Shabanu: Daughter of the Wind*. Random, 1989. 240 pp.

Shabanu has grown up in relative freedom with her family in the Cholistan desert of Pakistan: Her parents have let her play and work with the camels she loves rather than insisting that she confine herself to housework as is proper for a young Muslim girl. Now that

Books that encourage gender dialogue

Avi. *The true confessions of Charlotte Doyle.* Avon, 1990. 232 pp. Readability Grade 7. Historical fiction.

Baczewski, Paul. *Just for kicks.* Lippincott, 1990. 182 pp. Readability Grade 6. (Caution: Out of print.) Realistic fiction.

Creech, Sharon. *Chasing Redbird.* Harper Trophy, 1997. 261 pp. Readability Grade 7. Realistic fiction.

Cushman, Karen. *Catherine, called Birdy.* Harper Trophy, 1994. 212 pp. Readability Grade 8. Historical fiction.

Duder, Tessa. *In lane three, Alex Archer.* Bantam, 1987. 259 pp. Readability Grade 7/8. Realistic fiction.

L'Engle, Madeline. *A ring of endless light.* Laurel Leaf, 1980. 332 pp. Readability Grade 7. Fantasy.

Levine, Gail Carson. *Ella enchanted.* HarperCollins, 1997. 232 pp. Readability Grade 6. Fantasy.

Levy, Marilyn. *Run for your life.* Houghton Mifflin, 1996. 217 pp. Readability Grade 5/6. (Caution: Out of print.) Realistic fiction.

McCaffrey, Anne. *Dragonsinger.* Bantam, 1977. 240 pp. Readability Grade 6. Fantasy.

McCaffrey, Anne. *Dragonsong.* Bantam, 1976. 176 pp. Readability Grade 7. Fantasy.

Paterson, Katherine. *Lyddie.* Puffin, 1991. 182 pp. Readability Grade 6. Historical fiction.

Paterson, Katherine. *Jacob have I loved.* Harper Trophy, 1980. 244 pp. Readability Grade 7. Realistic fiction.

Spinelli, Jerry. *There's a girl in my hammerlock.* Trumpet Club, 1991. 191 pp. Realistic fiction.

Staples, Suzanne Fisher. *Shabanu: Daughter of the wind.* Random, 1989. 240 pp. Readability Grade 6. Realistic fiction.

Tate, Eleanora E. *The secret of Gumbo Grove.* Yearling Books, 1987. 199 pp. Readability Grade 4. Realistic fiction.

Voigt, Cynthia. *Dicey's song.* Fawcett Juniper, 1982. 211 pp. Readability Grade 6. Realistic fiction.

Voigt, Cynthia. *Come a stranger.* Aladdin, 1982. 248 pp. Readability Grade 7/8. Realistic fiction.

Voigt, Cynthia. *Izzy, willy-nilly.* Aladdin/Simon & Schuster, 1986. 280 pp. Readability Grade 7/8. Realistic fiction.

Walter, Mildred Pitts. *Trouble's child.* Lothrop, Lee & Shepard, 1985. 157 pp. Readability Grade 4, although dialect makes it more difficult. (Caution: Out of print.) Realistic fiction.

Wreade, Patricia. *Dealing with dragons.* Scholastic, 1990. 212 pp. Readability Grade 8. Fantasy.

she is 12 and approaching the age of marriage, however, her parents insist that she dress, speak, and behave in a more conventional manner. As loving and thoughtful Muslim parents, they have arranged marriages for Shabanu and her older sister to two brothers who are farmers, but when one brother is killed the family must keep the peace by marrying Shabanu to a rich landlord who lives in the city. This superb novel presents a fascinating look at daily life in an unfamiliar culture; Staples portrays her characters with great admiration and sympathy, with depth rather than stereotypes. Topics for discussion include the contrasts between the life of the protagonist and the lives of its readers, as well as in how Shabanu must find a way to value herself within the role of women in her culture. Realistic fiction.

Tate, Eleanora E. *The Secret of Gumbo Grove*. Yearling Books, 1987. 199 pp.

Eleven-year-old Raisin Stackhouse lives in South Carolina and loves history. She wonders why there isn't more information about the African American community of Calvary County. When she is asked to help clear an old cemetery by the church's secretary, Miss Effie, she begins to find out stories about her ancestors. The black community is not sure they want to revive the old stories. The book raises interesting questions about the effect of the past on the present, and how girls are stronger when they have a clear sense of their history. Realistic fiction.

Voigt, Cynthia. *Izzy, Willy-Nilly*. Aladdin/Simon & Schuster, 1986. 280 pp.

Izzy is "a nice girl" who seems to have everything she could want: She has a loving family, does well in her classes at school, is pretty and popular enough to have made the cheerleading team even though she's only a sophomore, and gets asked out on a date by a senior football player. But when she loses her leg in an automobile accident caused by a drunk driver, her world falls apart. Though she tries to stay cheerful and brave to please her family, she changes in profound ways as she discovers the differences in how her family, friends, and schoolmates treat her. As she loses the easy superficial friendships of the past based on looks and popularity, she finds more substantive relationships, especially with her classmate Rosamund, who is neither conventional nor pretty but is intelligent and far more compassionate than the girls with whom Izzy had spent her time. The novel presents excellent opportunities to discuss the basis of Izzy's friendships, the way her family handles her disability, and Izzy's own evolving attitudes toward what has happened to her. Realistic fiction.

Wreade, Patricia. *Dealing With Dragons*. Scholastic, 1990. 212 pp.

In this light-hearted fantasy, the princess Cimorene rejects her expected role as wife of a prince and instead takes the job of housekeeper for a dragon. She rebuffs suitors who try to rescue her from this task, and instead uncovers a plot to undermine her dragon's authority. She becomes more and more needed by the dragon society. The plot lends itself to questions about the expected role of girls and how unconventional choices are viewed by others. Fantasy.

Teaching the Literature

There are a number of ways to teach these books. The first way is to teach the book as a whole-class activity. All students read through the chapters at approximately the same pace, and whole-class discussions are held to examine the questions of gender and identity. We believe this is probably the least productive. First of all, the reality of a whole-class discussion is that very few people have the opportunity to speak, or, if there is a system in place that ensures equal distribution of responses, then no one gets to speak very often. This represses the opportunity for students to engage in deep dialogue about gender issues, particularly students who already are uncomfortable with the topic. We recommend alternate methods, as follows.

Cooperative Group, Single Sex

In this approach, students are placed in cooperative groups for the duration of the literature unit. Groups are single sex and consist of three or four students. All students read the same book and meet each day to discuss what they have read. The teacher provides a reading guide that focuses on the issues of identity and gender in addition to the normal literary questions about plot, theme, characters, and so on. Students discuss the questions, and a rotating recorder summarizes group consensus. (It is usually desirable to have these notes collected and counted for points or grades throughout the unit.) The teacher's role during the group discussions is to monitor student engagement, clarify confusions, and answer questions.

After the groups have finished reading, the teacher may want to have different groups share their analysis of the reading. As the differing responses emerge, the teacher asks students to analyze the responses of males and females and to hypothesize reasons for the differences. This discussion should lead to better understanding of the ways in which males and females view common events. The discussion in the cooperative groups is in itself powerful, allowing both males and females to examine their attitudes about gender issues. This approach provides not only a protected space for girls to share their ideas, but also for both sexes to confront societal expectations and norms about adolescent girls.

Literature Circle

In this format, students select one of the books to read, choosing from four to six selected by the teacher from the list. This means that a group of four or five students will be reading the same book. Presumably, boys and girls will be in each group. The students in each group set up a schedule for reading and then meet intermittently to discuss their reactions to the book. The schematic can serve as a source of questions that must be answered, or the teacher can design discussion questions or activities. The teacher should meet periodically with each circle to review progress. If desired, a time can be set aside for the groups to share their reading experiences with the whole class. This is a wonderful opportunity to study how the different female characters compare and contrast in the ways they negotiate their struggle for expression. The mixing of boys and girls may constrain the discussions within the group; however, it may also encourage a sharing of disparate viewpoints.

Book Club

Another option is to hold an extracurricular book club—before or after school, during a lunch period, or even in the summer. In this scenario, students (presumably a small group) all read the same book, discuss it, and then proceed on to the next. The teacher or student leader guides the discussion of the book using the schematic. The club reads as many of the books as time and resources allow. This permits students to compare and contrast the various heroines and to consider the different paths they have taken to self-expression. Because this is a voluntary activity, it is assumed that mostly girls will join the club. This may provide for more honest and in-depth discussion of the developmental challenges experienced by the girls in the club, as was found in a group led by Irwin-DeVitis and Benjamin (1995). In their summer discussion group centering on *The Diary of Anne Frank*, the authors confirmed that the focus on a literary female character struggling through adolescence did indeed provoke intense and helpful dialogue among girls.

Caveats and Cautions

The selection of books used in the classroom must contain a variety of cultural contexts. Clearly, the experiences of minority girls in the United States are different from those in the majority. Pipher (1994) narrates the discrepant experiences of American girls of different ethnicities due to the differing expectations of their families, as well as the challenges the girls may face in combating racism. The books *Come a Stranger* and *The Secret of Gumbo Grove* are both rich sources of discussion about the experiences of African American adolescents. It would be helpful to identify other books that speak to the experiences of Asian and Hispanic girls. Girls from low socioeconomic classes have additional challenges and issues. The effect of differing social classes on gender identity in British and Australian society, respectively, has been studied by MacRobbie and Thomas (as cited in Gilbert & Taylor, 1991). The novels *Lyddie* and *Run for Your Life* both deal with girls living in poverty. And girls in completely different societies are constrained by totally different rules: *Shabanu* is an excellent resource for exploring some of them.

Discussions of sensitive issues such as gender and cultural identity are sometimes painful for adolescents. The discomfort and dissension that arise during these discussions may raise tensions in the classroom. The use of smaller groups will reduce but may not completely dispel the tensions. One suggestion is to add a writing component to the experiences: After discussion, students could reflect on the discussion in writing, describing what their sense of the issues is and why it might be different from their classmates. The teacher will also need to be sensitive to the tensions and to continuously remind students that everyone's ideas need to be listened to respectfully.

A last concern is the proposal of having boys read books that feature girls as the central character. Cherland (1994), in her ethnography of a middle school in Ontario, describes the resistance that boys feel in reading "girls' books." Although it is considered acceptable for girls to like "boys' books" (such as Walter Farley's Black Stallion series) it is somehow shameful for boys to reciprocate. Even worse, Cherland found teachers complicit in this practice. Yet she quotes Segal (1986, as cited in Cherland) in arguing, "Many boys are missing out on one of fiction's greatest gifts, the chance to experience life from a perspective other than the one we were born to—in this case from the female vantage point" (p. 183).

The goal of the process is not to solve the problems of individual adolescent girls, but to provide a protected space where girls (and boys) can share ideas about what society expects of females and consider ways to handle the pressures of conforming to those norms.

Creating Opportunities for Discussion

Teachers and parents of adolescent girls know that early adolescence is a difficult time, with little opportunity to discuss issues faced by girls. A number of researchers have demonstrated the devastating toll that these years have on many girls in terms of depression, eating disorders, and poor academic performance. The typical school curriculum provides few opportunities for either girls or boys to consider cultural expectations of females, and to think about constructive ways to negotiate these expectations. Through reading and discussing novels in which girls meet varying challenges, the reading or language arts teacher can assist students in examining crucial issues. This article recommends a number of books and provides a variety of formats for their use in schools. In addition, the questions we developed may be helpful in selecting additional books for classroom use.

REFERENCES

Adler, E., & Clark, R. (1991). Adolescence: A literary passage. *Adolescence, 26,* 757–768.

American Association of University Women (AAUW) Educational Foundation. (1993). *Hostile hallways: The AAUW survey on sexual harassment in America's schools.* Washington, DC: American Association of University Women.

American Association of University Women (AAUW) Educational Foundation. (1995). *How schools shortchange girls: The AAUW report.* New York: Marlowe & Company.

Brown, L.M., & Gilligan, C. (1992). *Meeting at the crossroads: Women's psychology and girls' development.* New York: Ballantine Books.

Brumberg, J. (1997). *The body project: An intimate history of American girls.* New York: Vintage Books.

Cherland, M. (1994). *Private practices: Girls reading fiction and constructing identity.* London: Taylor & Francis.

Christian-Smith, L. (Ed.). (1993). *Texts of desire: Essays on fiction, femininity and schooling.* London: Falmer Press.

Gilbert, P., & Taylor, S. (1991). *Fashioning the feminine.* North Sydney, Australia: Allyn & Unwin.

Gilligan, C., Lyons, N., & Hammer, T. (Eds.). (1990). *Making connections: The relational worlds of adolescent girls at Emma Willard School.* Cambridge, MA: Harvard University Press.

Irwin-DeVitis, L., & Benjamin, B. (1995). Adolescent girls' development and *Anne Frank: The Diary of a Young Girl. ALAN Review, 33,* 10–15.

Meece, J., & Jones, G. (1996, February/March). Girls in mathematics and science: Constructivisim as a feminist perspective. *The High School Journal, 79,* 242–247.

Odean, K. (1997). *Great books for girls.* New York: Ballantine Books.

Orenstein, P. (1994). *Schoolgirls: Young women, self-esteem and the confidence gap.* New York: Anchor Books.

Pipher, M. (1994). *Reviving Ophelia: Saving the selves of adolescent girls.* New York: Ballantine Books.

Research for Action, Inc. (1996). *Girls in the middle: Working to succeed in schools.* Washington, DC: American Association of University Women.

Rothenberg, D. (1997). *Supporting girls in early adolescence.* (ERIC Document Reproduction Service No. 408 031)

Sadker, M., & Sadker, D. (1994). *Failing at fairness.* New York: Touchstone.

A Commitment to Challenging and Supportive Instruction

The phrase "reading wars" may characterize the recent history of beginning reading instruction, but experts agree to a remarkable degree about the characteristics of effective literacy instruction for adolescents. *Adolescent Literacy: A Position Statement* (Moore, Bean, Birdyshaw, & Rycik, 1999) identifies a wide range of teaching techniques that would help students to grow in their ability to read complex material. These include prereading strategies such as introducing technical vocabulary, during reading strategies such as study guides and self-questioning, and postreading strategies such as mapping concepts. The position statement particularly emphasizes the explicit teaching of reading and study strategies that students can learn to apply independently. The CRISS (Creating Independence Through Student Owned Strategies) program developed by Carol Santa is also built around this idea of modeling and guiding strategies that students will gradually learn to use themselves (LPD Video Journal of Education, 1997).

Mizelle (1997) identified important characteristics of classrooms that engage and sustain students' interest in reading. These include relevant and challenging tasks, authentic assessment that focuses on progress, opportunities to work in heterogeneous groups, longer periods of time for reading and writing, and student choice in the topics they will pursue and the materials they will read.

Considering the number of recommended instructional strategies available and the relative absence of controversy about their effectiveness, one would expect secondary teachers to be satisfied with their ability to guide the reading progress of their students. Unfortunately, this is not the case. Bintz (1997) explored the "reading nightmares" of secondary content teachers and concluded that

> Increasing numbers of middle and secondary school students do not perceive reading as meaningful, and thus do not value the act or the process. These students are apathetic, almost disdainful about reading. As a result, increasing numbers of teachers are left feeling bewildered and frustrated, almost paralyzed about how to teach. This situation is further exacerbated for teachers working in a climate of high-stakes assessment where the improvement (or lack thereof) in test scores across individual content areas determines the extent to which schools and teachers are rewarded or punished. (p. 16)

Bintz found that teachers tended to blame others (for example, teacher preparation programs, elementary teachers, and parents) for their students' struggles. He also found that a general feeling of gloom and frustration existed even though most teachers could identify one or more approaches for responding to the problem. He reported, for instance, that many teachers were seriously questioning the advisability of using a single textbook that might be too difficult or lack interest for many students. He concluded, however, that those same teachers felt poorly prepared and inexperienced in selecting alternative texts or balancing student-selected materials with the mandates of the curriculum.

Teachers, like students, require reassurance that new skills they learn are useful, and they need feedback that shows they are using new methods effectively, particularly when public scrutiny discourages risk taking. Students cannot reach their goal of reading independence without the help of teachers, but teachers need reasons to believe their efforts can make a difference. Recent research by Langer (2000) may help in this regard. Langer studied two sets of middle schools and high schools. The schools were the same in every possible way, including students' socio-economic status. Nevertheless, students in one group of schools had high levels of achievement in reading and writing, and students in the other group did not. Langer carefully studied the high-achieving schools and identified six interrelated features that characterized effective instruction:

1. Students learn skills and knowledge in multiple lesson types.

2. Teachers integrate test preparation into instruction.

3. Teachers make connections across instruction, curriculum, and life.

4. Students learn strategies for doing the work.

5. Students are expected to be generative thinkers.

6. Classrooms foster cognitive collaboration.

These findings provide support for teachers to renew their commitment to teaching methods that both challenge students to take control of their learning and support their efforts to do so. Langer found, for instance, that effective classrooms included support for reading skill development through "separated" or explicit instruction in particular skills, and "simulations" that provided guided practice. On the other hand, she concluded that these practices were ineffective unless they were used during challenging, meaningful, "integrated" activities such as literature discussions. This mix of activities is consistent with the "gradual release of responsibility" model of instruction advocated by Pearson and Gallagher (1983).

Langer's research also provides encouragement for teachers who are concerned that increased emphasis on student engagement will conflict with the school's effort to raise scores on high-stakes tests. She found that short-term test preparation or instruction that addressed test objectives without integrating them into meaningful activities were ineffective. She found that the more effective schools identified the important literacy skills that were assessed by the test and then selected instructional strategies that would develop those skills over the course of the year or across several years. In other words, the skills on high-stakes tests that are genuinely important can only be developed through steady application in real literacy activities. "Teaching the test" will only turn many students against reading and writing.

Rather than focusing on very specific instructional strategies such as K-W-L (Ogle, 1986) or Reciprocal Teaching (Palincsar & Brown, 1986), Langer describes the kinds of learning environments that teachers in the effective schools created. These classroom structures and procedures allow teachers to provide opportunities to address the differing needs of students while keeping the whole class involved. They include

- making explicit connections between the curriculum and students' lives,
- providing rubrics that show students how to evaluate their own learning,
- using discussion and writing to help students extend and clarify ideas, and
- collaborating with students so they share and challenge each others' ideas and responses.

The articles in this section provide concrete illustrations of instructional environments such as those Langer describes. Many of the specific techniques that are described are no longer new and the materials used range from traditional textbooks to computers. It is important to remember, however, that these methods have not been cooked up in a lab or dreamed up in an ivory tower. They are used on a daily basis by many good teachers in middle schools and high schools, and that is why they warrant a closer look. These teachers have already found a way toward more "meaning-full" literacy experiences. They offer both reassurance that change is possible and a challenge to use the best of what we know to gradually move students toward greater literacy independence.

Gay Ivey emphasizes the importance of choice for middle grade readers. She shows how environments such as reading workshops and theme units allow teachers to adapt instruction to the needs of individuals. Barbara McCombs and Mary Lee Barton provide examples of ways that even traditional textbook assignments can be transformed though the application of techniques grounded in cognitive psychology. Mary Santerre, on the other hand, provides an in-depth look at the many ways in which new technology is woven through the challenging reading and writing tasks her students do. One of the most powerful tools adolescents have for improving their literacy is knowledge of their specific strengths and weaknesses. As they learn to reflect on their performance, they come to see that by identifying goals and applying the strategies used by effective readers, they can improve noticeably. Portfolios promote this kind of reflection, and Bonita Wilcox demonstrates how it can be done. Finally, Rebecca Joseph describes the elements of choice, collaboration, and connection that can be incorporated in an urban school when reading instruction focuses on young adult literature.

REFERENCES

Bintz, W.P. (1997). Exploring reading nightmares of middle and secondary school teachers. *Journal of Adolescent & Adult Literacy, 41*, 12–24.

Langer, J.A., Close, E., Angelis, J., & Preller, P. (2000). *Guidelines for teaching middle and high school students to read and write well: Six features of effective instruction.* Albany, NY: National Research Center on English Learning and Achievement.

LPD Video Journal of Education. (1997). *Student centered reading and learning strategies* (Volume VI, Issue Eight). Salt Lake City, UT: Linton Professional Development Corporation.

Mizelle, N.B. (1997). Enhancing young adolescents' motivation for literacy learning. *Middle School Journal, 28*(3), 16–23.

Moore, D.W., Bean, T.W., Birdyshaw, D., & Rycik, J.A. (1999). *Adolescent literacy: A position statement.* Newark DE: International Reading Association.

Ogle, D.M. (1986). K-W-L: A teaching model that develops active reading of expository text. *The Reading Teacher, 39*, 564–571.

Palincsar, A., & Brown, A.L. (1986). Interactive teaching to promote independent learning from text. *The Reading Teacher, 39*, 771–777.

Pearson, P.D., & Gallagher, M.C. (1983). The instruction of reading comprehension. *Contemporary Educational Psychology, 8*(3), 317–344.

Discovering Readers in the Middle Level School: A Few Helpful Clues

Gay Ivey

Several years ago a group of students in seventh and eighth grade were surveyed about their most memorable schoolwork (Wasserstein, 1995). Not surprisingly, students named hands-on science projects, independent research projects, and performance activities as their favorite school experiences. Reading was a serious but not surprising omission. Other research has painted a similarly bleak picture, revealing that middle level students do not like to read (McKenna, Kear, & Ellsworth, 1995) and seldom choose to read on their own (Ley, Schaer, & Dismukes, 1994; Morrow, 1991).

It is not difficult to hypothesize about the prevalence of negative reading attitudes in the middle school years. Teacher-selected reading materials and activities still predominate in middle schools (Alvermann & Moore, 1991), despite the fact that advocates of middle school reform have called for more student-centered curriculum and instruction.

Middle school students probably have very little voice in creating the reading curriculum; consequently, they either become resistant to reading or they keep their dissatisfaction to themselves (Bintz, 1993). Thus, the decline in positive attitudes toward reading as students move through the middle grades may be the result of a mismatch between the type of reading that interests middle school students and the kinds of reading typically assigned to them in school.

Three Recurring Themes

What educators are learning about middle school students, however, is that there are indeed texts and contexts that motivate them to read and to do so enthusiastically. Despite the widespread belief that young adolescents dislike reading, I believe thousands of potential avid readers sit undiscovered in middle school classrooms. There are three recurring themes in the research that ought to serve as guiding principles for uncovering what fosters middle school students' ability and desire to read.

From the *NASSP Bulletin*, *82*(600), 48–56, October 1998. Reprinted with permission of the National Association of Secondary School Principals.

1. Middle level students need time to read in school.
Since time spent reading is strongly tied to reading success (Anderson, Wilson, & Fielding, 1998; Stanovich, 1986), motivating students to read ought to be a priority in middle level schools. The key to motivating students to read may be in getting them personally involved in reading (Nell, 1988). For students to become personally engaged in reading, however, they need significant amounts of time to get involved with books (Allington, 1994); this time ought to be provided in school.

Many middle level schools already schedule built-in voluntary reading times—such as Sustained Silent Reading (SSR) and Drop Everything and Read (DEAR)—but the effectiveness of these programs may depend on school level and classroom level factors (Wiesendanger & Birlem, 1984). If middle level students are to benefit from voluntary reading programs, they need access to materials they can read and want to read, as well as teachers who model engagement in pleasure reading, and this is probably not the case in every classroom. Moreover, reading time needs to be a priority.

Perhaps the most likely place for free-choice reading is the language arts classroom, particularly if the daily schedule is arranged into extended block periods. While it would be difficult to build a 20-minute reading time into a 45-minute period, teachers could easily set aside at least 20 minutes for pleasure reading within a 90-minute language arts block.

Unfortunately, language arts teachers encounter additional barriers to providing time for sustained reading. Despite compelling evidence that time spent reading leads to growth in reading ability, many middle level teachers feel that free-reading time is a luxury they cannot afford. Sixth-grade teachers interviewed by Worthy, Turner, and Moorman (1998) admitted they were conflicted about how best to use instructional time. Although they were convinced that free-choice reading was important, they felt external pressures to spend time preparing students for standardized tests. They also feared that "activities such as self-selected reading were not always viewed by the public as real instruction" (p. 302).

Worthy and her colleagues explain how students' long-term reading development and motivation to read is often sacrificed for temporary achievement gains: "When teachers are told, either explicitly or implicitly, that their major responsibility is to improve test scores, they may understandably be driven to spend precious class time on the option that leads to short-term results" (1998, p. 302). Thus, the message from administrators ought to be clear: Time spent "just reading" is a critical component of middle level instruction, and that conviction should be reflected in both scheduling and curricular decisions.

2. Middle level readers need good reading materials.

A group of sixth-grade reluctant readers interviewed by Worthy and McKool (1996) suggested that neither the school library nor their classroom collections contained books that were relevant to their personal interests, and this is probably typical of most middle level schools. Students reported they liked magazines (e.g., *Seventeen, Sports Illustrated*), popular series books (e.g., Stine's Goosebumps books), and scary books (e.g., *Scary Stories to Tell in the Dark*, Schwartz, 1981), but these were rarely available in school.

Bintz (1993) found that many of the resistant readers in his study were reluctant to read in school, but read extensively at home, and they were also drawn to magazines, popular books, and information books specific to their interests (e.g., romance novels, race cars, science fiction). Even high-achieving students who love to read may be secretly bothered by the kinds of texts they are required to read in school (Ivey, 1999), which may eventually lead to negative feelings about reading.

For many middle level students, particularly those who struggle with reading, having the right kinds of materials means not only having access to interesting texts, but also finding materials they *can* read. Unfortunately, textbooks and literature anthologies, which are the books middle level readers are most often assigned to read, are far too difficult for struggling readers and even many average readers.

Having to endure the task of reading books that are too hard not only makes struggling readers feel helpless (Kos, 1991) and unmotivated, but also may deter any progress in reading. Many struggling middle school readers who get frustrated when reading grade-level texts become enthusiastic about reading when they are given picture books, magazines, and easy-to-read chapter books that are close to their instructional reading levels. One should not assume that young adolescent readers will be embarrassed to read easy books in front of their peers. Worthy and her colleagues (1997) found that older struggling readers in their tutoring program read easy books "with gusto and not a hint of embarrassment" (p. 5).

Middle level readers also want opportunities to choose their own texts for reading (e.g., Atwell, 1987). Worthy and McKool (1996) reported that teachers and students they interviewed suggested there were few opportunities for choice in their curriculum. On the rare occasions when students were allowed to select their own topics (sharks, Martin Luther King), they reported positive experiences with reading.

Seventh- and eighth-grade students in another study (Stewart et al., 1996) identified choice as a factor in their overall reading improvement.

It is important to note that middle level students need real choice, including texts that span the gamut of genres and difficulty levels, and not just the opportunity to choose one novel from a selection of three or four books available in multiple-copy class sets. Although common reading experiences for all students in a class are important, particularly for purposes of discussion and critical thinking, one cannot escape the fact that any one grade-level novel will be either too difficult or uninteresting to a significant proportion of the class, especially for those students who most desperately need good instruction.

Teachers and administrators can create learning environments in which all kinds of texts are valued, especially if they adopt a principle of making difficult books accessible and easy books acceptable (Fielding & Roller, 1992) in their classrooms. In other words, they would demonstrate appreciation for a wide range of texts, from very easy to very sophisticated, and they would offer instructional support for students to read the more difficult books they cannot access on their own. Given the wide range of interests and abilities in any one middle grades classroom, access to an equally wide range of reading materials makes perfect sense.

3. For middle level readers, one size fits no one.

The wide range of development that exists in early adolescence is a generally accepted notion. When it comes to reading, however, individual differences take on two distinct dimensions.

First, there are notable differences between students. For instance, the range of reading achievement in any one middle level classroom may span from the early elementary level to the high school level (Pikulski, 1991). Certainly there is diversity in ability at all grade levels, but by the time students reach the middle level, instruction may have further widened the differences between students (Smith & Barrett, 1974). In addition, students who have not read much may have fallen even further behind both academically (Anderson, Wilson, & Fielding, 1988) and cognitively (Stanovich, 1986).

Second, there are inconsistencies and complexities within individual readers. A multicase study of sixth-grade students (Ivey, in press) revealed that regardless of achievement, individual middle level students were multidimensional as readers, and their reading abilities and dispositions toward reading varied with different contexts.

- Casey, who was a fluent and motivated reader, owned many books, read without hesitation at school and at home, and was quite confident in her ability. However, she was troubled by the mismatch between what she wanted to read and what she was asked to read in school, and this often affected her attitude about reading.

- Ryan seemed at first to be an average but reluctant reader. However, a closer examination showed that he actually used effective strategies for comprehension as long as the material he read was conceptually familiar to him and that his oral reading fluency was developing, particularly under the instruction of his teacher. He was quite motivated to read materials that he selected on his own.

- Allison, a struggling reader, appeared on the surface to be both unskilled and unmotivated as a reader. However, her reading was complex in a number of ways. Although her limited word identification skills prohibited her from reading most grade-level texts independently, she was very strategic in making sense of texts when they were read to her, and she became quite engaged when she listened. Whereas reading aloud in front of the class frustrated her, she was much more relaxed and willing to read in one-on-one and small-group settings. Finally, although she was not able to name many books she had read, she knew a small number of books well, and she had definite reading preferences.

These two dimensions of variability—both the wide range and differences between students and the complexities within individual students—have important implications for the reading curricula in middle level schools.

1. Given the variability that exists along both these dimensions, it is clear that students in the middle grades are still developing as readers, so their reading programs ought to include the teaching of skills and strategies, but only when it is appropriate and when it is based on ongoing assessments of their development.
2. No one curriculum or set of instructional strategies is suitable for all students all the time. Rather, teachers need to diversify their teaching in response to individual abilities and interests.
3. Given the multifaceted nature of young adolescents as readers, the reading curriculum ought to be multidimensional.

In practice, this means that students, rather than the curriculum, should be placed at the center of the middle level reading program. Since there is no one-size-fits-all plan, instruction must be driven by the learners. This is not to say the teacher relinquishes the responsibility for instruction. She or he must still ensure that students receive instruction in essential literacy skills and strategies (e.g., reading fluency, comprehension, spelling) and that students have a rich literacy environment in which to pursue their reading and writing interests. But, in a student-centered reading program, the teacher's role becomes more critical, because tailoring instruction to individuals requires that she or he act as an informed and careful decision maker, adopting a flexible perspective toward the curriculum. Spiegel (1998) recommends that teachers use student variability to their advantage: "Rather than trying to shoot each child with the same silver bullet, we need to recognize, celebrate, and work with this wonderful diversity."

Most teachers would probably agree that different students need different instruction. However, results of a recent survey (Tomlinson, Moon, & Callahan, 1998) indicate that middle level schools are not responding to this concern. Reports from teachers and principals suggest they do not organize for instruction in a way that addresses the wide range of developmental needs in middle level classrooms and that the curricula are far from being individualized. Furthermore, teachers were uncomfortable with the idea of differentiating instruction.

Principals of middle level schools can help facilitate and ease the transition away from a one-size-fits-all curriculum toward a more individualized, student-centered approach in at least three ways.

First, given the likelihood that textbooks are a major barrier to diversifying instruction (Bintz, 1997), principals ought to allocate resources for purchasing a wide range of reading materials across all the subject areas that accommodate varied reading abilities and interests among students. At the same time, teachers need opportunities to explore what materials are available and to familiarize themselves with ways to incorporate multiple texts into instruction.

Second, principals can resist the temptation to buy or mandate the use of commercially packaged materials (e.g., phonics programs, software packages) that claim to have a cure-all for reading problems. No one program matches the needs of all struggling readers or addresses the multifaceted nature of individual readers. A "quick fix" does not exist (Allington & Walmsley, 1995). Rather, for middle level schools the most sensible solution is a long-term commitment to professional development in literacy learning and teaching. When teachers begin to understand how literacy develops, they will be in the best position to find the right instructional fit for students.

Third, principals can support teachers' efforts to explore alternatives to the traditional whole-class instructional format. Formats such as the reading/writing workshop (e.g., Atwell, 1987; Roller, 1996) and flexible grouping (e.g., Radencich & McKay, 1995) are potentially good alternatives because they allow for both student choice and one-on-one and small-group instruction. However, teachers need to be assured that other members of the school community value classrooms in which different students are engaged in a variety of literacy activities at once, and in which the teacher and students share control of the curriculum and instruction. In addition, principals can both decrease the teacher-student ratio and increase the level of expertise for addressing diversity in classrooms by encouraging collaborative in-class relationships between regular classroom teachers and teachers of special populations (e.g., special education, reading resource programs).

Conclusion

In this article I have offered three basic suggestions for getting middle school students to read: giving them time to read; giving them access to books and other materials they want to read; and adopting a flexible, student-centered perspective on the curriculum. To suggest that implementing these three propositions would create a school full of readers would be naïve, overly optimistic, and overly simplistic. But I believe these principles form the basis for a major first step in building an environment that fosters the inclination to read.

The message to administrators and teachers is not a new one: Curriculum and instruction in middle level schools ought to be aligned with the complex nature of young adolescents as learners. For years, middle level schools have been reconceptualized and reorganized in response to research on the physical, social, and cognitive development of the students they serve. It is time to make significant advancements in what and how middle school students learn. The most promising direction for reading instruction seems to parallel broader recommendations for middle school reform. If we are to find the best ways to teach students, we must first pay attention to what they need.

REFERENCES

Allington, R.L. (1994). The schools we have. The schools we need. *The Reading Teacher, 48,* 14–29.

Allington, R.L., & Walmsley, S.A. (1995). *No quick fix: Rethinking literacy programs in America's elementary schools.* New York: Teachers College Press; Newark, DE: International Reading Association.

Alvermann, D.E., & Moore, D.W. (1991). Secondary school reading. In R. Barr, M.L. Kamil, P. Mosenthal, & P.D. Pearson (Eds.), *Handbook of reading research* (Vol. 2, pp. 951–983). White Plains, NY: Longman.

Anderson, R.C., Wilson, P.T., & Fielding, L.G. (1988). Growth in reading and how children spend their time outside school. *Reading Research Quarterly, 23,* 285–303.

Atwell, N. (1987). *In the middle: Writing, reading, and learning with adolescents.* Portsmouth, NH: Heinemann.

Bintz, W.P. (1993). Resistant readers in secondary education: Some insights and implications. *Journal of Reading, 36,* 604–615.

Bintz, W.P. (1997). Exploring reading nightmares of middle and secondary school teachers. *Journal of Adolescent & Adult Literacy, 40,* 12–24.

Fielding, L., & Roller, C. (1992). Making difficult books accessible and easy books acceptable. *The Reading Teacher, 45,* 678–685.

Ivey, G. (1999). A multicase study in the middle school: Complexities among young adolescent readers. *Reading Research Quarterly, 34,* 172–192.

Kos, R. (1991, Winter). Persistence of reading difficulties: The voices of four middle school students. *American Educational Research Journal.*

Ley, T.C., Schaer, B.B., & Dismukes, B.W. (1994). Longitudinal study of the reading attitudes and behaviors of middle school students. *Reading Psychology, 15*(1), 11–38.

McKenna, M.C., Kear, D.J., & Ellsworth, R.A. (1995). Children's attitudes toward reading: A national survey. *Reading Research Quarterly, 30,* 934–956.

Morrow, L.M. (1991). Promoting voluntary reading. In J. Flood, J.M. Jensen, D. Lapp, & J.R. Squire (Eds.), *Handbook of research on teaching the English language arts* (pp. 681–690). New York: Macmillan.

Nell, V. (1988). The psychology of reading for pleasure: Needs and gratifications. *Reading Research Quarterly, 23,* 6–50.

Pikulski, J.J. (1991). The transition years: Middle school. In J. Flood, J.M. Jensen, D. Lapp, & J.R. Squire (Eds.), *Handbook of research on teaching the English language arts* (pp. 303–319). New York: Macmillan.

Radencich, M.C., & McKay, L.J. (1995). *Flexible grouping for literacy in the elementary grades.* Boston: Allyn & Bacon.

Roller, C.M. (1996). *Variability not disability: Struggling readers in a workshop classroom.* Newark, DE: International Reading Association.

Schwartz, A. (1981). *Scary stories to tell in the dark.* New York: HarperCollins.

Smith, R.J., & Barrett, T.C. (1974). *Teaching reading in the middle grades.* Reading, MA: Addison-Wesley.

Spiegel, D. (1998). Silver bullets, babies, and bath water: Literature response groups in a balanced literacy program. *The Reading Teacher, 52,* 114–124.

Stanovich, K. (1986). Matthew effects in reading: Some consequences of individual differences in the acquisition of literacy. *Reading Research Quarterly, 21,* 360–407.

Stewart, R.A., Paradis, E.E., Ross, B.D., & Lewis, M.J. (1996). Student voices: What works in literature-based developmental reading. *Journal of Adolescent & Adult Literacy, 39,* 468–478.

Tomlinson, C., Moon, T.R., & Callahan, C.M. (1998, January). How well are we addressing academic diversity in the middle school? *Middle School Journal.*

Wasserstein, P. (1995). What middle schoolers say about their schoolwork. *Educational Leadership, 53*(1), 41–43.

Weisendanger, K.D., & Birlem, E.D. (1984, Spring). The effectiveness of SSR: An overview of the research. *Reading Horizons.*

Worthy, J., & McKool, S. (1996). Students who say they hate to read: The importance of opportunity, choice, and access. In D.J. Leu, C.K. Kinzer, & K.A. Hinchman (Eds.), *Literacies for the 21st century: Research and practice* (Forty-sixth yearbook of the National Reading Conference). Chicago: National Reading Conference.

Worthy, J., Patterson, E., Turner, M., Prater, S., & Salas, R. (1997). *Coming to love books: Reading preferences of struggling readers.* Paper presented at the 47th annual meeting of the National Reading Conference, Scottsdale, Arizona.

Worthy, J., Turner, M., & Moorman, M. (1988). The precarious place of self-selected reading. *Language Arts, 75*(4), 296–304.

Motivating Secondary School Students to Read Their Textbooks

Barbara L. McCombs and Mary Lee Barton

How can we motivate secondary school students to read their textbooks? The statistics cited in the *Report in Brief: NAEP 1996 Trends in Academic Progress* (NAEP, 1997) indicate that teachers' concerns about student reading are justified. Fifty-six percent of students age 13 and 47% of students age 17 reported reading 10 or fewer pages per day in school and for homework. In contrast, 61% of our nation's 13-year-olds and 46% of our 17-year-olds report watching at least 3 to 5 hours of television each day.

What has happened to young peoples' motivation to read? How can we create a school environment and curricula that will help motivate our students to want to read and learn?

We will attempt to answer these questions by examining

- what we know about students today and what they need,

- what current research says about motivation and the conditions that best promote motivation to learn and read, and

- what changes are needed in schools and classrooms to support student needs and promote higher levels of motivation for literacy learning.

Who Are Our Young People? What Do They Need?

Most educators and parents are aware of the tremendous changes that have taken place in our families, workplaces, and society in the past two to three decades. How have these changes affected this generation of school-aged children, and, in particular, how have they affected motivation for reading and learning in school? In our research on these issues (McCombs, 1997; McCombs, Peralez, & Lauer, 1998; McCombs & Whisler, 1997), we have identified a "bad news-good news" picture of who youngsters are and what they need.

On the bad news side, today's youth are being called the "Y Generation" and have been contrasted to both the "X Generation" and the

From the *NASSP Bulletin*, *82*(600), 24–33, October 1998. Reprinted with permission of the National Association of Secondary School Principals.

"Boomers" by Kreck (1998). Members of the Y Generation feel basically hopeless about the future; feel they deserve what they want; don't worry about being fired today because chances are good they'll be rehired somewhere else tomorrow; think that parents is no longer a plural concept; and believe teen death and killing are everywhere.

Many young people know only too well the reality of survival in an increasingly hostile and violent world. National statistics tell us suicide and homicide are now leading causes of adolescent death (Children's Defense Fund, 1998). In a study of 272,400 teenagers reported in *USA Weekend*, May 1998, teens reported that depression is common, with half saying they are occasionally really depressed. Nearly 1 in 3 teens say they have a friend who has discussed or attempted suicide. Friends are said to be most understanding, with 1 in 3 teens saying adults do not value their opinions. They also say they spend little time talking with their parents, with 1 in 5 saying they never talk to their parents more than 15 minutes a day.

In spite of these grim statistics, the good news is that our work and that of others (e.g., Johnson, Farkas, & Bers, 1997) indicates the current generation of school-aged children still do care about school and learning. Teens state, however, that they need more than they are getting from school right now. A survey of 10,000 high school students on what factors would motivate them to stay in school (Strong, Silver, & Robinson, 1995) reported their motivation would increase if schools were places where they could experience success (the need for mastery); curiosity (the need for understanding); originality (the need for creativity); and relationships (the need for positive involvement with others).

While the standards movement rightly has shifted the focus of education from the teacher to the learner, or from what teachers should teach to what students should learn, focusing on standards is not enough. Motivation and achieving challenging standards are possible only when there is a corresponding focus on the learner and his or her needs (McCombs & Whisler, 1997). Without this, we ignore students' calls for help when they say they think school is irrelevant, report feeling disconnected from their teachers and peers, or drop out mentally and/or physically because they just do not want to be in school.

When students feel a sense of belonging, feel competent, respected, and trusted to make choices—when these basic human needs are met in the classroom—it contributes significantly to healthful development, motivation for learning, and strong character. Meeting these needs is essential not only for eliciting motivation to learn but also for promoting a sense of personal responsibility for learning.

Meeting Students' Motivational Needs

We believe it is essential for administrators and teachers to work together to construct a climate and instruction, curriculum, and assessment that enhance motivation to learn. Research on the *Learner-Centered Psychological Principles* (APA, 1997; Presidential Task Force on Psychology in Education, 1993) tells us that students need to be supported personally in a classroom climate by teachers who

- believe in each student's capacity to learn,
- understand the research base on learning and learners,
- care about and get to know each student personally, and
- hold high expectations and challenge students to their highest levels of learning.

A schoolwide climate conducive to motivation and learning is created through a mission and organization that allows time for students to form meaningful relationships with teachers, administrators, and peers; and opportunities for mentoring with one significant adult who also helps connect with students' families and other support systems. If these conditions are created, students have been shown to develop positive views of themselves, each other, adults, and their personal and collective futures—all necessary to reach and teach the current generation successfully (Glenn, 1998; McCombs & Whisler, 1997).

Instruction, according to the *Learner-Centered Psychological Principles*, should allow for

- formation of meaningful adult and peer relationships,
- dialogue, collaboration, and expression of personal and collective views, and
- acknowledgment and respect for unique abilities and talents.

Curriculum should allow for

- connections to life issues and personal interests,
- challenge and talent development, and
- cooperative teaming when appropriate.

Assessment should allow for

- evaluation of and accountability for personal growth and progress,
- affirmation of and respect for unique skills and talents,

• reflection on learning process, and

• planning of next actions.

Applying Learner-Centered Principles to Literacy

The *Learner-Centered Psychological Principles* include a number of factors that have implications for motivation and reading in the content areas. One of these involves the impact that the learner's prior knowledge, experience, and perceptions have on the construction of meaning.

A reader's experience with, perceptions about, and prior knowledge of a topic act as a framework through which he or she filters new information and tries to make sense of what is read. Prior knowledge also acts as a structure to which the reader can attach new information (Barton, 1997). When students' prior knowledge of or experience with a topic is well developed, they understand and remember more of what they read (Anthony & Raphael, 1989). Moreover, when they are presented with strategies such as analogies that compare new information to be read with something familiar, comprehension and retention also improve (Alexander & Murphy, 1998; Hayes & Tierney, 1982).

Teachers can use many prereading strategies to help students access prior knowledge. Among these are K-W-L (Know, Want to Know, Learning strategy) (Ogle, 1986, 1989); Directed Reading/Thinking Activity (D-R-T-A) (Moore, Readence, & Rickelman, 1982); and the Pre-Reading Plan or PreP (Langer, 1981). Each of these strategies requires students to answer two essential questions:

1. What do I really know about this topic?

2. What new information do I need to learn about this topic?

The first question provides a structure to which the student can attach new information. The second question prompts readers to make predictions about what they will read and to set purposes for reading, two metacognitive skills that effective readers use (Vacca & Vacca, 1993).

The *Learner-Centered Psychological Principles* also recommend that learning tasks should stimulate curiosity, creativity, and higher order thinking. "Problematic Situations" is one strategy that fulfills those requirements; it activates what students already know about the topic, motivates them to want to read the text, and helps them to focus on the main ideas presented in the text as they read (Vacca & Vacca, 1993).

Before assigning a text passage that deals with a problem/solution relationship, the teacher designs a problematic situation similar to the one about which the students are going to read. For example, social studies students who will be reading about the problems Pilgrims faced settling in North America might be given the following problematic situation:

> You are leading a group of people who are traveling to the New World in the year 1612. You need to find a suitable location where there will be enough resources to support your group of 25 adults, where you can practice your religion as you wish, and where you will be able to establish your own form of government. Based upon what you know of the New World, explain where you would settle your group, why you would choose that location, and how your solution would ensure freedom of choice.

Language arts students who are going to read the short story "The Most Dangerous Game" by Richard Connell might be asked to discuss the following:

> A man is trapped on a small island covered with jungle vegetation. He has a three-hour head start on someone who is trying to kill him. The killer is well armed but the man has only a knife. The killer will be pursuing the man with hunting dogs.
>
> What could this man do to try to save himself? (Buehl, 1995)

In cooperative groups, students generate possible answers or solutions and justify their decisions. They compare their decisions with what they read in the assigned text material and refine or modify their solution as they gain new information from their reading.

Writing-to-Learn

Another type of learning task that encourages the use of originality and creative thinking is writing-to-learn. These short writing activities require students to reflect on and explore content area concepts about what they have read, which helps them to extend and refine what they learned. At the end of a unit, for example, the teacher might ask students to create an analogy, using the concepts or topics studied during the unit. After students spend time brainstorming a list of topics, the teacher displays a variety of common household objects, such as a broom, a calendar, a sponge, and a package of yeast. Students then write for 5 minutes, comparing in as many ways as possible how a concept studied in this unit is similar to one of these objects. Student responses require higher order thinking and are a thought-provoking review of what they have read.

Learner-centered practice also reflects the belief that learning is optimized when the learner finds what is being studied relevant and meaningful (McCombs & Whisler, 1997). Therefore, content area reading should provide a mix of "considerate" text (Armbruster, 1996)—well-organized, coherent, developmentally appropriate textbook material—and excellent trade books. The latter can provide in-depth, well-written, visually appealing, and timely information on concepts being studied. Schallert and Roser (1996) recommend using a range of trade books; this ensures that, regardless of reading level, students in the same classroom can choose to read material they like, which answers their questions about the topic being studied.

Allowing students to choose text material and to select from a range of performance tasks not only motivates them to learn, but also helps them become self-directed and self-regulating learners. As Ridley, McCombs, and Taylor (1994) have argued, responsibility begins with making choices and decisions, and with facing the consequences of those decisions. Providing students with an opportunity to choose gives them a sense of ownership over their actions. In fact, Zimmerman's (1994) research demonstrates that intrinsic motivation and self-regulation are only possible in contexts that allow choice and control. Zimmerman argues that if students are not given some choice and control, they are not likely to learn strategies for regulating their learning; they will not see any value to self-regulation strategies or willingly initiate and control the strategies.

Self-regulation is critical to effective reading and metacomprehension. If students are unable to regulate their behavior during reading, they will not engage in those metacognitive behaviors essential to effective comprehension; they will not plan for, monitor, modify, or evaluate their reading. Self-regulation is a natural outcome of motivation, promoted by providing students of all ages with appropriate choice and control that matches personal interests to required learning goals and standards.

Changes in Classrooms and Schools

We believe there must be a transformation in how we think about today's students, the kinds of classroom and school practices and policies that can best support their learning and motivation, and the roles that administrators and teachers play in the schooling and learning process. Our suggestions for a starting place follow.

Transformed Thinking About Youngsters and Motivation

The kinds of solutions that are needed to enhance student motivation to read go beyond the technical domain (e.g., the content, standards, curriculum) and organizational domain (e.g., management structures, decision-making strategies, policies) to focus on the personal domain (e.g., beliefs, assumptions, interpersonal relationships). One focus must be on helping all adults connected with today's students to examine their basic beliefs and assumptions about learners, learning, and teaching. Teachers, in particular, need permission and support to

- slow down and achieve a balance between spending quality time with students and focusing on standards, learning, and achievement;
- get to know all students personally and provide secure, caring environments for learning;
- build trust and communities of learning in classrooms and schools; and
- work with parents and community members to help them see who young people really are, what issues and pressures they face, and what they need.

New Practices, Structures, and Policies

Research has shown that the types of school and classroom level practices needed to best support high levels of learning and motivation are those that provide

- opportunities for active learning that address continuous academic and social growth;
- individualized performance expectations, support, and structures appropriate to the learner's needs and maturity;
- varied learning environments and reward systems that foster respect, trust, caring, and cohesiveness among students and school staff members;
- opportunities for student voice and input, including classroom and school rules cooperatively determined by faculty and students; and
- flexible curriculum and cocurricular activities that help students connect school learning with life goals and purpose.

Conclusions

In examining what we know about our current generation of school-aged children and what we know from research on motivation, we believe the following issues should be addressed to achieve the goal of enhancing reading engagement for all learners:

1. The need to consider personal, technical, and organizational influences within schools, families, and communities that influence

learners' beliefs, attitudes, and perceptions of their motivation to read.

2. The need for a research-based philosophy based on the best available knowledge about learning in general and the specific kinds of learning (literacy learning) as well as cognitive and affective individual differences in learners that must be considered to enhance motivation to read.

3. The need to align practices, programs, structures, and policies with this learner-centered and research-based philosophy in curriculum, instruction, organizational decision making, and management across classroom, school, and family contexts.

The key to motivating our students to learn, read, and develop unique and needed talents is to see that their needs for a healthful, safe school environment and for effective, stimulating, learner-centered instruction are met. We all need purpose and direction to foster optimistic views of ourselves and our future as well as motivation to learn and grow. Teachers and school administrators must share the responsibility for providing leadership and commitment to their role in setting up the conditions and connections today's students need to foster motivation. We must act on what we know about the needs of today's young people and how they can be met in our classrooms and schools.

REFERENCES

Alexander, P.A., & Murphy, P.K. (1998). The research base for APA's Learner-Centered Psychological Principles. In N. Lambert & B.L. McCombs (Eds.), *How students learn: Reforming schools through learner-centered education.* Washington, DC: American Psychological Association.

American Psychological Association. (1997, November). *Learner-centered psychological principles: A framework for school reform and redesign.* Washington, DC: Author.

Anthony, H.M., & Raphael, T.E. (1989). Using questioning strategies to promote students' active comprehension of content area material. In D. Lapp, J. Flood, & N. Farnan (Eds.), *Content area reading and learning: Instructional strategies.* Englewood Cliffs, NJ: Prentice Hall.

Armbruster, B.B. (1996). Considerate texts. In D. Lapp, J. Flood, & N. Farnan (Eds.), *Content area reading and learning: Instructional strategies.* Toronto: Allyn & Bacon.

Barton, M.L. (1997, March). Addressing the literacy crisis: Teaching reading in the content areas. *NASSP Bulletin, 81*(587), 22–30.

Buehl, D. (1995). *Classroom strategies for interactive learning.* Schofield, WI: Wisconsin State Reading Association.

Children's Defense Fund. (1998). *Every day in America: A report from the State of America's Children Yearbook.* Washington, DC: Author.

Glenn, H.S. (1998, June). *Developing resilient, capable youth.* Keynote speech at the Seventh Annual Rocky Mountain Regional Conference on Violence Prevention in the Schools and Communities: Building Assets and Leadership Skills for Youth, Denver, Colorado.

Hayes, D.A., & Tierney, R.J. (1982). Developing readers' knowledge through analogy. *Reading Research Quarterly, 17,* 25–80.

Johnson, J., Farkas, S., & Bers, A. (1997). *Getting by: What teenagers really think about their schools.* Washington, DC: Public Agenda.

Kreck, C. (1998, June 3). Talkin' to teens. *The Denver Post,* pp. 1F, 10F.

Langer, L.A. (1981).From theory to practice: A prereading plan. *Journal of Reading, 25,* 152–156.

McCombs, B.L. (1995). Alternative perspectives for motivation. In L. Baker, P. Afflerbach, & D. Reinking (Eds.), *Developing engaged readers in school and home communities.* Hillsdale, NJ: Erlbaum.

McCombs, B.L. (1997). Commentary: Reflections on motivations for reading— Through the looking glass of theory, practice, and reader experiences. *Educational Psychologist, 2,* 125–134.

McCombs, B.L. (1998). Integrating metacognition, affect, and motivation in improving teacher education. In B.L. McCombs & N. Lambert (Eds.), *How students learn: Reforming schools through learner-centered education.* Washington, DC: APA Books.

McCombs, B.L., Peralez, A., & Lauer, P.A. (1998, June). *Who are our kids? (And what do they need from us?).* Presentation at the Seventh Annual Rocky Mountain Regional Conference on Violence Prevention in the Schools and Communities: Building Assets and Leadership Skills for Youth, Denver, Colorado.

McCombs, B.L., & Whisler, J.S. (1997). *The learner-centered classroom and school: Strategies for enhancing student motivation and achievement.* San Francisco: Jossey-Bass.

McCombs, B.L., Whisler, J.S., & Lauer, P.A. (1997). *Maximizing the effectiveness of standards-based and standards-referenced educational models.* Aurora, CO: Mid-Continent Regional Educational Laboratory.

Moore, D.W., Readence, J.E., & Rickelman, R.J. (1982). *Prereading activities for content area reading and learning.* Newark, DE: International Reading Association.

National Assessment of Educational Progress. (1997). *Report in brief: NAEP 1996 trends in academic progress.* Washington, DC: Author.

Ogle, D.M. (1986). K-W-L: A teaching model that develops active reading of expository text. *The Reading Teacher, 39,* 564–570.

Ogle, D.M. (1989). The Know, Want to Know, Learn strategy. In K.D. Muth (Ed.), *Children's comprehension of text: Research into practice* (pp. 205–223). Newark, DE: International Reading Association.

Presidential Task Force on Psychology in Education. (1993). *Learner-centered psychological principles: Guidelines for school redesign and reform.* Washington, DC: American Psychological Association and the Mid-Continent Regional Educational Laboratory.

Ridley, D.S., McCombs, B.L., & Taylor, K. (1994).Walking the talk: Fostering of self-regulated learning in the classroom. *Middle School Journal, 2,* 52–57.

Rhule, P., & Soriano, C.G. (1998, May 1–3). 11th annual special teen report: Teens and self-image—Teens tackle their identity crisis. *USA Weekend,* p. S7.

Schallert, D.L., & Roser, N.L. (1996). The role of textbooks and trade books in content area instruction. In D. Lapp, J. Flood, & N. Farnan (Eds.), *Content area reading and learning: Instructional strategies.* Toronto: Allyn & Bacon.

Strong, R., Silver, H.F., & Robinson, A. (1995). What do students want? *Educational Leadership, 1,* 8–12.

Vacca, R.T., & Vacca, J.L. (1994). *Content area reading* (4th ed.). New York: HarperCollins.

Zimmerman, B.J. (1994). Dimensions of academic self-regulation: A conceptual framework for education. In D.H. Schunk & B.J. Zimmerman (Eds.), *Self-regulation of learning and performance: Issues and educational applications.* Hillsdale, NJ: Erlbaum.

One Teacher's Use of Computers and Technology: A Look Inside a Classroom

Mary Santerre

"**H**ey, Ms. Santerre, did you know there was a high school in Houston that's all online—no desks no building, no tardies, and *no dress code?*"

"No, Matt, I don't know which school you are specifically talking about, but I'm sure there is one because I'm aware of the existence of Web-based courses."

"Well, it does exist, Ms. Santerre. We got a brochure in the mail the other day about it, and I kind of think you might want to work there...but we sure would miss you in class everyday...you know, your literary insights, your laugh, your oom-pa-pa moments?"

Matt's question, made rather off-handedly one day as class was beginning, very much interests me and makes me ponder what the eighth-grade classroom of 2020 (the year of my projected retirement) will be like. Will our literature circles routinely include students from London, Paris, or Tokyo? Will our students be in conferences with literacy specialists and authors from all over the world? Even more basic, I wonder if we'll just occasionally meet in places with wired circuits for our laptops, or will conversations about literature never require our face-to-face meeting? I rather hope not, reflecting on Matt's appreciation of laughter and spontaneity in our place we now call school. There's a part of me that wants to believe that nothing will ever replace the immediacy of a shared physical space where two human beings come together in time and express their admiration of Atticus Finch, their outrage at Brother Jacques, or their empathy for Louie Banks. But perhaps that's a rather naïve hope on my part and a lack of understanding of what the world of technology will offer in 2020.

Regardless of what will come in the 21st century, I am quite aware of the impact of technology in my own teaching and learning at the close of the 20th century. If someone had told me in 1977—when I graduated from college and starting teaching—that within my career, I'd be teach-

From *Voices from the Middle,* 7(3), 33–40, March 2000. Reprinted with permission of the National Council of Teachers of English.

ing short story elements embedded in my own multimedia presentation, I would have simply shaken my head and said, "I don't even understand what you're saying." I could have never envisioned how abandoning the red-inked markers and overheads could give way to a Pentium 3 attached to an LCD projector for classroom presentations. And I could have never dreamed that I would be able to have a poet like Sharon Olds read her poem through Internet access as if she were standing behind the podium of our own classroom. Indeed, technology has changed my world of teaching and learning in a variety of ways, including,

- Professional growth
- Word processing
- Presentation of information
- Research on and access to the Internet
- Electronic literary magazines and portfolios
- E-mail and online discussions

Although I'm proficient in the use of technology, I am by no means an expert or a "techie." I am, however, a learner, and I am constantly exploring and working to improve my knowledge in all areas of my teaching, including technology. I depend daily on my students to help me navigate the information highway as I journey further into this age of information. My journey as a user of technology began in 1994 when I took my first class in Microsoft Word. I started using the computer as a storage place for all my Word documents—in a sense replacing my traditional manila folders with folders on the computer. Next, I began to experiment with multimedia and took a course in PowerPoint and HyperStudio. At about the same time, I began to explore the Internet and found that "surfing" took much time and energy. As time has passed these last 5 years, I've continued to grow in my knowledge of the computer and its uses in the language arts classroom. Now I realize that a computer, technology, and the information highway are an integral part of my teaching and my students' learning. That journey continues as I find that my own professional growth is occurring through online classes. Not only does this type of course work push me further into technology, it allows me to have conversations with teachers from all over. I'll continue to learn about technology, learn about teaching, learn about language arts through online discussions. As I do, I'll learn more about connecting my students to computers and technology, finding more ways to use these tools in my classroom. But I'm not at all disappointed with how I am using computers and technology in my classroom now, so step inside and see where computers have taken us.

Connecting the Writing Process With Word Processing

The whole process of writing has changed due to the word processing software now available. My students often grin at me or just look bewildered as I convey my utter delight in the copying and pasting functions of these programs. When I try to explain to them what liquid paper and the old Smith-Corona typewriter experience was like, they just don't get it, but of course, how could they? So, I just keep telling them how lucky they are to be able to rearrange text, delete, revise, insert, and spell check with just the click of a mouse.

While my students use Word to write papers, I use other features of word processing in our daily lessons. By using a projector that transfers my computer's screen image to a large screen at the front of the room, I am able to sit at my computer and type things that immediately appear on the large screen behind me for students to read. I use this capability as I make changes on their assignment sheets and class notes, as we brainstorm topics for writing assignments, as we look at drafts (mine and theirs), as we confront usage and style questions, as we practice daily edits, or as I deliver minilessons on the topic of the day. Since I type much faster than I write, this ability to "sit and deliver" keeps our lessons moving at a pace I never dreamed possible.

Of all the ways I use Word with students, I think I most enjoy my ability to share my writing process with students. Now I can keep my drafts of writing on my hard drive. As we move from brainstorming to drafting to revising, I can show them what my writing looked like at each stage as a model. For example, this past summer I read Donald Graves's *How to Catch a Shark*, which is a fabulous collection of essays on literacy, learning, and life. I knew as I read this book that I'd use several of Graves's topics and questions to help my students develop their own literacy stories. That meant I needed to write some of my own literacy stories. One such story was my recollection of those early reading experiences when we visited the bookmobile that came to our little town every summer. As I remembered, drafted, revised, and polished, I kept each draft in a folder on the computer. When school started and I wanted students to create the same type of stories, I simply pulled out *How to Catch a Shark*, accessed my folder, prompted students (as Graves odes) with a series of questions that focused them on their earliest memories of visiting books, then let them write. The combination of Graves's stories, my own writing, and the questions created powerful writing. I'll never forget the opening line to Doug's story: "The echoing screams fill the room, but the silence of the library is never broken."

Students like Doug bring their various drafts to class in their different stages for conferences and revisions. Students either work on drafts on their home computers or in our computer lab during lunchtime or after school. All of my students have a file on the network where they may store various works in progress and then simply pull their work up and print it out in our classroom writing sessions. Most students save their work on a disk and carry their work back and forth from home to school. The computer has changed this process of writing in fundamental ways, and now the presence of our one classroom computer is absolutely essential to our daily writing! (That's right—just one computer in our classroom; however, with the large screen projection ability, I use that one computer in remarkable ways.)

From Posters to PowerPoint

In Jane Healy's *Failure to Connect*, Healy says that for effective integration of technology to occur in schools, teachers must "build learning from what is known for teachers as well as students. Introducing teachers to new technologies is most effectively done by reducing the implicit threat of change" (1999, p. 68). In other words, start with what you know and move from there. That's good advice. For me, that advice just means that my presentation (done traditionally on overheads or written on the board) evolves, as one student put it, from poster to PowerPoint. Healy continues, "For example, emphasize that multimedia is not an end in itself, but rather one more means to accomplish familiar educational goals" (p. 68). PowerPoint or HyperStudio presentations are just new ways to dress up how information is delivered.

So, I've kept the message and changed the delivery system. For example, I teach short story elements now with a PowerPoint presentation instead of chalk and a blackboard. When I want students to understand the process of story from precipitating event to denouement, I use a PowerPoint slide presentation on *The Empire Strikes Back*. To make this lesson the grabber I know it needs to be, I have incorporated imported sound waves and stunning graphics downloaded from the Web. Similarly, PowerPoint has helped me present introductory lessons on authors we will study as well as poetry and yes, even minilessons in grammar.

PowerPoint teaching is powerful and, at first, time consuming. Time consuming for me, at least, because I didn't know what I was doing! But with continued practice, some good classes in PowerPoint, and time in the summer to build my presentations, the job of constructing a PowerPoint slide presentation became more and more routine. Also, I've found colleagues who are creating their own PowerPoint presentations. What we do now is what we call B&B—barter and beg! I beg for Karen's parts of speech presentation and she barters with me for my short story elements presentation.

While my use of PowerPoint is important, I have another goal: I want my students to use it as they share their knowledge with the class. They need these multimedia skills as much or more than I do. Returning to Healy's belief that we build learning from what is known, I ask my students to start our year together by writing a poem about the things they prefer. This "I Prefer" poem helps us learn who we are as we begin to build our community of learners and gives students a piece of text to use for their first PowerPoint presentation. After their poems are written, we head off to the computer lab to learn how to create slides for their presentations. For many of my students, creating a PowerPoint slide presentation is nothing new; for others, it's a move into the unknown. In the end, though, after all poems are built into PowerPoint presentations, the students save their work on the network drive. The next week, I ask the students to pull up their "I Prefer" presentations to share with the entire class from one classroom computer. (See Figure 1 for a copy of Sean's slide presentation.)

In addition to having interesting, moving text, many students insert sound files and fascinating graphics to enhance their presentations. I have devised a rubric that assesses the technical aspects of presentation since I've already assessed the writing during the previous week. Figure 2 is a copy of the rubric we used for the "I Prefer" PowerPoint presentation. The first venture into PowerPoint opens doors for students. They spend the rest of the year designing card stacks for HyperStudio presentations and slides for PowerPoint presentations in our language arts classroom as well as other courses. They become adept at inserting sound files and graphics. They move with ease from posters to PowerPoint and show me constantly that multimedia is the presentation mode they prefer.

Let's Go Surfin' Now: Electronic Options

I drive to school humming that Beach Boy classic, "Let's go surfin' now, everybody's learnin' how, come on and surfari with me…" and smile as I know that the surfin' I've got in mind doesn't need an ocean. It will require a computer and access to the Internet and I've got both. With those two things, Internet access has become a daily occurrence in our classroom.

Figure 1
A condensed version of Sean's PowerPoint presentation

For example, recently I was talking to my students about the heightened sense of one's place in the universe when one is ill or maimed. Our discussion was a result of our reading the scene in *April Morning* (Howard Fast) when Adam Cooper witnesses his father's death. From that discussion, we talked about the writer's or poet's ability to sense the essence of life and its uncertainties. One of my students referred to the "brief candle" speech from their reading of an abridged *Macbeth* in the seventh grade. Then, in a flash, I thought of John Keats's "When I Have Fears That

---

Figure 2
Rubric for PowerPoint "I Prefer" poem

Title Slide (slide 1):

I Prefer...

By: (Student's name)

4   3   2   1

Slides 1–8
Do print and graphic move on each slide?

Slide 1_____   Slide 2_____   Slide 3_____   Slide 4_____

Slide 5_____   Slide 6_____   Slide 7_____   Slide 8_____

Overall assessment of slides 1–8 for placement of text, movement, etc.

4   3   2   1

End slide (Does it state "The End" with a review of graphics used as an optional feature?)

4   3   2   1

Edited text? (Is the text edited and does the text cover the text box completely?)

4   3   2   1

Overall creativity and presentation of PowerPoint

4   3   2   1

Overall score: _____

Comments: _____

I May Cease to Be." In the old days, I would have had to crack open my *Norton Anthology of English Literature* and photocopy the page and share the next day with my students, or at best do an oral reading of the text. With the immediacy of the Internet, I was able to quickly locate the poem (http://portico.bl.uk/exhibitions/keats/reputation.html) with a voice file attached, project it on the screen, and have the students hear the text read from Real Time Player and then read the words of Keats's poem—without any delay in our discussion. Now that's a teachable moment!

Later in the year, on the Friday before the Martin Luther King holiday, we came to one of my favorite lessons. We accessed a variety of sites that I had researched, allowing us to take a virtual tour of the significant places involved in his life and death, from the steps of the Lincoln Memorial to the balcony of the Lorraine Motel.

In addition to using the Internet to access sites that complement what we are studying, students use the Internet to help with assignments and research. For instance, the eighth-grade students do online research to find out about poets for our poetry unit or about the Revolutionary War for information to use in their Revolutionary War newspapers, or to preview Williamsburg and Washington, D.C. in preparation for the annual eighth-grade trip to these cities of historical significance.

When students use the Internet to conduct research, the issue of authenticity of source must be examined carefully. I think it is my responsibility as a language arts teacher to help students learn to be critical readers of Web sites. To learn to do this, we constantly study sites together and ask ourselves questions about who the author is, when information was updated, what the purpose of the site is, and what information is at the site. These simple, basic questions remind my students that when knowledge is only a click away, careful reading must be a part of every click. When students learn to access information from the Internet, the Internet truly becomes (to borrow Doug's title from his piece about the magic of libraries) a "vault of knowledge." Indeed, it's a library at our fingertips with knowledge only a keystroke away!

Electronic Literary Magazines and Electronic Portfolios

Two years ago at The Village School, we made a decision to stop printing the literary magazine in hard copy and go to an electronic literary magazine that could be accessed from a link on our Web page (www.thevillageschool.com). It has saved a great deal of money in publication costs, and it is readily accessible for all of our students at any time. In addition, students and parents may view the types of writing that are available in the language arts classrooms whenever they wish.

In addition to the electronic literary magazine, the existence of the electronic portfolio looms in our near future. Since students are also including an extensive array of multimedia text in their portfolios, it only makes sense that the traditional writing portfolio move from the filing cabinet to a zip drive disk for future access. Contained on the zip drive will be all of their multimedia work and their files of Word documents that would include their poetry, critical analysis, response writing, and miscellaneous pieces of work. E-literary magazines and e-portfolios fit into this electronic world we all inhabit.

E-mail and Online Discussions

I remember waiting for the mail when I was a child. I wanted something in the mailbox just for me. I'm still waiting for the mail—but now my mailbox is on my computer and the mail I'm looking for is sometimes mail from my students. My students are able to e-mail me messages with attachments of their papers as well as correspond with me if they are absent. The most recent e-mail that I required my students to send was a postcard constructed from a link off the Kodak home page (www.kodak.com); the postcard's message was written from the point of view of one of their characters in their independent reading (see Figure 3). It was interesting to see what snippet of information was shared on the postcard since the message space was limited. The Kodak exercise forced my students to become succinct in their analysis of what message would best indicate the "heart" of their character's voice.

Perhaps the most significant impact of electronic communication has been in the area of online discussions about the books that my students read. I first learned about online computer conversations from Marilyn Jody and Marianne Saccardi at the International English Convention held a few years ago in New York City. When I read their statement, "We believe that computers can become a powerful force, one as powerful as books themselves became with the advent of printing, in creating the universally literate community of our dreams" (xvii), I was fascinated with the prospect of what our own classroom community could become.

So, this past summer I finally got busy and decided this was the year the online discussions with my students were going to happen. With tremendous help from my technology coordinator and support technology staff, we decided the best method was to rent space on a Web bulletin board that could be accessed from our home page. We began by having our own online discussions about a professional book we were reading; that familiarized us with the process.

Next, I allowed my students to choose the books they were reading in groups. The technology coordinator "keyed" in the names of the group members so that only those members could have access to that discussion group. This was a necessary security step to ensure that our conference areas would be private to our school community.

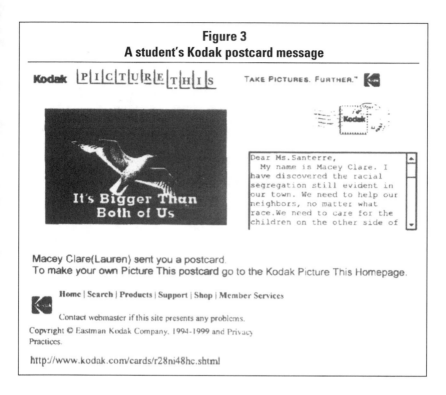

Figure 3
A student's Kodak postcard message

Kodak ⌊P⌋⌊I⌋⌊C⌋⌊T⌋⌊U⌋⌊R⌋⌊E⌋⌊T⌋⌊H⌋⌊I⌋⌊S⌋   TAKE PICTURES. FURTHER."

It's Bigger Than
Both of Us

Dear Ms.Santerre,
   My name is Macey Clare. I
have discovered the racial
segregation still evident in
our town. We need to help our
neighbors, no matter what
race.We need to care for the
children on the other side of

Macey Clare(Lauren) sent you a postcard.
To make your own Picture This postcard go to the Kodak Picture This Homepage.

Home | Search | Products | Support | Shop | Member Services

Contact webmaster if this site presents any problems.
Copyright © Eastman Kodak Company. 1994-1999 and Privacy
Practices.

http://www.kodak.com/cards/r28ni48hc.shtml

Students have enthusiastically embraced this method of discussion. It doesn't mean that we don't have our rich classroom talk as well, but it provides a vehicle where the group members may discuss the book as they read. The conference area may be accessed from our computer lab, any classroom, the library, or from home. Figure 4 is an excerpt of a discussion on Julius Lester's *Othello* that shows the type of discussion that occurs through e-mail.

Online conversations are fascinating because of the ways students respond in their own time. Recently, one of my students said, "Ms. Santerre, you know what's great about this method of talking? I don't have to come up immediately with a witty, intelligent thought. Actually, now I just stare at the Web board and read what others say…and then when I'm ready, I type in my thoughts and post them. Wow—I like being able to think about what I want to say." That comment really got my attention. It's so "eighth gradish" to want to be perceived as witty and intelligent.

Another aspect that I've enjoyed from a teacher's perspective is that I can participate in all the conversations of the groups, whereas in traditional reading literature circles, I usually could only hear bits and pieces of the conversations. Keeping up with all the postings is easier since I've

Figure 4

Matthew, Jackie, and I "talk" about Lester's book *Othello* via our online discussions

Topic: Othello's Trust
Conf: Power - Period Two
From: matthewD@thevillageschool.com
Date: Tuesday, October 26, 1999 08:20 PM

sup, y'all
Why do you think Othello places such implicit faith in Iago, yet he doubts Desdemona so easily? Is it because of D's and Michael's friendship? And is Michael really worthy of Othello's trust, especially as a lieutenant?

Matthew

Topic: Othello's Trust
Conf: Power Period Two
From: JackieO@the villageschool.com
Date: Tuesday, October 26, 1999 10:21 PM

I think that Othello trusts Iago and doubts Desdemona because he has known him longer, has always known him to be faithful (but he doesn't know that he's wrong) and because what Iago says seems to hold some truth in it, and as the saying goes, better safe than sorry. However, I think that Othello would be sorry if he acted safe. I also think that Michael is worthy of his post as lieutenant even though he loves Desdemona because I believe him loyal to Othello and Desdemona. Since he loves Desdemona he would never do anything to lose her good opinion of him (unless, of course, he was deceived, inveigled, or obfuscated) and since he respects Othello he wouldn't jeopardize his lowered reputation.

Btw the quote "deceived, inveigled, and obfusticated"[sic] (I think that was the word they used) came from X-files and I think I got music to work this time! The song sorta applies to Othello and Desdemona...

[*Editor's note:* Jackie inserted a sound file as a part of this mail. The song he chose is about loving someone forever.]

Topic: Othello's Trust
Conf: Power - Period Two
From: Ms.Santerre@thevillageschool.com
Date: Wednesday, October 27, 1999 03:54 PM

Oh my goodness...Jackie...this is SOOOO cool! That you inserted the sound file...fabulous...

Your thoughts...are so interesting that precede the sound file...your response to Matthew...very interesting...reasoning...   *(continued)*

Topic: Othello's Trust
Conf: Power - Period Two
From: MathewD@thevillageschool.com
Date: Thursday, October 28, 1999 12:50 PM

Nice music. Another song that might be somewhat pertinent would be that "My Guy." Ya know, "Nothin' u can do would make me…" Well anyway, it's just a thought. Don't laugh. Personally, Jackie, I don't think Michael is really deserving of the rank of lieutenant. He is supposed to make firm decisions, yet he is so easily enticed to get drunk by Iago. True, he is loyal to Othello, but he is soooo easily manipulated. Also, one thing that I think causes Othello to trust Iago, would be his color, as well as their long "friendship." Des is white; in her innocence, she can look past colors, but Othello has lived w/ so much discrimination that he cannot learn to trust, or truly love.

Matt

Topic: Othello's Trust
Conf: Power - Period Two
From: Ms.Santerre@thevillageschool.com
Date: Wednesday, October 27, 1999 03:47 PM

Ah….Matthew…this is such an interesting question…and gets to the heart of character motive…which is such an imp. skill to analyze…I think you've suggested an interesting proposition…Des. And Michael could potentially have a relationship…and that might put Othello ill at ease…but…go back to what you already know from the tragic flaw study…from Macbeth…Is there something just inherent in him that makes him doubt? And is this part of human nature in general?

Topic: Othello's Trust
Conf: Power - Period Two
From: MatthewD@the villageschoo.com
Date: Thursday, October 28, 1999 12:57 PM

As a soldier, Othello is naturally alert. He needs to be prepared for any contingency. Though he is overwhelmed with his "love," it subsides, and the suspicion lurking in his heart again arises. Both Emily and Des are soo unaware of anything. Emily thinks of Des as a child, yet she has no doubt of her husband's motives. Des is completely oblivious to her husband's doubts. They, though total opposites, are still unenlightened of their husbands' mindsets. I doubt that Des will ever realize what's happenin'.

Matt

had students print out their posts once a week and place them in their writing folders. We then use these printouts as a basis for their in-class discussions. Finally, I enjoy reading the comments of the "quiet" students, those students whose voices are rarely heard in class. Some of their thoughts and commentary online have been fabulously insightful.

My future online discussion plans have my students teaming up with other eighth-grade classes to create an even larger literature circle. We'll begin by including other eighth graders in our own city, and later branch out to hear the voices of eighth graders from all around the United States, as so many of my colleagues are doing already. What a great frontier of literary discussion awaits us!

And so...

Returning to Matthew's question about the classroom without walls and space, I sit here and ponder technology's impact on me, our classroom, and our collective future. I would have never dreamed that I would be such an active participant in this digital world—from the use of Word to multimedia presentations to Internet use and online discussion groups. I love the computer and all that it offers my students and me in our journeys in literacy. I can't imagine life without technology now!

The use of technology, though, requires a willingness on my part to be a learner, a commitment from school budgets to purchase equipment and train teachers, and, of course, time. Just as there is a learning curve for any new skill, learning to manipulate a computer and travel on the information highway has been challenging—but I wouldn't go back to a world of typewriters and isolation from the outside world for anything! Each new day when I arrive at school, the first order of business is to turn on my computer, check my e-mail, and pull the files from the computer filing cabinet that I will access and use to share reading and writing with my students.

I think about Matthew's deeper question: Will there ever be a day when I'm not needed? I can say unequivocally, "No!" Even though the Web texts are fabulous and the online conversations are alive and the access to places or people is unlimited in our technologically advanced world, somehow I just have to believe that we'll all gather in a place and share our stories and our lives, and my presence will continue to act as a guide to my students. I think it's not only the laughter that Matthew would miss, but it's our collective experience of seeing a pair of eyes roll when I tell a corny joke, or hearing an aha sigh and seeing a nod of understanding when we all finally understand something we've read or talked about. Our classroom is a place where we will continue to share worlds and expressions together, but it's technology that will allow us to travel to places we once only dreamed of knowing.

REFERENCES

Fast, H.M. (1983). *April morning.* New York: Bantam.

Graves, D.H. (1998). *How to catch a shark and other stories about teaching and learning.* Portsmouth, NH: Heinemann.

Healy, J.M. (1999). *Failure to connect: How computers affect our children's minds— and what we can do about it.* New York: Simon & Schuster.

Jody, M., & Saccardi, M. (1998). *Using computers to teach literature: A teacher's guide.* Urbana, IL: National Council of Teachers of English.

Lester, J. (1998). *Othello* (adapted from William Shakespeare). New York: Scholastic.

Writing Portfolios: Active vs. Passive

Bonita L. Wilcox

> All we can say for certain is that our definition of portfolios ought to move, grow, and change as we see what portfolios can do and as we continue to apply them in practice for ourselves and for our students. (Donald Graves & Bonnie Sunstein, *Portfolio Portraits*, 1992)

The passive portfolio has earned recognition as a method of assessment; however an active portfolio that can generate ideas and teach new ways of thinking offers unlimited possibilities for teachers and learners. While the passive portfolio sits on its laurels, the active portfolio is a place to record, collect, and fine-tune thinking as perceptions and ideas are formulated and reformulated. A passive portfolio is a "showcases" portfolio out of the writer's hands, while an active portfolio is a "working" portfolio that changes and grows with new input as it creates and generates new output. The learning is in the process itself, and teachers need to show students how to think about the process more carefully.

The Passive Portfolio

Although passive portfolios may be vivid and colorful, they lack the creative spirit of the active, working portfolio. For example, think about the collections parents put together, saving all the important papers their children carry home from school. I, for one, took the best pieces of writing from each year, added those precious notes preschoolers write to Mom, and put them together in a folder. In addition to this writing folder, I had some other documents in a scrapbook, newspaper clippings, certificates of achievement, birthday cards, photos, etc. I combined the artifacts in a three-ring binder. This was the first portfolio I ever put together. It tells a good story, but it is a passive portfolio. For posterity's sake, it is great; but it cannot change or grow or help its creator learn new information or to become more literate.

Many states have writing portfolio assessment programs in place. Determining beforehand what students should know and be able to do and agreeing on guidelines for collecting and scoring examples is considered to

From the *English Journal*, *86*(6), 34–37, October 1997. Reprinted with permission of the National Council of Teachers of English.

be a significant improvement on multiple-choice testing. Moreover, the idea of having the teacher, the parent, the curriculum specialist, the school administrator, textbook publishers, and teacher educators all working toward the same goals certainly seems like a sound approach.

Unfortunately, these portfolios are of little long-term benefit to individual learners even when they have selected and defended their best pieces. Portfolios with high stakes are collections of past work rather than projects that increase learning and improve performance. This kind of large-scale assessment portfolio is passive. It cannot change and grow.

Many teachers-in-training use a showcase portfolio to organize and highlight their successful experiences when they are ready to interview for a teaching position. The contents typically include reference letters, a teaching certificate, a transcript, the student's philosophy of teaching, an A paper, a supervisor's evaluation, a scholarship award, etc. Administrators seem to appreciate this extra effort because, aside from the information that the portfolio contains, they feel that the portfolio reflects organizational skills, decision-making skills, and literacy skills as well as indication of classroom experience. Although this requires creativity and is a reflection on past achievements, this portfolio is also passive. It is not a learning tool.

Another kind of portfolio used by junior faculty during the early years at the university requires that novice professors gather evidence of their accomplishments for promotion and tenure. Portfolio assessment is used at the university level as assistant professors approach third-year review and tenure (Edgerton, Hitchings, & Quinlan 1991; Seldin, 1993). Documents and materials related to teaching, scholarship, and service are displayed and explained for others to evaluate. Somewhat like an artist's portfolio, the professor's best works can be examined through student evaluations, tests, course syllabi, speaking opportunities, and especially publications. The content and organization of this portfolio can determine the professor's future. Its importance as an evaluative tool is obvious, but it too is passive. Its purpose is for making personnel decisions, not for improving performance.

When the National Board for Professional Teaching Standards began looking at "what classroom teachers should know and be able to do," portfolio assessment was the choice for making some of those decisions (Petrosky, 1994). School Site Portfolios were used to help in the assessment of teacher knowledge in order to determine whether teachers meet the requirements for certification by the National Board for Professional Teaching Standards. However, a recent article in *English Journal* clearly demonstrated the need for teachers to oppose efforts toward the "standardization" of teacher assessment (Petrosky, 1994). A passive, "rank and sort" portfolio would not be helpful to teachers attempting to learn from their own experiences in order to improve their teaching practices.

Moving to the Active Portfolio

Historically, we have come a long way in a very short period of time. In reviewing the last 10 years when little has been published on portfolios, researchers in writing assessment at the university level were investigating better ways to assess (Burnham 1986; Camp 1985; Elbow 1987).

Roberta Camp was exploring the writing portfolio for placement in the transition from high school to college. Peter Elbow was concerned with writing proficiency and portfolios with college writers. Donald Graves described the reading/writing folder, conferencing, and keeping track of younger students in *Writing: Teachers and Children at Work*. Nancie Atwell described a reading/writing workshop (process) approach for middle school students. In secondary classrooms, we wondered how a collection folder could be more helpful to writers in high school.

Teachers began to question the folder's contents. When carefully chosen, the contents could illustrate a developmental story of a student's writing over time. But upon close examination, it also told a story about writing instruction. It was useless to argue that a 45-minute writing sample could be as informative as a collection of long-term artifacts. Teachers soon discovered that by imitating the process used by "published" writers, students became more engaged in their writing. When students made decisions and judgments about particular pieces of writing, they gained a sense of ownership in their writing. When students were asked to share their writing, they became more responsible writers.

Whether the teacher was looking for evidence of growth and development or indicators of skill levels and writing competency in a variety of genres, the process portfolio was obviously more informative for the teacher and more helpful to the writer. The most significant change, however, came from the initiation of prewriting strategies and thought-provoking journal prompts.

You may wonder how a journal can magically transform a passive writing folder into an active portfolio. Consider the following scenarios. Miss Passiviti is a traditional teacher. She knows about journals. Her students take notes in their journals. They outline chapters and write summaries. When she gives an overview and tells the students about the important aspects of texts, they record everything. The students use this information to write papers, and the best ones are placed on the bulletin board.

Mrs. Activiti, on the other hand, takes a different approach. She has the students doing double-entry journals: They record text notes in one column and their questions or comments in the other. She tells the students that this is the next best thing to having a conversation with the author. Instead of lectures and quizzes, she uses journal prompts and questions to encourage reflective thinking. Students discuss, debate, and share their ideas before Mrs. Activiti assigns group projects where problems are solved and projects presented. Students make handouts to illustrate their ideas and explain their thinking. Their formal papers are sent to real publishers after self-assessment, peer assessment, and teacher assessment. Students can look at their thinking and learning patterns and connections in a final reflective journal write.

With a thinking journal at the heart of the portfolio, it can be magically transformed into a thoughtful, active portfolio. The developmental process can be seen as the journal changes and grows with each experience, interaction, and reflection. Consider the outcomes outlined in Figure 1.

Figure 1
Passive to active outcomes

PASSIVE

1. Students have read a text and taken notes or written a summary.
2. Teacher gives quiz on reading, consisting of five recall questions.
3. Teacher goes over quiz and begins a discussion emphasizing the important aspects.
4. Students write a paper from one of the important aspects of class discussion.
5. The teacher hangs the best papers on the bulletin board for parents' night.
6. Final assessment is done by the teacher, or raters will holistically rank and sort the unknown students' papers.

ACTIVE

1. Students have written a double-entry journal response of dialogue with text, using questions and comments to clarify and extend their thinking.
2. Students are asked to draw their responses to the text. Papers are evaluated in groups of four students.
3. Students still in groups are asked to explain their thinking as they evaluate peers. Students articulate what they know while making sense of the drawings.
4. Students prepare a presentation for the class using their own drawing incorporating the new ideas and thoughts recently gathered from others.
5. Students work in pairs to put a publishable piece together. Peers assess the work, suggesting ways to improve it. The best pieces are sent to a publisher, and the rest are bound for use in the classroom.
6. Students assess their own work with checklists. They review the work of their peers. They defend and justify their assessment strategies. Thus, they learn to monitor and manage their own learning.

Figure 2
Artifacts in an active portfolio

Reading Artifacts
Making connections through reading.
Diagrams
Booklists
Booknotes
Summaries
Outlines
Sketches/drawings

Thinking Artifacts
Constructing our own knowledge base.
Dialogue
Responses to prompts
Process memos
Tracing thinking charts
Steps to problem solving
Mind maps

Writing Artifacts
Making meaning through writing.
Self-evaluations
Formal papers
Poems/letters
Publication piece
Reflections on learning
Written plans

Interacting Artifacts
Sharing and scaffolding ideas.
Peer assessments
Group consensus
Brainstorming charts
Arguments
Defending/justifying
Problems and solutions

Demonstrating Artifacts
Application and transfer of learning.
Video
Speech
Oral interpretation
Creative drama
Project
Exhibition

Active Portfolios

The active portfolio has a diversity of artifacts that are assessed in a variety of ways (see Figure 2). Although tests are not mentioned as an outcome of the active portfolio, traditional tests can be added to any portfolio. The point is that when different artifacts are evaluated in different ways by different evaluators, the chances increase for one more authentic assessment of the final portfolio. Furthermore, classroom assessment strategies become models for students to follow as they learn to manage and monitor their own learning. Students who actually use a variety of peer- and self-assessment tools begin to understand how assessment and learning connect.

Active portfolio strategies increase student learning. The reflective, meaning-making process is evident in the artifacts. The learning process itself is the most valuable feature; the active working portfolio enables students to see their learning progress, while at the same time it allows them to understand that the assessment process is in itself a learning experience. From a teacher's perspective, the active portfolio becomes a more accurate tool for assessment, but primarily it focuses on an individual's learning process.

An active portfolio that can generate ideas and initiate new ways of thinking offers unlimited possibilities for enhancing teaching and learning. Creating an active portfolio enables students to know what they know and how they came to know it. The processes of recording, collecting, and selecting are not enough; constant and continual assessing, interacting, reflecting, and sharing are processes that engage students and lead to personal growth and change.

The active portfolio is a powerful process resulting in meaningful connections that enable students to take the responsibility for their own learning. The active portfolio lets students see that learning is what portfolio assessment is really about.

REFERENCES

Atwell, N. (1978). *In the middle: Writing, reading, and learning with adolescents.* Upper Montclair, NJ: Boynton/Cook.

Burnham, C. (1986). Portfolio evaluation: Room to breathe and grow. In C. Bridges (Ed.), *Training the new teacher of college composition.* Urbana, IL: National Council of Teachers of English.

Camp, R. (1985). The writing folder in postsecondary assessment. In P. Evans (Ed.), *Directions and misdirections in English evaluations.* Urbana, IL: National Council of Teachers of English.

Edgerton, R., Hitchings, P., & Quinlan, K. (1991). *The teaching portfolio: Capturing the scholarship in teaching.* Washington, DC: American Association of Higher Education.

Elbow, P. (1987). Using portfolios to judge writing proficiency at SUNY Stony Brook. In P. Connolly & T. Vivlardi (Eds.), *New methods in college writing programs: Theory and practice.* New York: Modern Language Association.

Graves, D. (1983). *Writing: Teachers and children at work.* Portsmouth, NH: Heinemann.

Petrosky, A. (1994, November). Schizophrenia, the National Board for Professional Teaching Standards' policies, and me. *English Journal, 83*(7), 33–42.

Seldin, P. (1993). *Successful use of teaching portfolios.* Bolton, MA: Anker.

"Is This Really English?": Using Young Adult Literature in an Urban Middle School

Rebecca J. Joseph

*"I*s this really English?" one of my students asked me recently during class. When asked to clarify his question, Jerrard, an eighth grader, replied: "We can talk about anything in here."

Jerrard's comment followed a lengthy class discussion about breast-feeding that resulted from reading a section in Mary E. Lyons's *Letters From a Slave Girl: The Story of Harriet Jacobs* (which I will refer to as *Letters*) where 19th-century Harriet remembers that her grandmother had to stop breast-feeding her own daughter to feed her owner's daughter. A class discussion about the injustice of the situation expanded to a general conversation about breast-feeding and reasons why mothers do and don't breast-feed.

Each year, I try to start off with a provocative young adult novel that will not only help students develop their reading and writing abilities but will also help sharpen their abilities to connect the literature with their own life experiences and will initiate great conversations. For the 3 years I taught at a racially integrated middle school, I began the year with Jerry Spinelli's *Maniac Magee*, which enabled my classes to investigate and question racism initially through the character of Maniac and eventually through themselves.

This year I am at a brand new city middle school with a 100% African American population and with a schoolwide commitment to explore the African American experience. I chose to begin with *Letters* because I felt the issues covered in the text would spark lively and meaningful classroom discussions as well as provide lots of fodder for reading and writing assignments.

From *Voices from the Middle*, 5(2), 21–25, April 1998. Reprinted with permission of the National Council of Teachers of English.

Conversations

When reading and discussing a novel, I encourage students to discuss any issue arising from the book that interests them. I never know where classroom discussions will go. One student, Brandon, was so stunned by the horrific treatment of Harriet by her owner Dr. Norcom that he asked me if my relatives ever owned slaves. I answered with the truth that my relatives had not come to the country until the late 1880s when slavery was over. Not deterred by my response, he countered with, "But what would you do if you found out that you were related to Dr. Norcom?" I replied that if I had lived during the period there was slavery, I would have done everything in my power to oppose it. Brandon seemed satisfied with my answer, saying, "You're lucky you're white. If I was alive back then, I would not let anyone touch me. I wouldn't have lived long."

Provocative questions like Brandon's delight and at times stump me. Young adult literature and the vibrant young characters that come to life in them help my students become active participants in their reading. Other conversations have centered on Nat Turner and the effect of his revolt on other slaves in the country, the underground railroad and reasons why slaves did and did not escape, and the reasons why people keep journals. One class began a 15-minute debate about whether Harriet's brother should have escaped from slavery like he did or should have stayed behind to take care of Harriet, his grandmother, and his nephew and niece.

"He better not have left me behind," Joniece stated to begin the conversation. "It's his own life, Harriet can take care of herself," countered Kenneth. "She has no right to be mad at him."

"But what if Samuel does get made at Harriet's kids. I know they better not come near me or my children," exclaimed Marquita. This lively conversation weaving personal reactions in with specific analysis of the text continued until I asked the students to finish their thoughts in their journals.

Using young adult literature has enabled me to talk about sensitive topics in the classroom. A 20-minute conversation about the use of the word *nigger* resulted from reading a passage from *Letters*. We talked about how uncomfortable it is to see the word in print, how saying the word aloud doesn't mean you use the word, and how black people often call each other nigger but don't like it when white people do. The novel offered a safe haven for discussing this topic.

Other sensitive topics included discussions about premarital sex and Harriet's decision to have relations with a white man. In the neighborhood where I teach, 5% of eighth-grade girls become pregnant, and many more are sexually active. The boys and girls in all of my classes began to squirm when Harriet talks about her decision to have sex with an older white man as a way to stop another man from harassing her. Debating Harriet's decision enabled us to begin a discussion about current peer pressure to have sex. Boys and girls alike began to admit their concerns with feeling pressure to have sex when they weren't ready. Talking about the pros and cons of Harriet's decision helped the students relax and enabled them to discuss situations they personally had experienced.

Parent/Guardian Permission

While the city school system approved my teaching of the text, I sent a letter home before we read the book informing parents about the book's mature content and asking for their permission to use the book with their children. Every parent/guardian agreed to let his or her child read the book. If a parent said no, I was prepared to use an alternative text.

In fact, so many children went home and described their daily reading and conversations with their relatives that I began to receive requests from students to borrow copies of the book for their parents. I fortunately had 40 extra copies of *Letters* from a grant I had received 2 years ago. That way, when parents began to ask if they could read the book, I was able to send copies home with their students. At a parent night, one woman told me she had read the book until two in the morning, she found it so interesting. Another student informed the class that her mother had read the book in one night and wanted to know if I could recommend any other books.

I have an open door policy for parents to borrow books from my lending library. In fact, I have submitted a grant to begin a parent/child book discussion group.

Relating to Other Facets of English

Reading

While we read a book in class, students have a comprehension packet of questions in front of them that they need to answer by the end of each section of the book. I try to use the questions as guides for their reading and to help keep their focus on the text. Even when students read independently or with partners, I want them to have packets to help guide their reading. During the year, I design fewer and fewer of the packets; the students design their own.

Moreover, each October all middle school students in Maryland take a functional reading test that they need to pass to graduate from high school. Questions center on locating information, reading maps, following directions, and identifying the main idea of a passage. There are no official practice materials so I center all our practice time on questions relating to *Letters*. In the back of the book, the authors included a series of maps, family trees, and pictures all directly drawn from Harriet Jacobs's life. I use all of these documents in our practice sessions for the functional test.

Writing

All year long, teachers are expected to assign narrative and expository writing prompts to students in preparation for a January statewide writing test for seventh and eighth graders. I introduce the different prompts through the literature we are reading and help the students learn to develop fully detailed and organized essays through their responses to the text.

A typical city prompt about attending a dinner party left many of my students confused. Few had even been to a dinner party. I adapted the prompt for the students to describe a dinner party they would give to Harriet if they had been alive during her lifetime. Then I was able to connect this writing assignment back to the original one, explaining that if they hadn't ever experienced what was asked for in the assignment, they should use their imaginations to generate a complete essay.

I also ask my students to connect the reading to their own lives in their writing. I assign many open-ended writing activities with no right or wrong answers. Even though we spend much of our class time discussing the differences between Harriet's experiences and ours, I think it is important for the students to begin to probe possible similarities.

Their responses are amazing. Chantelle wrote, "We both talk to our mothers about everything even though my mother is still alive and hers isn't. We both look out for our brothers...." Her classmate Ryan responded, "We are similar because we have dreams, emotions, and feelings. We are also similar in heritage. Another way we are similar is in our beliefs."

After reading their comments, I photocopy several to share with all the students. The students meet in small groups to discuss their own responses to the question and to come up with examples to support the general ideas.

Journals

Students write daily in their journals, either in class or as homework. Sometimes I assign topics related to our readings in class. Topics have included designing their own wills, giving Harriet advice about running away or staying, or charting the improvement of her spelling and overall writing. Other times students write about their reactions to the text.

Students design the cover of the *Letters* sections of their journals with their own adaptations.

Valantina called hers "Letters from Valantina" and wrote her journal entries to different important people in her life. Her anger at Dr. Norcom's behavior toward Harriet caused her to write directly to him: "Dear Dr. Norcom: Dr. Norcom I think you should keep your hands off of Harriet."

Another student, Sam, called his journal "Letters from King Sam," and wrote an entry describing how lucky he was to live in a time where there was no more slavery because "I would be dead now because I couldn't allow my relatives to be treated so badly."

Other times students become critical of the protagonist's actions. "I disagree with Harriet. I would go back," Shante wrote, "I would not put my kids or family in jail no matter what."

Grammar

I have a class set of grammar texts and am expected to cover intermediate grammar skills with my students. Rather than use the texts directly, I first read students' writing assignments and select the skills they need to improve, adapting the grammar text assignments to fit with the novel we are reading. For example, my students needed work on writing in complete sentences. After introducing the difference between fragments and complete sentences, I gave them a series of fragments from *Letters* to make into complete sentences. I do the same with other grammar-related activities.

Vocabulary/Spelling

Rather than introduce unrelated vocabulary or spelling words, I take the words directly from the young adult novel. Words like *emancipation*, *oppression,* and *fidelity* become our weekly vocabulary/spelling words. When the students see the words directly in the context of their readings, they are able to retain the words and use them in their own writing.

Poetry

I use *Letters* as a way to introduce my students to the wonderful poetry of many African American poets including Langston Hughes and Nikki Giovanni. Langston Hughes's poem "Baby" connects wonderfully with Harriet's concern for her brother and the use of dialect. In Hughes's poem "Dreams," he compares a dying dream to a bird with a broken wing, which complements Harriet's description of herself in hiding as a bird with a broken wing. (Both are in *The Dream Keeper and Other Poems*, 1994.) Giovanni's poem "Legacies" (from *The Selected Poems of Nikki*

Giovanni, 1996) explores the difficulty relatives have communicating with each other and caused students to revisit the text of the novel to look for places where Harriet and her grandmother had trouble communicating.

Interdisciplinary Connections

During one of our opening teacher meetings, I did a brief book talk on *Letters*. All of the teachers expressed a strong interest in reading the book, as did the office staff. I provided each one with a copy and requested that each teacher plan to include a lesson or two related to the book in their own classes. Everyone agreed to participate. The social studies teacher taught several lessons related to the novel. She focused on the geography of the setting along with the key political movements that laid the backdrop for the novel. The science teacher did a fascinating lesson on the muscles of the body, explaining why Harriet's legs deteriorated during her years in hiding in her grandmother's 3-foot-high attic.

Other Readings

There are many other wonderful texts that supplement *Letters*. I use excerpts from Julius Lester's collection of slave narrative, *To Be a Slave*, to give students an opportunity to look at other slave writings. I also do a book talk on *Incidents in the Life of a Slave Girl*, the autobiography Harriet Jacobs wrote from which Lyons drew most of the information for her novel. I provide the students with selections from this text to compare with Lyons's writings. This way they are able to distinguish between nonfiction and historical fiction, a separation they had a difficult time making at the beginning of our reading of the novel.

Mary E. Lyons also wrote *Keeping Secrets: The Girlhood Diaries of Seven Women Writers*. I introduce this book to the class via a book talk. Her new novel, *The Poison Place*, examines the life of Moses Williams, a former slave of Charles Willson Peale. While all of the boys in my classes have been fascinated with *Letters*, they like to look at a book that centers on a man.

Other related books that I give book talks on include two of Ann Rinaldi's historical fiction books. The first is *Wolf by the Ears*, which explores the life of another Harriet, Harriet Hemings, the alleged daughter of Thomas Jefferson and one of his slaves. One of the students asked during a class discussion whether Harriet's children would have been slaves if they had looked white. I referred her to *Wolf by the Ears*, and 2 weeks later, she made a class presentation about the dilemma Harriet

Hemings faced about staying with her family or assuming the life of a white woman and leaving. In response to a question about what other kinds of writing slaves did, I introduced Rinaldi's book *Hang a Thousand Trees With Ribbons*; the novel explores the life of Phyllis Wheatley, the first African American woman to publish. It focuses on the challenges she experienced while trying to publish her writing and deciding whether to live as a slave in Boston or a free woman in England.

I also invite the local librarian in at the end of each novel. At the end of *Letters*, she brought in a wide variety of books that related to the novel.

Literature Matchmaking

Inviting students to read is never very difficult. Wherever I teach, my classroom is always filled with young adult literature ranging from biographies to novels to short stories to anthologies to poetry collections. I take my reading matchmaking responsibilities seriously. I use classroom time to help develop students' abilities to analyze and respond to novels. Encouraging them to read independently is a major goal. Using adolescent literature in my curriculum is a great starter.

In addition to exposing students to a wide variety of books related to the novel we are reading, I also try to discover my students' previous reading experiences and preferences by having them fill out a reading survey at the beginning of the year—often I am shocked by their limited reading experiences in elementary school, and the high number of them who put Goosebumps books on their list of favorite books. However, I look at their interests and attempt to introduce them to books they might like.

I constantly add to my collection through purchases from my favorite local children's bookstore or from books I review for a local children's literature newsletter. I do weekly book talks about my new library additions along with old favorites. I use the book talk model Hal Foster recommends in his text *Crossing Over: Whole Language for Secondary English Teachers*. My book talks start with a personal connection with the text, a quote, a brief summary, and a review. The personal connection with the book always brings the students in. I extend the option for students to do books talks on their independent readings for extra credit.

My lending library is constantly in flux. I have a library book sign-out that has no due date but I do encourage students to return the books as soon as they finish them. Certain books disappear for good. I watch other students pass popular novels from one to the other before the books make their way back to the library. Some of my young adult books have adult content. I ask my students to bring in a note from their parent saying they have permission to read before letting them sign out the book.

Conclusions

Young adult literature is a wonderful way to encourage my urban students to read. By selecting books that pique their interest, I am able to help develop their fundamental skills along with encouraging them to participate in lively conversations. There is nothing better than having students realize that talking about books is not an isolated classroom activity, but a way to connect with their entire lives.

REFERENCES

Foster, H. (1994). *Crossing over: Whole language for secondary English teachers.* New York: Harcourt Brace.

Giovanni, N. (1996). *The selected poems of Nikki Giovanni.* New York: William Morrow.

Hughes, L. (1994). *The dream keeper and other poems.* New York: Alfred A. Knopf.

Jacobs, H. (1988). *Incidents in the life of a slave girl.* New York: Oxford University Press.

Lester, J. (1968). *To be a slave.* New York: Dial.

Lyons, M.E. (1992). *Letters from a slave girl: The story of Harriet Jacobs.* New York: Aladdin.

Lyons, M.E. (1995). *Keeping secrets: The girlhood diaries of seven women writers.* New York: Henry Holt.

Lyons, M.E. (1997). *The poison place.* New York: Atheneum.

Rinaldi, A. (1991). *Wolf by the ears.* New York: Scholastic.

Rinaldi, A. (1996). *Hang a thousand trees with ribbons.* New York: Scholastic.

A Commitment to Comprehensive and Collaborative Programs

There is no "silver bullet" program that will inoculate schools against reading problems just as there is no one "right method" for teaching (Duffy & Hoffman, 1999). Successful literacy programs for adolescents are the result of creation, not imitation, but the process of creation must be guided by an awareness of the literacy needs of adolescents and a vision of the literacy demands they will face as adults. A set of broad criteria can be derived from theory, research, and experience.

Literacy programs for adolescents begin with curriculum objectives. They form the "what" of a literacy program, and instructional strategies such as those described in the last section provide the "how." Developing and evaluating programs also requires answering questions about *who* should be involved, and *when* and *where* literacy growth should be expected to occur. What roles, for instance, should be played by parents, by content area teachers, and by reading specialists? Are the literacy experiences students have outside of school a useful part of their development, or are they distractions that compete with the school for the student's attention?

The goals of a literacy program for adolescents should be comprehensive. They should go beyond a handful of objective, testable outcomes. As critics of the standards movement often point out, standards tend to embody the knowledge and skills that today's "educated" people find most valuable (Brady, 2000), but they do not guarantee that adolescents will be prepared for the literacy needs of tomorrow. As they mature, adolescents can construct meanings using their rapidly accumulating personal experiences and learn to use reading and writing to help them define who they are and how they relate to their communities. An instructional emphasis on displaying "basic" skills may conflict markedly with these developmental needs.

Library media centers and cyberspace are important locations for literacy learning if students are to go beyond a narrow canon of classic literature and "one-size-fits-all" textbooks. Given an adequate budget, sufficient time, and Web access, library media specialists can help teachers deliver instruction that encourages students to use and create a wide range of language genres from classic books to popular media. A comprehensive literacy program cannot be confined to a few classrooms. It must permeate instruction and the learning environment of the school. If respect for the usefulness of literacy is demonstrated both tacitly and explicitly throughout the building, students will come to accept and expect reading and writing as part of their learning lives.

Resources outside the building and beyond the school day are also worth considering. After-school activities involving parents, community organizations, and businesses can help to close the gap between in-school and out-of-school lives of adolescents. Such activities can stretch the literacy program beyond its usual limitations.

Moore (1998) uses the analogy of "full-service programs" to characterize comprehensive literacy programs that are focused on the personal, social, and literacy needs of all adolescents, including those who are "at-risk." He notes that full-service reading programs help students accommodate potentially limiting identities with literate academic identities, and he includes a wide range of interpersonal collaborations and interactions under the umbrella of literacy. These include mediating between students and teachers, involving parents, publicizing achievements, and mentoring students' transitions to college or the workforce.

Collaboration is an important element in comprehensive programs. Just as it is important to use all the available time and materials, it is important to make use of all the available human resources to support students' literacy development. This may mean renewing or reinventing the relationships between teachers and subjects in middle schools and secondary schools. All teachers may not see themselves as teachers of reading, but every teacher does, in fact, teach lessons about the place of reading and writing, even if those lessons are taught through silence. Content teachers need to be a part of the effort to improve students' literacy, but their role cannot be mandated from the outside. Teachers need time to explore how literacy can enhance teaching their favorite content, and they need to be convinced that the school's literacy goals do not contradict a regard for content. This may mean that content teachers, principals, and reading specialists, among others, need to work together around broad goals such as improving communication skills, problem solving, or higher level thinking in ways that integrate literacy rather than place it in the foreground.

The articles in this section have been chosen to aid anyone who is attempting to reexamine or reinvent a program to develop adolescent literacy at the classroom, building, or district level. Strauss and Irvin provide an overview of comprehensive programs at the middle grade level. Although all aspects of successful programs are included, the article pays special attention to showing how the "what" of a program—the overarching objectives—should be based on an understanding of adolescent development. Jack Humphrey's article highlights the crucial role played by a well-supplied and well-staffed library media center in expanding students' access to a wide range of materials. Feirsen argues that schools must create a "culture of literacy" and shows how every aspect of the school program can contribute to the message that literacy learning is important, enjoyable, and attainable.

Patricia Anders and Geraldine Henwood both focus on the "who" of the reading program as they demonstrate ways in which educators can collaborate in pursuit of broad goals that are intended to benefit all students. James Rycik expands the view of people involved to include the still-important contribution of parents, and Martha Magner focuses attention on the possibilities for meaningful reading and writing that can come from involving students with members of the community through service learning. Taken together, these articles show how schools can provide a "full-service" literacy program by making use of all the resources that are available.

REFERENCES

Brady, M. (2000). The standards juggernaut. *Phi Delta Kappan, 81*(9), 648–651.

Duffy, G., & Hoffman, J.V. (1999). In pursuit of an illusion: The flawed search for a perfect method. *The Reading Teacher, 53,* 10–16.

Moore, D.W. (1998). Metaphors for secondary reading: Choosing one or choosing several. *NASSP Bulletin, 82*(600), 10–15.

Exemplary Literacy Learning Programs

Susan E. Strauss and Judith L. Irvin

Young adolescents entering the middle grades are faced with multiple challenges to proficient literacy learning. First, the amount of reading and writing required for successful academic progress in the middle grades increases substantially from that required of elementary school students. Second, content area courses such as social studies, science, language arts, math, music, art, and technology are likely to require that students read and understand texts in each academic area. These texts are primarily expository and often complex, detailed, and filled with difficult vocabulary. The reading demands of such expository texts are often quite different than those of the narrative text that comprises the bulk of elementary school reading (Irvin, 1998). "Students in the middle years face increasingly complex literacy challenges as they move from a curriculum where acquiring initial literacy knowledge and competencies permeates their school day, to a time when their literacy skills and interests are prerequisites for success across the school curriculum" (Hosking & Teberg, 1998, p. 332).

The complex processes of literacy do not occur in a vacuum; they are negotiated within and influenced by a social and cultural context (Bloome, 1989; Cazden, 1988; Delpit, 1995; Finders, 1997; Gee, 1990; Heath, 1996; Hynds, 1997). Interactions with peers, teachers, and parents form the framework within which students in the middle grades practice and develop as literacy learners. During the course of early adolescence middle grades students are deeply involved in the process of forming an identity. This identity formation, affected by the developmental tasks of early adolescence, is "constructed and constrained" (Finders, 1997) by literacy. Hynds, in a 3-year ethnographic study which focused on the literacy development of nine adolescents in their middle school language arts classroom, concluded that "rather than mastering a set of discrete, decontextualized skills, students engaged in a complex array of social practices that defined and developed their identities as readers, writers, and language users" (1997, p. 26).

Literacy learning is a complex and fluid act; it is determined by the demands of the task and influenced by the communicative style and lan-

From the *Middle School Journal*, *32*(1), 56–59, September 2000.

guage experiences the learner receives in the home. Furthermore, as the young adolescent progresses through the rapid and profound stages of physical, moral, emotional, social, and cognitive development, literacy learning can "facilitate the young adolescent's progress through these essential stages; conversely, as the young adolescent works through these developmental tasks, they [sic] become more adept at literacy" (Irvin & Strauss, 2000, p. 116).

Effective literacy learning programs in middle grades schools are informed by the developmental tasks of early adolescence; they are student centered, flexible, and responsive to students' needs (Davidson & Koppenhaver, 1993; Strauss, 2000). The responsibility for teaching and encouraging literacy learning is shared by all teachers and administrators; it is not the sole domain of those who teach language arts classes. Student writing is encouraged across the curriculum, and school staff members have been trained in writing strategies and assessment. Students are provided with school environments in which literacy learning thrives: A variety of appropriate and interesting text is available to them, and they are given regular opportunities to read and interact with other readers. Students in effective literacy programs are provided with knowledge about and practice with reading and comprehension strategies. In these programs, the needs of struggling readers are not ignored. They are provided with appropriate instruction by trained reading teachers who believe that struggling readers can become successful readers.

A Student-Centered Philosophy

Too often school structure is determined by tradition and routine; it is important for school staff and administrators to examine the way students are scheduled, taught, and treated within the school program and adopt a willingness to change according to the individual needs of the students. Students should be allowed "credible and autonomous voices at school" (Powell, Skoog, & Troutman, 1996). Bean (Bean, Bean, & Bean, 1999), through "intergenerational conversations" with his two teenage daughters regarding various forms of discourse they used regularly, offers a definition of content literacy as a "concept of functionality [that] suggests that adolescents allocate varying levels of energy and interest to literacy activities serving particular functions in their lives" (p. 445).

School staff and administrators in schools that demonstrate academic success believe that all students can learn and that it is the responsibility of all those in the school program to facilitate that success. Rather than dismissing some students as unwilling or unable to learn, they actively seek ways to structure their classroom activities and their school-wide program in ways that support a diverse array of student needs and learning styles. Time at school and staff expertise are used to the fullest: Students in homeroom or advisory group might be involved in remediation work, academic games, or schoolwide silent reading. Teachers and administrators share knowledge and skills with each other, engage in ongoing assessment of student needs and ways to address them, and work together to design and redesign an effective school program (Strauss, 2000).

Students in the middle grades progress through the rapid and profound changes in development that define early adolescence. These changes affect every aspect of their lives and most certainly their school experiences. Young adolescents work through the developmental tasks of adolescence within a primarily social framework so there is a tremendous need to belong to a group, to feel accepted, to communicate, to compare, and to share with each other and members of the school staff. "When teachers present non-motivating course work, create a mismatch between [a] student's learning preferences and instructional practice, or have as their primary focus 'covering the course' with little recognition of individual student needs, the results are often student disengagement" (Hosking & Teberg, 1999, p. 3).

Literacy Learning Is Emphasized Across the Curriculum

Language arts teachers whose responsibilities include the teaching of reading, writing, spelling, grammar, vocabulary instruction, and oral language skills cannot possibly design opportunities for in-depth study in one 50-minute class period per day. Students in effective programs are afforded more time throughout the school day for literacy learning; some possibilities are flexible scheduling to afford students larger blocks of time for more in-depth study, a reading class in addition to a language arts class so that more instructional time can be spent on reading and writing, incorporating reading into a content area course like social studies, or an integrated curriculum that incorporates reading and writing activities throughout the school day. Literacy learning is encouraged throughout the curriculum by regularly including reading and writing activities in other content areas (Strauss, 2000).

To address the reading needs of middle grades students, effective literacy programs include multiple opportunities to engage in literacy learning: Students are asked to read different types of text regularly, and they are involved in reading-related activities such as written or creative responses to literature, research projects, or discussion groups. Time is scheduled for silent reading, and students have choices in what they read (Davidson & Koppenhaver, 1993).

Class reading selection reflects knowledge of the interests and concerns of young adolescents; the availability of quality young adult literature that is relevant, interesting, and challenging to young adolescents increases the likelihood that students will become actively engaged as readers. This is supported by the Adolescent Literacy Committee of the International Reading Association which in *Adolescent Literacy: A Position Statement* declares, "Adolescents deserve access to a wide variety of reading material that they can and want to read" (Moore, Bean, Birdyshaw, & Rycik, 1999, p. 25). Likewise, Moje, Young, Readence, and Moore (2000) state that "even marginalized readers and writers often read popular texts [such as comic books and magazines] with fluency and enthusiasm" (p. 406).

In effective middle grades literacy programs, reading strategies are taught to facilitate student comprehension of demanding text (Davidson & Koppenhaver, 1993; Farnan, 1996; Irvin, 1998; Moore, Bean, Birdyshaw, & Rycik, 1999; Oldfather, 1995; Walker-Dalhouse, Dalhouse, & Mitchell, 1997). Comprehension strategies are used across the curriculum, and "may be as simple as underlining a main idea or as complex as organizing an entire chapter into a graphic organizer" (Irvin, 1998, p. 168).

The Needs of Struggling Readers Are Addressed

Students need to be engaged in literacy events, but they also must be enabled (Roe, 1997). Much of the academic success in schools is based on students' ability to read and comprehend text, so when students struggle with reading demands, they experience frustration and failure in most classes. Struggling readers need attention, and they benefit from a reading expert who can assess their reading needs and offer appropriate instruction and practice. (Moore, Bean, Birdyshaw, & Rycik, 1999; Strauss, 2000). Small classes taught by a trained reading professional and which offer students opportunities to read and be involved with text allow these less confident readers to see themselves as readers and writers. In a 5-month naturalistic investigation of sixth-grade readers, Ivey (1999) found the following recurring themes: Struggling readers "like to read when they have access to materials that span the gamut of interests and difficulty levels...want opportunities to share reading experiences...need real purposes for reading...and...want to be and can become good readers" (pp. 373–378). Effective teachers of struggling readers also help their students manage the reading demands from other classes as they grow as readers and literacy learners.

Conclusion

What do literacy programs in academically effective middle grades schools look like? They are organized around teacher and student teams that facilitate collaboration and communication between teachers who share the same students, which, in turn, are supported by a leader within the school community. Effective literacy programs in the middle grades emphasize literacy learning across the curriculum; reading and writing are not relegated to one language arts class, but are taught and encouraged in other content areas and/or a reading class scheduled in addition to language arts classes. Classes are scheduled and designed to meet the needs of struggling readers. Faculties include trained reading professionals. Evidence that literacy is valued in these schools can be found in interesting and accessible materials, instructional methods, beliefs about literacy learning, school organization, and school culture.

Effective middle grades literacy programs are student centered. As Davidson and Koppenhaver (1993) describe successful compensatory literacy programs, "they are both good literacy programs and good adolescent programs" (1993, p. 221). The needs of individual students drive the school schedule, curriculum, and instruction; students are treated with respect and are rewarded and recognized for their achievements. Literacy is celebrated in an exemplary middle grades program, and everybody wins.

REFERENCES

Bean, T.W., Bean, S.K., & Bean, K.F. (1999). Intergenerational conversations and two adolescents' multiple literacies: Implications for redefining content area literacy. *Journal of Adolescent & Adult Literacy, 42*, 438–448.

Bloome, D. (1989). Beyond access: An ethnographic study of reading and writing in a seventh grade classroom. In D. Bloome (Ed.), *Classrooms and literacy* (pp. 53–106). Norwood, NJ: Ablex Publishing.

Cazden, C.B. (1988). *Classroom discourse: The language of teaching and learning.* Portsmouth, NH: Heinemann.

Delpit, L. (1995). *Other people's children: Cultural conflict in the classroom.* New York: The New York Press.

Davidson, J., & Koppenhaver, D. (1993). *Adolescent literacy: What works and why.* New York: Garland.

Farnan, N. (1996). Connecting adolescents and reading: Goals at the middle level. *Journal of Adolescent & Adult Literacy, 39*, 436–445.

Finders, M.J. (1997). *Just girls: Hidden literacies and life in junior high.* Urbana, IL: NCTE.

Gee, J.P. (1990). *Social linguistics and literacies: Ideology in discourses.* London: The Falmer Press.

Heath, S.B. (1996). A lot of talk about nothing. In B.M. Power & R.S. Hubbard (Eds.), *Language development: A reader for teachers* (pp. 55–60). Englewood Cliffs, NJ: Merrill.

Hosking, N.J., & Teberg, A.S. (1998). Bridging the gap: Aligning current practice and evolving expectations for middle years literacy programs. *Journal of Adolescent & Adult Literacy, 41*, 332–340.

Hosking, N.J., & Teberg, A.S. (1999, April). *Structuring support for change in the middle years literacy program*. Paper presented at the American Educational Research Association, Montreal, Canada.

Hynds, S. (1997). *On the brink: Negotiating literature and life with adolescents*. New York: Teachers College Press.

Irvin, J.L. (1998). *Reading and the middle school student: Strategies to enhance literacy* (2nd ed.). Boston: Allyn & Bacon.

Irvin, J.L., & Strauss, S.E. (2000). Developmental tasks of early adolescence: Foundation of an effective literacy program. In K. Wood & T. Dickinson (Eds.), *Promoting literacy in grades 4–9: A handbook for teachers and administrators* (pp. 115–127). Boston: Allyn & Bacon.

Ivey, G. (1999). Reflections on teaching struggling middle school readers. *Journal of Adolescent & Adult Literacy, 42*, 372–381.

Moje, E.B., Young, J.P., Readence, J.E., & Moore, D.W. (2000). Reinventing adolescent literacy for new times: Perennial and millennial issues. *Journal of Adolescent & Adult Literacy, 43*, 400–409.

Moore, D.W., Bean, T.W., Birdyshaw, D., & Rycik, J.A. (1999). *Adolescent literacy: A position statement*. Newark, DE: International Reading Association.

Oldfather, P. (1995). Commentary: What's needed to maintain and extend motivation for literacy in the middle grades. *Journal of Reading, 38*, 420–423.

Powell, R., Skoog, G., & Troutman, P. (1996). On streams and odysseys: Reflections on reform and research in middle level integrative learning environments. *Research in Middle Level Education Quarterly, 19*(4), 1–30.

Roe, M. (1997). When middle level students don't read and write well enough: Combining enablement and engagement. *Middle School Journal, 28*(3), 35–41.

Strauss, S.E. (2000). Literacy learning in the middle grades: An investigation of academically effective middle grades schools. Unpublished doctoral dissertation, Florida State University, Tallahassee, Florida.

Walker-Dalhouse, D., Dalhouse, A.D., & Mitchell, D. (1997). Development of a literature-based middle school reading program: Insights gained. *Journal of Adolescent & Adult Literacy, 40*, 362–370.

Supporting the Development of Strong Middle Grades Readers

Jack W. Humphrey

In all curricular areas except reading, schools demonstrate continuous support for young people's learning. Basic mathematics skills are a prelude to geometry and calculus. Children learn how to turn on computers and use the keyboard in lower grades and engage in elaborate computer activities in higher grades. Band members learn to play their instruments in lower grades and then perform in higher grades. Sports in lower grades prepare students for competition in higher grades.

In reading, however, we often act as if students are competent by the sixth grade and place the burden on them to continue to improve their skills and to choose to read without encouragement. As a result, almost every measure of voluntary reading shows a decline from elementary to the middle grades.

A recent example is the number of students who participate in the Young Hoosier Book Award Program, an Indiana program sponsored by school librarians to promote voluntary reading. A total of 56,720 students voted for their favorite book in the grades K–3 category. Participation dropped to 17,535 in the grades 4–6 category, and further dropped to 7,239 in the grades 6–8 category (Fall 1997, 1998).

Library circulation tells the same story. During the 1997–1998 school year for the same students, the average library book circulation for Indiana K–5 schools was 46.1 books per student. This compares to 15.3 for students enrolled in 6–8 schools and 8.5 for students enrolled in 7–12 schools (*Young Hoosier*, 1998).

There is also strong evidence that reading scores begin to decline when students leave the elementary grades. This decline in reading scores appears to correspond to the recent decline in support for young adolescents reading development. In a study conducted by researchers at Indiana University, the Iowa Test of Basic Reading Skills results from 1944–1945 were available. When the same tests were administered in 1976 and 1986, sixth-grade scores increased from 6.2 to 6.6 while tenth-

From the *NASSP Bulletin, 82*(600), 87–92, October 1998. Reprinted with permission of the National Association of Secondary School Principals.

grade scores dropped from 10.2 to 9.7 (Farr, Fay, Myers, & Ginsberg, 1987).

Fifty years ago, prior to the change from K–8 schools to junior high or middle schools, sixth, seventh, and eighth graders had one period a day for reading activities and one period a day for English. Today's students may have considerably less time for reading. This is due in part to movement in middle grades schools toward a block of time called English or language arts, with reading eliminated and, thus, only half the time previously provided for reading and English.

Missing, as a result of reduced time, is attention to the development of the complex range of skills necessary for becoming an adept reader of many kinds of materials, as well as the practice time necessary to perfect these skills. Appropriate reading classes for young adolescents provide ample time to read and encouragement to do so. There are opportunities to discuss the books read and to develop understanding through interactions with peers and teachers.

The decline of reading time in the school day can also be attributed to the perception many have that young adolescents are already adequately proficient in reading and, thus, studying areas such as foreign language or computers is a better use of their time. Yet, 40% of 9-year-olds scored below the basic level in reading on the *1994 National Assessment of Educational Progress* (Bradley, 1998). At the same time, many middle grades students have *no* reading or literature course during an entire school year (Humphrey, 1992).

The lack of time devoted to reading is often accompanied by a lack of access to the school library. The media center may not be open at convenient times for students, and they may not be encouraged to use the library for voluntary reading as well as class assignments. Most elementary schools provide time for weekly class visits to the library, where students are encouraged to check out books. In middle grades schools, where no weekly class visit occurs, many students visit their school library infrequently. It is no coincidence that voluntary reading decreases for these students.

Many young people are in danger of academic failure because they lack the reading skills needed for assignments in the middle grades. Young adolescents who are in this at-risk category are not receiving the help they need (Humphrey, 1992).

Role Models

Adults at school, at home, and in the community should serve as role models to ensure that reading becomes a priority in the life of students. Many schools provide neither programs that encourage teachers to share and discuss books nor programs that allow them to stress the value of reading books. Similarly, few schools help parents encourage their children to read, despite the existence of several national models that encourage parental involvement (Humphrey, 1992).

When students enter a middle grades school, they look to older students as role models. Unfortunately, the example many younger adolescents receive from older students in their schools is often not a positive model for reading.

Learning to read is like learning to play basketball. First you learn the skills and then you need lots of practice. Students need access to new books and magazines and encouragement to read them. The Center for the Study of Reading at the University of Illinois found that

> Independent silent reading is one of the most important activities for the reading development of students of all ages. Research shows that students who do a lot of reading on their own become better readers because independent reading
>
> • enhances their reading comprehension,
>
> • provides them with a wide range of background knowledge,
>
> • accounts for one-third or more of their vocabulary growth, and
>
> • promotes reading as a lifelong activity. (Center for the Study of Reading, n.d.)

Libraries and Reading

For middle grades students, libraries and reading are indispensable partners. School libraries should contain the books that middle grades students want to read. There is overwhelming evidence that school libraries make a difference in providing access to books for students. School libraries that have larger, quality collections; that are available to students more hours; that provide comfortable and relaxing reading environments; and that are staffed with qualified school librarians produce students with higher reading achievement (Krashen,1993). There is clear evidence that the size of a school library's staff and collection is the best school predictor of academic achievement (Lance, Welborn, & Hamilton-Penell, 1992).

From 1981 to 1987 the amount of federal support for school libraries declined by 49%, following a steady downswing from the high of school library spending in the 1960s and 1970s. At one time a considerable amount of federal money was restricted to purchasing books and related print materials for use in school libraries; during the 1960s and early 1970s, libraries purchased an extensive supply of books with federal funds.

With the consolidation of various federal programs and site-based control of the allocation of funds, however, most of the nation's school systems opted to purchase fewer and fewer books in favor of other needed items (Hopkins & Butler, 1991). As a result, the majority of the books in most school libraries are now outdated and of little use to students. Whatever the source of funds, schools need to purchase two books per year per student to maintain the school library book collection at a current and useful level (Gerhardt,1986; Humphrey, 1990; Miller & Shontz, 1991).

Library books remain current, on average, for 10 years. Thus, most books that are more than 10 years old have limited current interest. In a library of 10,000 books in a school with 500 students, at an annual replacement rate of only one-half book per student, 75% of the collection would be more than 10 years old and out of date.

As school library book purchases have declined, family purchases at bookstores have increased. In fact, children's and young adult's book sales have had a history of extraordinary growth in the past few years. Book sales doubled from 1980 to 1985, and the future looks bright for book publishers (Roback, 1990).

This market-driven approach does raise issues of equity and quality. Families must provide books because school libraries are not providing copies of many new books, but many low-income families lack funds to purchase books for their children. These same families, due to lack of time or access, are relatively unlikely to use the public library. Needless to say, this means that students from low-income families do not have access to as many books as those from more affluent families. Access to attractive books supports the development of reading skills. Lack of access appears to be one of the factors that undermines the reading development of low-income students.

Suggestions for Middle Grades Principals

1. Conduct an assessment of the reading program.

Find out information such as the following:

- How many books per student were purchased in the past year?
- How many books were circulated in the past year?
- Is there enough time for reading?
- Do teachers and librarians know about and read books most popular with students?

- How many librarians and reading teachers participated in local, state, and national professional development meetings concerning the development of proficient and voluntary middle grades readers?
- How many students have public library cards?
- How are families encouraged to support reading for young adolescents?

Provide the same amount of time for reading as for mathematics. It costs no more to have classes in reading than in any other subject. If certified reading teachers are not available in a school, reading teachers can be added as positions become available.

The following are questions to ask when interviewing prospective reading teachers:

- What books are you reading?
- To what professional organizations do you belong?
- What college reading courses did you complete?
- Do you believe all middle grade students can read?
- How would you encourage parents to support the reading program?
- Can you name three of your favorite young adolescent books or authors?
- Do you have a public library card?
- As one of our reading teachers, in what ways would you promote reading throughout the school and community?

Reading teachers need a strong background in the areas they teach. The following courses would be helpful: developmental reading, content area reading, analysis of reading ability, corrective/diagnostic/remedial reading, and literature for young adolescents. If a prospective teacher has an incomplete background, a second question might concern the willingness of the candidate to complete further courses.

2. Increase library book acquisitions.

Many administrators and faculty members do not realize how much their school library book collections have aged. A library book inventory by copyright date will help. Determine the number of books with copyright dates up to 1940 and for each decade after that. Then determine the percentage of books with copyright dates for each decade. Chances are that the average copyright date for the collection is around 1970. Many of the older books have not been checked out for many years and are of no use to today's students. These books should be removed from the collection.

With knowledge of the present status of the book collection, along with current book circulation rates as compared to desired circulation rates, the case can be made for new books. If reading productivity is important in the school system, the school system's budget will be linked to the purchase of books that students will read. Sources other than the school system's regular budget include Title I, PTAs, and community groups. Just as important, make books a part of any proposal for new programs.

3. Create an environment for reading.

When students enter a middle grades school, they soon know whether or not it is a place where reading is important. Reading is seen as valued, promoted, and encouraged in middle grades schools in which

- Posters, material in display cases, and bulletin boards highlight reading.
- Libraries have high circulation of books voluntarily selected by students.
- Reading classrooms have collections of useful and current books for voluntary reading.
- Teachers read to students.
- The oldest students in the school are avid readers and pass that culture on to younger students.
- The principal promotes the importance of reading to new students during visits to feeder schools.

Conclusion

Students who possess strong reading skills will excel; those who do not will fail. The middle grades are the time when this final sorting out occurs, for decisions to drop out of school are often made during these years. Those who leave school or who complete basic schooling but leave without plans for further training or employment are, by and large, those with limited reading achievement.

Developing strong middle grades readers requires many different kinds of supports, including time, access, emphasis, skilled reading teachers, and a supportive administration. We know what a comprehensive reading program for young adolescents should include and we also know what the consequences are if we do not provide good reading instruction in the middle grades. Not supporting middle grades readers means, in the end, diminished opportunities for them and for our nation as we move into the 21st century.

REFERENCES

Bradley, A. (1998, February 18). Ed schools getting heat on reading. *Education Week.*

Center for the Study of Reading. (n.d.). *Teachers and independent reading.* Champaign, IL: University of Illinois.

Farr, R., Fay, L., Myers, J., & Ginsberg, M. (1987). *Then and now: Reading achievement in Indiana (1944–45, 1976, and 1986).* Bloomington, IN: Indiana University.

Gerhardt, L.N. (1986, March). Half-a-book onward. *School Library Journal.*

Hopkins, D., & Butler, R. (1991). *The federal roles in support of school library media centers.* Chicago: American Library Association.

Humphrey, J.W. (1990). Do we provide children enough books to read? *The Reading Teacher, 44,* 94–95.

Humphrey, J.W. (1992). *A study of reading in Indiana middle, junior, and senior high schools.* Paper presented at Youth Institute, Indianapolis, IN.

Krashen, S. (1993). *The power of reading: Insights from the research.* Englewood, CO: Libraries Unlimited.

Lance, K., Welborn, L., & Hamilton-Pennell, C. (1992). *The impact of school library media centers on academic achievement.* Denver, CO: Colorado Department of Education, State Library and Adult Education Office.

Middle Grades Reading Network. (1998, January). Fall 1997 information concerning libraries from Indiana schools enrolling students in grades K through 8. *NetWords.* Evansville, IN: University of Evansville.

Middle Grades Reading Network. (1998, May). Young Hoosier Book Award participation dramatically increases. *NetWords.* Evansville, IN: University of Evansville.

Middle Grades Reading Network. (n.d.). *Middle Grades Reading Assessment.* Evansville, IN: Author.

Miller, M.L., & Shontz, M. (1991, August). Expenditures for resources in school library media centers FY 1989–1990. *School Library Journal.*

Creating a Middle School Culture of Literacy

Robert Feirsen

Walk into an elementary school and take a look around. In all likelihood, the sights and sounds of literacy will barrage your senses. At one entrance, a bulletin board may display student writing under a catchy, alliterative title. In a classroom, students may be publishing their latest poems, while others are conferencing with peers and teachers as they work toward their final drafts. A stroll down a hallway may find a cluster of students sprawled outside a classroom, reading a book by a noted children's author. Over the main office door, a sign enlivened by a smiling face may greet visitors with the announcement, "Welcome to our school—a community of readers!"

Elementary schools often preach consistent messages about the importance of reading, writing, listening, and speaking. Daily routines are supplemented by special assemblies, contests, author visits, guest readers, reward systems, and parent workshops. Together, they focus attention on the central importance of becoming literate members of the community.

Follow elementary students into middle school, however, and observe a startling change: The zeal and enthusiasm noted during earlier days get tempered, and the drive for literacy appears to wither. Several factors account for this dramatic turn of events. Middle school students manifest a significant change in levels of motivation. Students once focused on pleasing the adults in their lives develop an emerging sense of independence and a greater need for acceptance by peers (Wolf, 1991). Emotional peaks and valleys consume much time and energy (Irvin, 1990). Social pressures and the media place an emphasis on being part of the crowd; no one wants to be labeled a "geek." Self-concept and confidence in one's abilities to master new challenges often take a nose dive (Eccles, Midgley, et al., 1993). Through all this turmoil runs an emphasis on action. Many middle schoolers therefore agree with Atwell's (1987) student Melissa, who commented, "I don't like to read because I think reading is boring." I like to do things. I'll read the sports pages and

From the *Middle School Journal, 28*(3), 10–15, January 1997. Reprinted with permission of the National Council of Teachers of English.

comic books but that's it because it's JUST SO BORING [emphasis in original]" (p. 187).

Reading, writing, and more formal forms of speaking also find themselves competing with a host of other endeavors during the day. Athletics, cocurricular programs, responsibilities at home, flirting, visiting with friends, and other early adolescent activities occupy much of the available free time. As a result, "When reading doesn't happen in school, it's unlikely to happen away from school, which means it's unlikely to happen at all" (Atwell, 1987, p. 156).

The picture, however, does not have to remain bleak. In fact, middle school educators have enormous potential to forge literate environments that encourage lifelong learning. As noted by the Carnegie Council on Adolescent Development, "Cognitive development during early adolescence is not on hold" (1989, p. 42). Research and experience confirm that middle level students are greatly interested in the world around them; they are eager to investigate such concerns as personal and group identity, morals and values, change and participation in the complexities of the adult world (George, Stevenson, Thomason, & Beane, 1992). Learning activities that encourage exploration of these intriguing ideas and that allow students to flex their newly discovered cognitive abilities for critical thinking and abstraction will create a student body that is "ripe to be hooked" (Atwell, 1987, p. 48) by academic matters.

The remainder of this article provides information that middle level educators can use to develop dynamic school cultures that feature a strong emphasis on literacy and actively engage students in the quest for growth. After defining "school culture," the article discusses how cultures are created and sustained. Middle school practices are then examined for the cultural messages they may communicate to students. In its final sections, the article describes how literacy may be enshrined as a core value of school life. Specific, age-appropriate practices that create excitement about literacy are presented as models for change.

The Elements of School Culture

Discussions of school culture assume that educational institutions behave in much the same manner as other organizations. In this view, schools are miniature societies and powered by a set of core understandings that guide and structure interactions among stakeholders. Accordingly, "organizational culture is a composite of the values and beliefs of the people within the organization" (Karpicke & Murphy, 1996, p. 26). Sergiovanni (1984) defines school culture as "the collective programming of the mind that distinguishes the members of one school from another" (p. 9).

Culture is composed of several elements, some relatively easy to discern, others well-hidden beneath the surface of day-to-day operations. Symbols of culture, for example, include organizational slang, memos, office arrangements, and objects and locations around the school building upon which special meanings have been conferred (e.g., a faculty lounge chair reserved for a veteran teacher). Heroes, another cultural level, serve as role models for the school; their accomplishments become part of an oral history handed down from one generation to another. Rituals and ceremonies establish mechanisms for conducting interactions; they acknowledge and celebrate notions of both what is central and what is only tangential to the school's mission. Social networks pass along and interpret information about members of the school community and events deemed significant. Beliefs, consciously held understanding about right and wrong, provide measuring sticks against which actions can be evaluated. At the deepest level, shared values represent broad feelings, usually held out-of-awareness, about what is good and what is bad, normal or abnormal, or appropriate or inappropriate. These values are not open to discussion; instead, they are taken for granted as natural parts of the environment. In short, culture defines what is and what should be (Corbett, Firestone, & Rossman, 1988).

Once established, organizational cultures tend to sustain themselves through the processes of socialization, affirmation, and recruitment. Stakeholders "learn the ropes" through such mechanisms as orientation programs; rule-setting; role modeling; formal and informal interactions with peers, supervisors, and subordinates; and a consistent set of sanctions and censures that defines what is acceptable. Group activities confirm core understandings through celebrations, rituals, verbal and nonverbal communication that interprets the meaning of events, and the anointment of heroes who personify attributes held in high regard. Those identified as villains, of course, receive condemnation with similar intensity for faults that violate beliefs and values held in common.

At the same time, an informal social network provides credit and support to those who conform to approved standards and criticizes those who push the boundaries beyond acceptable limits. This "cultural broadcasting system" transmits news and editorials about school activities through highly efficient channels.

In many schools, de facto historians on the staff recount previous innovations tried and found wanting, while power-broker "priests" offer or deny benedictions to the actions of various members of the school community (Deal, 1985). Over time, stakeholders develop a sixth sense that tells them whether or not a given action or idea will receive a warm collective greeting or a series of icy stares.

Once established, school cultures tend to perpetuate themselves. By defining what is reasonable and possible, cultures provide on-the-job satisfaction for staff members whose views are most aligned with shared practices, beliefs, and values. Those who find it difficult to blend their own needs and views with prevailing ideas may look for other jobs or be counseled to leave; others learn to squelch actions and statements that are incompatible with the mind-sets of supervisors and peers. When turnover occurs, potential replacements may be screened for their abilities to blend with others. Over time, this search for good matches tends to eliminate from hiring consideration those who might upset the cultural boat. The outcome is a set of common understandings that accepts current ways of doing things and constrains the search for alternatives.

Middle School Culture and Literacy

Without question, middle level programs have been heavily influenced by their secondary school heritage. In contrast to elementary schools, programs and practices have often reflected a traditional high school emphasis on the separation of content areas, tracking, teaching for coverage rather than deep understanding, formalized systems of midterms and finals, and lecturing as the dominant mode of instruction (George et al., 1992). These circumstances have made it difficult to sustain school-wide efforts to heighten literacy. Understanding the cultural significance of these influences is a necessary first step on the road to creating developmentally appropriate environments for learning.

When students enter middle school, they receive cultural messages about literacy that appear markedly different from the ones they encountered only a few months before. Gone are the highly visible symbols that enlivened elementary school corridors and classrooms. In place of the energetic mixture of reading and writing displays to which elementary teachers and students devote so much time are hallways dominated by lockers, perhaps interrupted by the occasional showcase holding neat, finished products from art or technology. Classroom bulletin boards may offer samples of student work, but they may just as easily appear lifeless with nothing except announcements, calendars, and commercially designed posters to occupy the space. Large areas such as the cafeteria, gymnasium, and auditorium may be similarly adorned with little of academic consequence; students accustomed to seeing invitations to join the school community in reading and writing may instead view school logos, pictures of team mascots, and statements of rules and regulations.

Activity patterns differ inside classrooms as well. The reading corner, a prominent feature of primary and intermediate grades, becomes an artifact of the past; and floor mats, classroom libraries, and reading charts are nowhere to be found. Imaginative reports on books, perhaps represented by dioramas, mobiles, and characters dress-up days, are replaced by the more traditional book reports, literary essays, and multiple choice tests. Spelling and vocabulary lists substitute for inventories developed from personal interactions with print; individual choice in reading and writing topics is often eliminated for the sake of covering the assigned curriculum and preparing for the demands of high school. Visits to the library become less frequent; and when they do occur, they are often dominated by an emphasis on teacher-directed research rather than exploration, oral reading, and book sharings of earlier years. Even the writing process, a validated cornerstone of many approaches to literacy instruction, may be jettisoned in order to accommodate the needs of 40-minute periods.

Middle school rituals and celebrations also may offer few connections to the theme of literacy. Sustained, silent reading periods may prove difficult to implement on a consistent basis without wreaking havoc with the master schedule or past practices. Similarly, guest authors and special assemblies devoted to literature and drama may become rare occurrences. Sadly, awards for reading, writing, and speaking, proffered with such frequency in the earlier grades, may lose their standing among students who no longer view these honors as "cool" and among faculty members hesitant to expose to potential embarrassment the strongest students in their classes.

Tracking, a common feature of many middle schools, adds further complications by separating students into the more challenging higher tracks and the bottom groups composed of reluctant readers and writers. Lower expectations follow these students; and they are frequently provided with skills-based exercises, rarely confronting an assignment that requires extended writing, independent reading, or formal speech (Wheelock, 1992). By the end of their middle school years, students from the lower tracks regard books as obstacles rather than facilitators to school success.

Report cards and parent-teacher communications send cultural messages as well. Regardless of the specific format utilized, elementary schools place considerable emphasis on reporting progress in reading. Grades and teacher comments specifically targeted toward reading, however, often disappear at the middle level, subsumed under the more general heading of "English" or "language arts." In addition, content area instructors frequently lack a good background in the teaching of reading, writing, and study skills (Thomas, 1993). Uncertain of the validity of their own suggestions for the improvement of performance, they send concerned parents to see specialists or English teachers (who often have similar gaps in their academic preparation) when literacy deficits are noted. As a result, the statement, "I'm not a reading teacher," often resonates through the halls by the end of parent-teacher conference day.

Middle schools do affirm some values with considerable emphasis and consistency, particularly the importance of teacher control and student discipline (Eccles, Wigfield, et al., 1993). Unfortunately, the expression of these values in daily school life may limit rather than encourage academic growth and the risk-taking essential for learning new habits of mind. When added to the volatile young adolescent mix of developmental challenges and social pressures, the culture of middle schools may therefore complicate an already difficult quest for enhanced levels of student literacy.

Creating a Culture of Literacy

Middle school cultures that promote literacy cannot be simply willed into existence; as Fullan (1993) notes, "You can't mandate what matters" (p. 125). Similarly, one-shot inservice seminars will not remove deep-seated skepticism about the feasibility of changing adolescent attitudes and behaviors. Above all, superficial change efforts will not reach down into murky layers of organizational culture, the "symbolic webbing" that holds together the many and varied aspects of schooling (Deal, 1990).

Educators concerned with the process of cultural change should instead utilize a wide-angle lens to determine how the elements of the school day interact with each other to create subtle messages about the place of literacy in middle school affairs. This examination of the social and institutional landscape should include assessments of the overt and covert effects of school activities, formal and informal communications, official and unofficial traditions, reward and penalty systems, status hierarchies, funding patterns, classroom design, leadership styles, decision-making structures, and stakeholder interactions. In this way, the "hidden" outcomes of actions may be identified and the implicit values and beliefs that drive collective behavior and structure the school environment may be discerned.

Armed with an understanding of the complexities of school culture, members of the school community can then draft plans that establish or reinforce the importance of literacy as a cornerstone of middle school life. Strategies should align all aspects of organizational behavior, including administrative activities (Sashkin & Sashkin, 1993), to create a powerful blend that surrounds students with continuous support for improvement. When successful, these efforts will create an ambience and vitality appropriate for middle schools yet reminiscent of the elementary school devotion to making every student a skilled reader, writer, speaker, and listener.

A blueprint for action might include or extend the following approaches:

- Encouraging adults to serve as role models by allowing themselves to be seen reading books and writing for a variety of purposes. For example, one middle school established a book club that enabled faculty members to read and discuss works of literature drawn from many genres. Students who caught teachers and administrators in the act of being literate recognized that a love for language can be a significant component of adult life.

- Establishing the library as a symbolic center of the school universe. Through motivating contests, dynamic programming that addressed student interests, faculty collaboration, the utilization of information technology, and the judicious use of available funds, a school created a "uscr-friendly" library that served as many students' second home.

- Encouraging research on subjects of interest to young adolescents. Allowing students in one middle school to select their own topics for a graduation exhibition communicated an awareness of pupil needs and aroused the motivation spawned by emerging interests (George et al., 1992).

- Using many formats to elicit reactions to books will encourage sharing, heighten interest in the world of print, and transmit the enthusiasm for reading and writing felt by adult role models. Parents in particular can provide invaluable assistance in this endeavor; good books can anchor a Parents and Children Read Together evening (Vossler, 1996) that reaffirms the strength of shared values and beliefs.

- Telling stories about students, teachers, and other members of the school community who have demonstrated a commitment to literacy or achieved success in areas related to reading, writing, and speaking. Stories are told around schools all the time, and they have extraordinary power to highlight cultural values (Deal, 1985). Harnessing this potential would create an oral tradition and a set of heroes that may inspire others.

- Developing celebrations that recognize achievements in literacy for individuals, families, interdisciplinary teams, and the school in general. Far from being trite, special assemblies, awards, and contests heighten engagement and remind members of the school community about what is considered important; a pep rally for reading can become as prized as one for athletics. Celebrations that applaud effort and involvement will encourage the participation of students from all points along the achievement continuum, not just those who are most skillful and practiced.

- Identifying literacy as an area of focus for site-based decision making teams. Group deliberations may produce practical, creative suggestions for achieving literacy goals; and dialogue with parent representatives may inspire efforts to create meaningful literacy experiences outside, as well as inside, the schoolhouse. A reading committee (Irvin, 1990), for instance, could plan special events related to reading, writing, and public speaking while affirming the importance of working cooperatively to raise student performance levels.

- Empowering teacher teams and facilitating dialogue across grade levels and subject areas (Clark & Clark, 1996). As faculty members share perspectives, they may recognize the need for collaborative efforts to solve problems. In addition, they may learn that strategies to teach reading and writing are not as mysterious as they once seemed. Team efforts to raise reading levels, for example, will almost certainly demonstrate that literacy is intimately connected with heightened mastery of subject content. Productive byproducts of such conversations may also include the redefinition of literacy efforts to include technical reading, writing, and speaking, as well as consensus-based commitment to reducing the stranglehold of "coverage."

- Focusing staff development initiatives on promoting literacy. Instruction in this area may reduce teacher hesitation to address student deficits. At the same time, it can provide teachers with an arsenal of tools, including flowcharts, webs, and sorting trees that have valuable, task-specific applications in the various content areas (Hyerle, 1996).

- Including reading and writing specialists in all aspects of instructional design. If greater literacy is our quest, we should encourage participation by those with the richest academic background in this area. Elevating the status of these staff members will inform decisions and simultaneously proclaim the importance of new goals.

- Conducting a "culture audit" on a regular basis. Examining organizational action and stakeholder behavior will provide the data needed to determine the extent to which values and beliefs are shared. Plans can then be drafted to enhance or support the drive for literacy (Champy, 1995).

Conclusion

Middle schools face serious challenges in their efforts to increase literacy levels among their students. As always, each building must respond to the developmental, academic, and social demands that confront young adolescents. In addition, educators must recognize that achieving basic competency in areas related to literacy is no longer sufficient; energies should be focused on attaining the high standards of pupil performance required for success in an increasingly competitive environment.

Our actions must also reflect the awareness that middle schools are not simply passive vehicles for students as they move from elementary to high school. The collective effects of school policies, practices, and implicit values transmit strong messages to teachers and students about the significance of literacy and the importance of increasing levels of achievement. To create environments that engage students in the consistent pursuit of ever-higher goals, middle schools must go beyond traditional staff and curriculum development approaches: They need to develop cultures that broadcast a clear commitment to literacy and support the attainment of this outcome in word and deed. In this way, they will define skillful reading, writing, listening, and speaking as "the way we do things around here" (Deal & Kennedy, 1982).

REFERENCES

Atwell, N. (1987). *In the middle: Writing, reading, and learning with adolescents.* Portsmouth, NH: Heinemann.

Carnegie Council on Adolescent Development. (1989). *Turning points: Preparing American youth for the 21st century.* New York: Carnegie Corporation.

Champy, J. (1995). *Reengineering management: The mandate for new leadership.* New York: HarperCollins.

Clark, D.C., & Clark, S.N. (1996). Building collaborative environments for successful middle level school restructuring. *Bulletin of the National Association of Secondary School Principals, 80*(578), 1–16.

Corbett, H.D., Firestone, W.A., & Rossman, G.B. (1987). Resistance to planned change and the sacred in school culture. *Educational Administration Quarterly, 23*(4), 36–59.

Deal, T.E. (1990). Reframing reform. *Educational Leadership, 47*(8), 6–12.

Eccles, J.S., Midgley, C., Wigfield, A., Buchanan, C.M., Reuman, D., Flanagan, C., & Mac Iver, D. (1993). Development during adolescence. *American Psychologist, 48*(2), 90–101.

Eccles, J.S., Wigfield, A. Midgley, C., Reumann, D., Mac Iver, D., & Feldlaufer, H. (1993). Negative effects of traditional middle schools on students' motivation. *The Elementary School Journal, 93*(5), 553–574.

Fullan, M.G. (1993). Innovation, reform, and restructuring strategies. In G. Cawelti (Ed.), *Challenges and achievements of American education* (pp. 116–133). Alexandria, VA: Association for Supervision and Curriculum Development.

George, P.S., Stevenson, C., Thomason, J., & Beane, J. (1992). *The middle school— and beyond.* Alexandria, VA: Association for Supervision and Curriculum Development.

Hyerle, D. (1996). *Visual tools for constructing knowledge.* Alexandria, VA: Association for Supervision and Curriculum Development.

Irvin, J.L. (1990). *Reading and the middle school student: Strategies to enhance literacy.* Boston: Allyn & Bacon.

Karpicke, H., & Murphy, M.E. (1996). Productive school culture: Principals working from the inside. *Bulletin of the National Association of Secondary School Principals, 80*(576), 26–34.

Sashkin, M., & Sashkin, M.G. (1993). Leadership and culture building in schools. In W.E. Rosenbach & R.L. Taylor (Eds.), *Contemporary issues in leadership* (pp. 201–211). Boulder, CO: Westview Press.

Sergiovanni, T.J. (1984). Leadership and excellence in schooling. *Educational Leadership, 41*(5), 575–591.

Vossler, J.M. (1996). When danger threatens. *Middle School Journal, 27*(3), 47–51.

Wheelock, A. (1992). *Crossing the tracks: How untracking can save America's schools.* New York: New Press.

Wolf, A.E. (1991). *Get out of my life, but first could you drive me and Cheryl to the mall? A parent's guide to the new teenager.* New York: Noonday Press.

The Literacy Council: People Are the Key to an Effective Program

Patricia L. Anders

A literacy council can respond to student's literacy needs by drawing on the available resources in the school—teachers, administrators, counselors, media specialists, and others who work with students. The people-oriented program framework suggested here can improve the overall school climate; provide a structure of professional growth and curricular activity that benefits the faculty and the students; and enhance relations with the local community.

People are key to this organizational framework for both theoretical and practical reasons. Successful school literacy programs reflect the purposes students have for reading and writing—deeply embedded, meaningful contexts of communication. By examining particular theoretical features of literacy and by comparing those with the literacy behavior of students, common ground can be found for developing a program that allows literacy to flourish. From what we know about literacy and about adolescents, the criteria for a literacy learning program are clear:

1. It would provide opportunities for all students to be a part of the program.
2. It would take advantage of the social nature of literacy and of adolescents.
3. It would take advantage of the "need to know" among secondary students.
4. It would respond to adolescents whose behavior suggests alienation.

The Literacy Council

The all-school literacy program is created, nurtured, and sustained by a "literacy council" founded on three assumptions. First, that the literacy program permeates every aspect of the curriculum and activities of the school. Literacy provides an avenue for students to engage in the multi-

From the *NASSP Bulletin, 82*(600), 16–23, October 1998. Reprinted with permission of the National Association of Secondary School Principals.

tude of learning opportunities and activities of the school. A sense of the purpose and value of literacy can be shared by the entire school community. Further, teachers need to know how to observe, evaluate, and describe their students' literacy activity.

Second, that each educator in the school can contribute to the literacy program. Reading and writing instruction is sometimes perceived to be the responsibility of the English teacher, the resource teacher, or the reading teacher, but when literacy is used across the curriculum, it becomes clear that each educator should and can be a part of the literacy program. The counselor, media specialist, allied arts teacher, administrator, and classroom teacher each have a contribution to make.

Third, when people have an investment in a project or activity, they are more likely to take responsibility for the quality of that project. For the most part, it is simply a matter of recognizing these talents and experiences and making a place for them to be expressed in the school. For example, one English teacher with whom I worked, Melissa, has extensive knowledge and experience of the writing process. She uses the writing process successfully in her English classes and is eager to help other teachers understand what she does and how they might adopt/adapt her ideas. She is teaching in a high school of more than 2,000 students, more than 85% of whom are either Hispanic or Native American. The school has limited resources and although there is a curriculum resource person, she has multiple duties and her curricular expertise is in math. A literacy council would give Melissa the opportunity to use and share her talents; students, teachers, and administrators would ultimately benefit.

Council Leadership

Ideally, the leader of the literacy council is a person who knows the reading and writing processes, who has experience teaching in the middle or high school, and who has at least a master's degree in reading, writing, or teacher education with an emphasis in reading/language arts. Whatever the academic qualifications, he or she needs to conceptualize reading and writing as part of the bigger picture of literacy; understand content area literacy; have a working knowledge of adolescent literature; and be well qualified to evaluate students' progress in literacy.

Equally important is the ability to work with peers and students. In most cases, and for very good reasons, the reading/literacy specialist is not an administrator and has no authority over teachers. She must cajole, demonstrate, argue constructively, and provide opportunities for her colleagues to gain intrinsic and sometimes extrinsic rewards for their efforts. She should be well organized, and have a good sense of humor and an outstanding work ethic. Most important, she must see herself as a problem-solving, inquiry-oriented colleague who has good ideas and professional resources to contribute to the effort of the council.

Council Membership

Members of the literacy council need to be caring and dedicated members of the faculty who share the literacy specialist's attributes of being inquiry-oriented, problem-solving types who are knowledgeable about their subject matter and enjoy their students. Generally, the members should be respected by their peers, but should not be department heads or nontenured.

The school administrator(s) and literacy specialist should decide on the best method for identifying members of the literacy council. In one school, the administrator called for volunteers and then appointed members from among those who volunteered. In another school, department heads invited nominations from their respective departments and then the principal, in consultation with the literacy specialist, made appointments.

The number of members should be decided by the literacy specialist and principal by taking into consideration the first-year goals of the program. In many schools the first year of the program is primarily dedicated to researching the needs of the school and to developing a common knowledge base among the literacy council members. If that is the case, the literacy specialist and the principal should consider who would best represent the various groups in the school.

If teachers are organized by teams, it might be sensible to have a representative from each team. A department organization might suggest one or two members from each department. The important points to remember are that all teachers should feel they are represented on the council and the number of council members should be manageable.

Scheduling might be a consideration in some schools. In one school, the literacy council meetings are held during lunch and into the planning period that follows. In another school, all the literacy council members share a common planning period. The schedule should be arranged so the literacy council members and the literacy specialist have common time to meet and work together.

A formal letter from the principal inviting membership on the council can go a long way to enhance its prestige. Some measure of privilege should also be provided for members of the literacy council. For example, the volunteers might be assured by the principal that time will be set aside for their additional duties. The literacy specialist and principal should take every opportunity to publicly thank and to acknowledge the contributions of the literacy council members.

Council Tasks

The tasks of the literacy council are multiple and are decided, for the most part, by the council. In one school, for example, the council decided that the first year would be devoted to professional development, and that all literacy council members would report the information they learned in the meetings to their departmental colleagues. The literacy specialist designed a curriculum, which responded to the council members' questions. The council met every 2 weeks for instruction and the members provided less elaborate professional development for their departments. The literacy specialist also arranged for the council members to earn district credit for their participation, thereby providing an extrinsic reward for the extra work.

Another middle level council decided to do a needs survey to determine the future of their literacy program. The members conducted interviews in the community, reviewed standardized test results, looked at students' performance on the state performance test, interviewed and surveyed colleagues in the school, and visited the feeder schools from which their students came and the high school to which their students graduated. This collection and analysis of data played a major role in helping the council members decide which of many directions they might take in the future. The members received district credit for their data collection. In addition, the school paid for a class in teacher research at a nearby university during the summer, where the collected data were analyzed and prepared to present to the faculty in the fall.

Each of these first-year activities provided the starting point for ideas during subsequent years. In the first school, after learning some basic information about literacy, the teachers were ready to learn about the status of literacy in their school community in the second year. They designed a study that helped them to decide on the direction of their program. The second school determined that they needed to develop a program to provide opportunities to learn content area literacy strategies. Teachers were taught strategies and the teachers and literacy council members decided on the scope and sequence of strategies that would be taught across the curriculum.

From each of these school's data gathering and analyzing activities, the literacy council set priorities and shared them with the school. They developed a plan to accommodate the needs of the students. In one school, the literacy council decided to promote wide reading among students. As a result, homeroom was extended to provide time for a sustained silent reading program and the librarian organized book clubs around the most popular books. Students could come to the library from their homerooms to discuss a particular book. The librarian kept track of the amount of recreational reading done by the students and found a 100% increase in just one year.

In another school, the literacy council assigned top priority to students for whom literacy was difficult. They did not want to fall into the trap of tracking students and they did not have the resources or desire to hire a special reading teacher. The problem was addressed by forming a partnership with the high school and the local college, and by calling for volunteers from the community. A tutoring program was set up and teachers allowed readers needing help to leave their class to work with a tutor. The literacy specialist trained the tutors and organized and monitored the tutoring.

Providing a Literate Climate

Through the years, these literacy councils have accomplished great things. As a result of the council's efforts, awareness of literacy and knowledge about literacy have both increased dramatically. The councils have led in-depth inservice training sessions with their faculties and have connected with businesses for materials and work-related literacy experiences.

Teachers and students alike have taken responsibility for providing a literate climate in the school. When new teachers are hired, they are asked about their background in literacy and the role literacy plays in their curriculum and pedagogy. Students in the school have sponsored neighborhood literacy drives to make sure preschoolers have picture books and adults know appropriate ways to share with preschoolers. Educators in the school have learned to recognize students who need instruction and know how to either offer the instruction, if appropriate, or find someone who can.

The life of a literacy council is typically 3 to 5 years, depending on the teacher turnover in the school. New people are cycled into the council every couple of years, thereby increasing the commitment of a larger and larger proportion of the faculty. Another way to disperse responsibility would be for the literacy council to appoint ad hoc task groups to accomplish specific purposes.

These examples serve to demonstrate that people, usually those already employed in the school or district, can respond to the needs of their students. When the resources and talents of these professionals are tapped and put to use, a tailor-made program is designed to meet the needs of the school. No purchased program or single person can accomplish what can be done by a literacy specialist and a council that represents the constituents and their interests.

Stumbling Blocks and How to Avoid Them

The Literacy Specialist

A literacy council needs to find the right literacy specialist. If a current member of the faculty is not available and if resources do not allow hiring a new person, a principal might consider hiring a consultant to help set up the council and to work with it until it is well established. In all likelihood, the consultant should be present at the school while setting up the council and then at the school every 2 weeks to meet with the council. One assignment of the consultant would be to locate a person within the district who could be taught to serve as the literacy specialist.

Finding the Time

Teachers rarely have enough time to do their job, let alone take on new responsibilities. Educators must carefully analyze the way time is being spent and reallocate time so literacy learning becomes a priority for all administrators, staff members, teachers, and parents.

The Pressure of High Stakes Testing

Teachers are sometimes hesitant to try innovations because they fear a decline in students' test scores (Anders & Richardson, 1992). This is a difficult issue and one about which many educators are ambivalent. Anders and Richardson found that even when a principal assured the faculty that she was not concerned with test scores and that the new ideas should be tried, the faculty was reluctant. The issue was addressed by closely examining what students were asked to do on the tests and the amount of correspondence there was with the types of strategies teachers were being asked to implement. Those strategies that showed the greatest correspondence to the activities required on the tests gained the greatest acceptance.

In another school, however, this practice backfired. The principal insisted that the purpose of the staff development was to raise test scores; hence, the staff developer designed the inservice program around strategies teachers could use to help students in the content areas and also to improve test scores. The teachers claimed they were not interested in test scores and resisted the recommended strategies. These two examples point to the importance of listening carefully to what teachers want and to what they believe they need. The literacy specialist and the council should not make assumptions about these expectations and needs.

Attitude

The literacy specialist and/or members of the council should be careful not to assume an attitude that suggests to others they alone possess the "right" answers. If a literacy specialist or members of the council adopt an attitude of superiority, others will resent and reject their suggestions. Teachers who have developed expertise in a content area and who have thought through their expectations for students in that content area resent those who are outside the context and have limited experience with the content area making recommendations. That is where the orientation toward problem solving and inquiry, or teacher research (Cochran-Smith & Lytle, 1993) is helpful. Rather than assuming that the answer to a problem is known, the literacy specialist and teacher(s) might pose a solution or response in terms of a research problem and then design a method to address the question. By doing so, the educator with the problem and the literacy specialist are able to each bring their expertise to bear on the issue.

The Value of Reflection

Another idea, related to teacher research, is the value of reflection for teacher change. Teachers do not change simply because they have heard another good idea. If a good idea fits in with their already established belief system, they are likely to adopt the idea. On the other hand, if the new idea does not make sense, or in the teacher's perception will not work it will not be tried. If the idea is tried, it will be changed to accommodate the teacher's belief system (Anders & Richardson, 1991). The solution to this challenge is to provide opportunities for teachers to reflect on their beliefs and to think of the new ideas in terms of their belief systems. If beliefs are to be changed to accommodate new ideas, time and opportunities for experimentation and discussion are necessary.

Finally, the notion of a literacy council is likely to be a departure from the normal ways of reading instruction at a school. The norm is to hire a reading teacher or specialist and turn the "problem readers" over to her. This is an approach that is doomed to failure because it is isolated from the culture and context of the school. It is limited to a narrow, linear skill view of reading and does not account for the multifaceted nature of literacy.

The literacy council idea is, however, consistent with movement toward site-based management and teacher control over the curriculum.

Like those reforms, the program created by the literacy council needs time to evolve, and should not be disbanded too quickly if the initial response is lackluster. Chances are, the faculty need time and experience to understand the potential of the council and to trust that the council really will have an impact.

Conclusion

Middle and high school literacy programs are exciting and necessary; they are often the last chance educators have for "catching" students and helping them to develop a love for reading and writing and the ability to learn through reading and writing. Commercial programs, machines, or special classes do not create a successful program; rather, the program must begin with the people—all professionals working with students—who are responsible for the literacy climate of the school and the learning of the students.

REFERENCES

Anders, P., & Richardson, V. (1991). Research directions: Staff development that empowers teachers' reflection and enhances instruction. *Language Arts, 68,* 316–321.

Anders, P., & Richardson, V. (1992). Teacher as game show host, bookkeeper or judge? Challenges, contradictions, and consequences of accountability. *Teachers College Record, 94,* 382–396.

Cochran-Smith, M., & Lytle, S.L. (1993). *Inside outside: Teacher research and knowledge.* New York: Teachers College Press.

A New Role for the Reading Specialist: Contributing Toward a High School's Collaborative Educational Culture

Geraldine F. Henwood

I n 1990, a suburban Pennsylvania school district in an affluent community near Philadelphia hired me to teach approximately 60 of the 1,200 students who attended the high school. My assignment was to address gaps in the comprehension skills of these students through direct instruction. During the 5 years I taught this course, colleagues often shared their concern about the reading weaknesses of additional students they taught. Their comments, along with overall declining performance scores on state reading assessments, made it clear that reading improvement of a much broader scope was needed. The challenge was how to meet the broader reading needs of the entire school population with only one reading specialist on staff.

The opportunity to explore this situation arose at the beginning of the 1995–1996 school year. Communicating his desire to promote collegiality by encouraging teachers to collaborate so as to further both student learning and professional growth, the principal of the high school released me from my teaching responsibilities to collaborate with content teachers. He noted that because of my nonthreatening, diplomatic interactions with staff and because of my understanding of the dynamics and interrelatedness of the teaching and learning process as a reading specialist, I could promote his vision of the school as a learning community (Barth, 1990).

I was left, however, to determine for myself the best way both to structure this new role and to evaluate its outcomes. There were no road maps available for me to follow because there was nothing in the literature about such a role for a reading specialist at the high school level; I had to function in this new role while at the same time creating it. Because of my years of teaching experience, my background in reading, and with knowledge from many recent graduate courses in the area of curriculum and instruction, I realized that the framework of this new po-

Reprinted from the *Journal of Adolescent & Adult Literacy, 43*, 316–325, December 1999/January 2000.

sition had to be based solidly on the concept of collaboration. In any form, collaboration is sharing, using, and reflecting on people's insights and expertise in order to improve pedagogical practice so as to promote student learning. While the focus is on improving student learning, collaboration sparks ideas between colleagues, invigorates these professionals, and ultimately improves their teaching.

My Approach: A Partner, Not an Expert

In beginning my efforts to collaborate with colleagues in paired relationships, I felt it was necessary that they not regard me as an expert rendering advice. Instead, I needed to be considered a partner in improving the learning of all students, one who complemented the teacher's knowledge of content with knowledge of the learning process that I possessed as a reading specialist. Costa and Kallick (1993) describe a similar role and characterize it as being a "critical friend." In valuing the work of colleagues, I hoped to share my teaching perspective while considering relevant approaches to student learning.

With this clear goal in mind, I distributed a letter to the faculty at the beginning of the school year, clarifying my new role and inviting staff members to collaborate with me. Of necessity a teacher's response had to be voluntary. We had to be coworkers, equal partners in an activity that by its nature is accomplished with a common effort and involves an ongoing openness to ideas. Collaboration requires freedom of choice to be most productive.

Although reasons for collaboration varied, the process became relatively consistent:

1. The colleague (a content teacher) identified in writing the reason for working with me.

2. I met with the content teacher and discussed strategies to deal with the teacher's concern.

3. The content teacher selected the strategy that was most comfortable and appropriate for his or her classroom setting.

4. I fulfilled the teacher-selected option for me to do any one of the following: model a teaching strategy, demonstrate a learning strategy, participate as a student, or observe the content teacher and offer feedback.

5. The content teacher and I shared reactions to the executed strategy, confirming what went well and refining the strategy to improve student learning.

6. The content teacher executed the revised strategy in a follow-up lesson.

This format is based on the elements or norms that affect school improvement and reflects the degree to which a culture is collaborative (Saphier, 1985). Specifically, the effective characteristics are providing tangible support, offering recognition and appreciation of teachers' efforts to improve and to change, involving colleagues in decision making, extending trust and confidence in them, and referring to knowledge bases and not to personal style when collaborating.

This last characteristic is a pivotal one that the reading specialist is uniquely qualified to provide. The instructional framework for promoting reading development is equally effective for learning in all of the content areas, including history, English, science, or math.

The "before, during, and after" reading format is valid for all of the subjects in the curriculum. Every teacher can design lessons to promote the use of reading strategies that prepare students for reading, help them to interact with text to construct meaning while they are reading, and enable them to extend meaning after they finish reading. For example, after formulating the goal of the lesson, the teacher can then select or create instructional strategies that activate students' background knowledge of the subject. One effective technique to elicit background information is having students complete the What I Know column of the K-W-L procedure (Ogle, 1986). After students have had an opportunity to share orally what they have written, they are in a stronger position to generate questions and list them in the Want to Know column, thereby setting their own purposes for reading. During reading, as students discover the answers to their questions, they note them in the Learned column of the K-W-L format. Finally, students may conclude after they finish reading the selection that there are additional questions they want answered, thereby extending their response to the text.

This specific example of a knowledge-based approach is well understood by reading specialists and can easily be related to the subject area and to the cooperating teacher in a collaboration. Additional approaches familiar to reading teachers for improving student learning and comprehension include previewing the meanings of the lesson's key vocabulary words, instructing the class in the various methods of notetaking to help make students active learners, and purposeful structuring of small-group settings.

During the first year I enjoyed the opportunity to interact with so many of my colleagues, who stimulated my thinking as I hope I did theirs. The length of time spent working with a teacher or other member of the staff was determined by what was needed to achieve the goal of the requested collaboration. The range of time spent extended from one or more class periods to a few weeks and even to an entire school quarter, and it may have involved sharing one or all of a colleague's assigned classes, depending on the focus of the consultation. The number of staff involved by department that year was a total of 34, distributed as shown:

English	8
Social studies	2
Science	4
Math	3
Special education	4
Health	2
Art	1
Challenge	3
Library	1
Counseling	1
Social services	1
Administration	4

Teachers sought collaborative support for the following reasons:

• Desire to learn how to individualize help, deal with large class size, and handle students' comprehension and decoding problems.

• Need to learn most appropriate techniques for including the special learner.

• Concern over poor notetaking skills and awareness of multiple reading levels within one class.

• Need to make directions/questions/discussion more direct and concrete, less abstract.

• Desire to develop a thematic unit.

• Need for concrete suggestions for parents who want to help their child improve in reading.

• Need for supplemental materials.

• Need for reading specialist to work with small student groups involved in a special project, to increase comprehension and facilitate research.

• Desire to develop more interactive teaching skills.

Learning to Collaborate

Perhaps the best way to describe my daily activities is to provide details of some of my collaborations with colleagues during the year.

• A master English teacher needed help in convincing his ninth-grade honors students that their reading ability could be improved. Working together we helped to change the values and beliefs that these students held about their reading ability. We did this in stages, and by using many different strategies. Initially, for about 3 weeks, I taught the class. I first involved the students in a discussion of what was involved in the reading process and how people came to understand what they read. Then it was time to challenge their claim that they knew all there was to know about reading.

The English teacher and I divided the class into cooperative groups, and after a surface reading of a short story asked each group to respond to a different set of factual questions about the reading. All did very well. Then we posed inferential questions to the groups, and asked them to reread specific sections of the text in order to develop answers. As anticipated, some could do this more easily than others. In the third round of reading, we gave them critical thinking questions that required them to synthesize information from the story and apply it to new situations. Most could not handle this level of assignment. This demonstration literally proved to them that they did have more to learn about reading.

• A special education teacher asked for help with her reading program. We discussed her program and I made suggestions, which I demonstrated with her students. We decided to focus on strategies to help students learn that they needed to pose questions, make predictions, and use contextual clues including illustrations and headings to improve their comprehension. We extended this focus to include reading a textbook, a newspaper, and a short story. The thrust was to change the students from passive to more active learners.

• Another colleague, recently hired to spearhead a new ninth-grade program for 10 special students, voiced interest in working with me in the early part of the school year. While not designated as special education students, these 10 nevertheless had difficulty fitting in socially with their peers. Their integration into the high school community was limited and controlled; she taught them English and social studies, had them for homeroom, spoke on the phone daily with their parents and other professionals who interacted with them, and counseled them frequently.

The opportunity eventually came to work with these students in their classroom, although not until the latter part of the school year. They were learning about the culture of China, and each student had been assigned a cultural category like religion or geography to research. Their teacher saw a need for them to learn the correct process for writing a research paper. Specifically, she wanted them to learn techniques for determining an approach to their pursuit of information, how to organize and to analyze the data, and how finally to write the report. Once a week I would come to their classroom and offer suggestions that addressed these broad areas, sometimes teaching the whole class, sometimes working with individuals. I shared ideas with the teacher about discussions to have with the students and projects to do with them. In particular, several students learned how to use graphic organizers and how to take notes along with improving their research papers.

• Good teaching practices as they relate to the most fundamental teaching tool, the textbook, were on the mind of one of the science teachers. In our after-class conversations I discussed the features of the textbook chapters and pointed out many things to him. Specifically, we talked about how, by examining the chapter's illustrations, students could generate questions about the new material that could motivate their reading. In the absence of motivation, this activity would at least give students a purpose for reading, essential for increasing comprehension. We also looked at the end-of-the-chapter questions that contained vocabulary or phrasing that would prevent many students from responding because they would not know what the question was asking. The usefulness of bold headings in sensitizing students to transitions and how the headings could be helpful in easily locating information also were part of our talks.

The science teacher often took notes during these discussions, asked questions, and retold what he had understood to be sure he had absorbed these new insights. Although our collaboration was based on only a month's observations of his first-period class (a general science class consisting of mixed grades) and while we did not participate in a lengthy collaborative relationship, he evidently felt that he had absorbed vital concepts during the reflections and discussions following each class. He revealed a degree of confidence that now allows him to use the textbook more comfortably in preparing for all of his classes.

• A history teacher was concerned about nothing less than learning to transform her professional practice from being teacher centered to pupil centered. Rather than be discouraged by what some colleagues might view as a daunting task, she invited me to observe her classes and to comment, as a colleague, on her teaching methods. She also invited me to model strategies recognized to increase student comprehension. She wanted to update her teaching skills, and so was willing to listen to my perspective as a reading specialist, to observe the teaching techniques I volunteered to demonstrate, and to reflect with me on the outcomes as she integrated new approaches into her teaching. Because our collaborative relationship lasted for 5 months, during which time I attended and for the most part observed her two classes 4 days a week, we had an opportunity to do many new things together. Unlike the science teacher, however, my history colleague did not have a preparation period we could use to discuss a day's lesson. Our exchanges took place either in the hall as she walked to her second class or in the evenings on the phone, in conversations that often lasted an hour.

The topics discussed ranged widely, and they included her adjustment to increasing noise levels in the room whenever students engaged in cooperative learning, the need to identify first the purposes in teaching content before developing lessons to accomplish these outcomes, and behavior management issues that seemed to persist with certain students. She picked up on prereading activities and on ways to turn a lecture into a group activity that is pupil centered, not teacher centered. I helped her devise ways to make students think critically, and presented the value of a rubric to grade term papers fairly. I encouraged her to use illustrations and editorial cartoons to exemplify issues and eras. I demonstrated the effect of preparing question sheets before showing a movie.

• A faculty member who is almost as much of a department unto herself as I am, and who often is a teacher within her domain, is the librarian. Our collaboration occurred when I joined a conversation she was having with a ninth-grade history teacher who was scheduling her class for an orientation session in the library. The session's purpose was to communicate the rules of the library to the students and to prepare them for a future library visit to learn about computer research programs. The librarian was open to hearing my ideas for making the first meeting with the students an interactive one and to incorporating her library assistants into the presentation. She also agreed that a student booklet had to be created so that students would have something concrete to use during the computer lesson, and as a reference after the session.

In meetings that occurred over 4 weeks, she and I planned the orientation sessions, all of which I attended, and later critiqued the content and method of presentation. The orientation booklet that she developed and asked me to critique became the focus of many of her comments regarding the outcome of our collaboration. The issue of reading levels triggered another outcome for the librarian and the students. I was able to help her select some books recommended from professional journals and from recent conferences I attended.

• To provide training that would enhance high school reading tutors' skills, I conducted a workshop prior to the tutors' meeting with their young charges. This session lasted about an hour, and the coordinator of community services reported that the students "seemed to get a better sense for how to tutor more effectively." The students were not getting that much guidance and leadership from the organizations in which they worked, so they turned to the coordinator, and he in turn came to me.

While these summaries of the responses to the pivotal questions provide a survey and analysis of the major part of my collaborative work, this discussion would not be complete without reference to my involvement with the ongoing ninth-grade collaborative team, an interdisciplinary group of colleagues consisting mainly of English and social studies teachers. In initial meetings during the spring of 1996, we as team members formulated our goals. The primary goal was to help students make a smoother transition between middle school and high school. To that end, during the summer of 1996 the team identified skills and behaviors the students needed to succeed in high school, and we then agreed to mutually reinforce them in our respective classrooms throughout the school year.

To assess the success of this first year's effort, I volunteered to develop a student questionnaire that reflected these skills and behaviors. Students would respond to the questionnaire at the beginning of the school year and again at the end. The results of this measure would help the team and the administration learn to what extent their attempts had succeeded in acclimating students to the high school community and to the rigors of its academic life.

From my perspective as the reading specialist, I frequently tried to bring the learner's interests to the table, and to that end, for example, offered my opinion of the new English and social studies texts to be adopted. I tried also to focus teachers on their purposes for teaching specific content so as to align evaluation with that purpose. I offered suggestions for dealing with the diversity of students in their classrooms and urged teachers to construct a summer reading assignment that was direct and that provided an example of a completed assignment done satisfactorily. My contributions as a resource to this group, while not measured quantitatively, nevertheless are reflected in the accomplishments of the ninth-grade collaboration to date.

As a result of this survey of my work with the staff, I believe that one can see clearly the potential of someone in my position making a significant contribution to the development of collaboration in a high school. While the role of an agent of collaboration should not be confined to a reading specialist, the advantage of selecting a teacher with such a background is evident.

Benefits of Collaboration

The benefits of my collaboration with colleagues to improve the reading and learning skills of all of their students were numerous. These colleagues, when queried at the end of the school year, reported positive outcomes relative both to their teaching and to student learning. Their reported results reflect both tangible, concrete benefits as well as intangible, intrinsic outcomes. For example, that science teacher in whose class I had worked for a month said this:

> I have a clearer understanding of how a textbook can be an effective teaching tool when all of the book's resources are used, for example pictures, bold type, section reviews, et cetera. Some students who avoided reading the textbook are now using it as an effective reference book.

The history teacher with whom I had collaborated for a semester cited specific changes in her pedagogy as a result of our collaboration:

> Instead of getting up and lecturing on a topic, I'll ask questions to elicit information that they knew before, to find out what they knew coming into the concept...and by having students review pictures, and go over them, talk about them, and I asked them many questions about the pictures, it elicited a lot of critical thinking responses.

These teachers and others also cited as benefits of collaboration the following: being able to employ these strategies in the noncollaborative classes they taught, using the two teachers in a collaborative relationship to individualize learning, and creating and using new assessment tools to measure student achievement. These specific and tangible outcomes occurred as a result of the collaborative relationship with the reading specialist. As noted by Hargreaves, Earl, and Ryan (1996),

> It is unfair, unrealistic and ineffective to expect or insist that teachers change their teaching dramatically, in a short space of time. But it is fair, realistic, and likely to prove more effective if we expect teachers to commit themselves to continuous improvement as a community of colleagues, and to experiment with new teaching strategies as part of that commitment. (p. 158)

The intrinsic benefits of collaboration mentioned by staff were also numerous. That English teacher whose ninth-grade honor classes I had cotaught for several weeks perceived a connection between the outcome of collaboration and the outcome of formal evaluation:

> Collaboration opens each teacher to challenge his or her own assumptions, values, approaches to teaching. I think that's always good. It seems to me that's what formal evaluation ought to be doing. It ought to be opening the possibilities where anyone can grow. And I think that is those very same ideas, and ideas are what teaching is all about. When you approach each individual's learning, it's the very same kind of thing: to open, to broaden, to extend, to help grow.

For this English teacher, the value of collaboration is the same for both teacher and student; the process challenges all alike and presents them with the possibility of continuous improvement.

Like the English teacher, the special education teacher made comments about the results of our coteaching the new reading class that applied both to herself as well as to the students:

> Collaboration gave me a bolstered sense of what I was doing in the classroom, that it wasn't something I was just making up, that it was being shared with the reading specialist, someone who was trained in what I had been working on. Students got feedback from more than one person; they got to look at different teaching styles. They also got to look at different learning styles, because the reading specialist and I had different styles of learning and teaching.

The special education teacher remarked further that while support and validation were anticipated and important outcomes of collaboration for her, an even more valuable offshoot was an enhanced reflective process:

> Collaboration forces you to reflect on your own practice...and true change and true growth really doesn't happen unless you are reflective. You may make a decision to make some changes, but if you don't reflect on everything you do, it will not become part of your teaching practice.

Although the outcomes they cited were to some extent different, the special education and English teachers nevertheless agreed that the major benefit of collaborative sharing is the reflection that in turn leads to positive changes in behavior. This changed behavior, whether in teachers or in students, is learning. For teachers, the learning can improve teacher practice; for students the learning can improve skill development. In either case, reflection creates learners, be they teachers or students. Collaboration brings a broad array of personal and educational benefits to both students and teachers that can transform the traditional system of a school.

Benefits of the Reading Specialist's Collaborative Role

Regardless of whether I had worked with colleagues for months, weeks, or only occasionally, their reactions to the benefits of collaborating specifically with a reading specialist clustered around three areas. The first area focused on reading as understood by most people, and involved both skill and comprehension acquisition by students. The remarks of the special education teacher are illustrative:

> I've seen their skills, not only in this particular class, the reading class, but also in their other courses because I do get to see them outside of this room. Their oral reading fluency increased; they were much easier to listen to. They understood more of what they themselves read and what others read. That was documented in this classroom by question sheets that we answered at the end of each chapter. I also was able to see the students taking other exams and doing other homework assignments where it was reflected that they had indeed learned to question before they read, as they read, and after they read with the skills learned in the reading course.

Through collaboration with the reading specialist, the special education teacher learned how comprehension occurs, and then taught her students comprehension strategies they could use to enhance their learning. The comments of an experienced teacher also demonstrate how skills she learned will help students improve their learning:

> The reading specialist gave me ideas about discussions to have with the students, projects to do with the students. In particular with the graphic organizers, several students learned how to take notes in their classes, and that's something I'll definitely teach, and am planning to as an opening unit to both English and history classes next year before the students go into a classroom and take notes.

Even if viewed only from this traditional stance, as the reading specialist collaborator I have the opportunity to contribute to the overall literacy development of students. Time taken at the beginning of the school year for me to teach or reinforce notetaking skill (instead of my assuming that students possess this skill) would signal an expectation that students will actively participate during future lectures or readings. This in turn would result in more active learners. Helping both teachers and students to become more critical and efficient users of textbooks should increase the probability of more effective teaching and enhanced learning.

Sensitizing teachers to the reading levels of written materials that could be problematic for some of their students would prevent frustration and alert them to needed adaptations to encourage and ensure learning. These are only a few of the outcomes that are likely to result from the pairing of a reading specialist and a content teacher, which the teachers themselves recognized as being valuable.

The second area identified by colleagues related to instruction, with some key staff recognizing that "reading" meant more than skills and comprehension and that it encompassed communication, learning styles, and the learning process. Those who acknowledged this felt that this unique knowledge and perspective, when shared with colleagues, had the potential to transform the current teaching practice of many teachers. The science district coordinator explained the instructional benefit of the reading specialist's collaboration with content teachers:

I guess I perceive the reading specialist as having tremendous potential because you deal with one of the basic cross-cutting skills. And because I know that reading also deals with much broader issues than just reading. It's communication; you deal with learning styles. Just to deal with sub-ject area, you deal with so many other things, like instruction. Instruction is much more important for you than for some of the other teachers. They think that knowledge is more important; you are more of a process person. So, there's two cross-cutting things. I think the strength of reading teach-ers is that it's learning process, a major domain that you deal with, and read-ing, and they cross over.

The science district coordinator's remarks relative to improved learn-ing through collaboration with the reading specialist were echoed by the building principal:

Well, regardless of what we talk about in schools regarding the changing nature of learning assessment, a great deal is still based upon information that's acquired and its use, and a lot of that, of course, relates to literacy. And I see a reading specialist who knows a lot about the acquisition of language and the use of language and getting meaning from text as being able to help classroom teachers to understand those issues, and by under-standing those issues to help their students, in some cases directly teach them how to get meaning from text, how then to do something with that meaning in order to organize it in a way that provides meaning for them, then to answer new questions that weren't originally in the text.

The principal acknowledges that the particular knowledge a reading spe-cialist has relative to the comprehension of language in all its forms— whether through listening, speaking, reading, or writing—is information he would like shared with all teachers. He sees the possibility for this information to transform teaching practice as teachers integrate learning strategies with their pedagogy.

The third area to appear in the responses of colleagues was that of team building or liaison. Since I have an open, flexible schedule, I am able not only to work with colleagues in their classrooms and with individual students, but also to attend meetings and share my perspective. A case in point was my being invited to attend the meeting of the science and mathematics departments because I could quickly apprise them of the efforts to date of the ninth-grade English/social studies teachers—known collectively as the "ninth-grade collaborative." These teachers are paired to promote an improved teaching/learning environment. They have a common planning period, meet as a group once a week, and also meet departmentally. I am a member of the collaborative and serve as a resource to them by regularly attending the latter two meetings. Being the link between the two groups, I not only provide information to one group, but also open communications between the groups in the future, and possibly provide the basis for more extended interdisciplinary work. Because reading is identified as a "cross-cutting skill," some colleagues felt that a natural contribution for me would be to serve among many groups as a "team builder."

A Resource for Teachers and Students

In addition to my collaborative work as a reading specialist with content teachers, there were others with whom I collaborated. They included a high school counselor who asked me to test one of his students at the request of the boy's parents. Not only did I test the student and speak with him about the results and the implications for improvement, but in a letter to the boy's parents narrated essentially what I had said to the student himself. On another occasion, in response to a letter from the father of a senior, the principal asked me to work with the young man to improve his study skills, notetaking ability, and test-taking skills. After meeting with him on a tutorial basis for a few months during his study halls each week, and prior to the student's graduation, I wrote a letter to his father apprising him of the efforts that had been extended on behalf of his son. The principal was appreciative, and commented in a note to me that "by keeping parents informed of our efforts with the students, we help to complete a circle of support that is essential to the success of schools and their mission."

This circle of support is a reference to the entire educational community that consists of students, school staff, parents, and the school board. The principal, along with many others in the school community, is interested in the school addressing its mission as it is reflected in the district's strategic plan. In order to do that, he has begun cultivating a collaborative school culture, one that reflects shared values and beliefs, where there is a "we" instead of an "I" mentality (Sergiovanni, 1993). Although this complex task takes time, successful efforts to nurture collaborative cultures (where teachers discuss teaching, plan and teach lessons together, evaluate their efforts, and are open to experiments) will have a positive impact on student achievement (Little, 1982).

The principal is doing his part to plant the seeds of change so that good cultures grow (Sergiovanni, 1993). In my role as a resource in the building, I support his efforts by helping teachers focus on the teaching and learning process. My response, coming through the lens of a reading specialist, brings to bear the unique framework that guides the approach to learning to which most reading specialists subscribe. Reading specialists are informed by theories and research related to language acquisition, literacy, and learning. Our feedback to colleagues would always be to encourage more active participation of students through strategies for instruction that reflect a "Before, During and/or After concept as an organizing structure" (Lytle & Botel, 1990, p. 35).

These new understandings basically mediate the argument between those who suggest that education should focus on knowledge acquisition and those who believe that the production or the process of learning should be emphasized. Arguing that process is just as important as content, Costa and Liebmann (1995) present compelling reasons for teachers concerned about "covering the curriculum" to modify their stance. They point out that knowledge is so rapidly increasing that it is doubling every 5 years. "If students are to keep pace with the rapid increase in knowledge, we cannot continue to organize curriculum in discrete compartments" (p. 23). Instead of having students concentrate on absorbing endless, isolated facts and concepts, they recommend that the teacher be selective about the content, distinguish between important and unimportant information, and teach content that will facilitate connection making and discernment of patterns. Teachers, they suggested, need to emphasize meaning making and help students to learn how to do this independently. "Learners need to discover that they can be self-referencing, self-initiating, and self-evaluating—that their capacity to comprehend comes from within" (p. 23). Sensitive to those who would accuse them of "dumbing down the curriculum," Costa and Liebmann clearly stated their position:

> Our recommendation is not that content be undervalued but, rather, that content be rethought as means, not ends. We must value content because it enhances the development of processes, and judiciously select content because of its generative qualities. (p. 24)

I have the opportunity, therefore, as a high school reading specialist serving as a resource, to be a change agent (Freire, 1993), someone from within the school organization who can help teachers examine their own practices and generate strategies that will enable students to comprehend more and to see learning as a perpetual endeavor. While not being the only influence in helping the educational culture evolve into that of a collaborative society, the high school reading specialist in a resource role to both colleagues and students nevertheless makes a significant contribution toward that end.

As a result of surveying and analyzing the responses of colleagues to my work with them, I see clearly the potential of someone in my position making a significant contribution toward the development of collaboration in the high school. Judging from my work with teachers across the disciplines and from dealing with a continuum of requests involving support for enhancing teaching and learning for both teachers and students, it is evident to me that the reading specialist can readily contribute to fostering and developing collaboration schoolwide. That the staff spoke of positive outcomes from their collaborations, and that they also communicated confidence in the process of collaboration for the future, should be encouragement enough to recommend this role for a reading specialist in every high school's effort to improve learning.

REFERENCES

Barth, R. (1990). *Improving schools from within*. San Francisco: Jossey-Bass.

Costa, A.L., & Kallick, B. (1993). Through the lens of a critical friend. *Educational Leadership, 51*(2), 49–51.

Costa, A.L., & Liebmann, R. (1995). Process is as important as content. *Educational Leadership, 52*(6), 23–24.

Freire, P. (1993). *Pedagogy of the oppressed* (2nd ed.). New York: Continuum.

Hargreaves, A., Earl, L., & Ryan, J. (1996). *Schooling for change: Reinventing education for early adolescents*. Washington, DC: Falmer Press.

Little, J.W. (1982). Norms of collegiality and experimentation: Workplace conditions of school success. *American Educational Research Journal, 19*(3), 325–340.

Lytle, S.L., & Botel, M. (1990). *The Pennsylvania framework for reading, writing and talking across the curriculum*. Harrisburg, PA: Pennsylvania Department of Education.

Ogle, D. (1986). K-W-L: A teaching model that develops active reading of expository text. *The Reading Teacher, 39*, 564–572.

Saphier, T. (1985). Good seeds grow in strong cultures. *Educational Leadership, 42*(6), 64–74.

Sergiovanni, T.J. (1993). *Building community in schools*. San Francisco: Jossey-Bass.

From Information to Interaction: Involving Parents in the Literacy Development of Their Adolescent

James A. Rycik

Most efforts to improve communication with parents have focused on increasing the volume of messages from the school to the parent. The assumption seems to be that if parents receive more information, they will understand the school program, which will lead to more interest in their children's schoolwork, more time spent helping them with assignments, and more efforts to convince their children of the value of an education.

Although this seems logical, many school administrators and teachers have been disappointed in the results of their ever-increasing efforts to inform parents. It may seem that either the information is not being received, or that parents' increased knowledge about school is not being translated into effective action with students.

Smith (1996) found the "regular communication" was one of parents' most frequently cited causes for the success of their youngster's secondary school. They particularly valued "Happy-gram" messages from teachers that told them about significant progress their young people had made. More important, however, is the observation that parents believed successful schools treated their children with respect as individuals and "teachers were concerned with their well-being and their personal interests in addition to their academic pursuits" (p. 114). Communication was important to these parents, but they wanted communication that went beyond information to say, "We think your child is important and interesting."

Information Is Not Enough

Cotton and Mann (1994) studied the attempts of middle level teachers and administrators to involve parents in the school. They found many involvement activities occurred, from homework hotlines to parent conferences, but that parents became genuinely involved only when their

From the *NASSP Bulletin*, *82*(600), 67–72, October 1998. Reprinted with permission of the National Association of Secondary School Principals.

children were directly involved in an activity. School personnel were dissatisfied. Apparently, none of their efforts resulted in the day-to-day involvement between parents, their children, and the curriculum they thought would be ideal.

Efforts to involve parents with the school and with their children's work should focus not only on sending information but also on fostering interaction. Interaction implies an equal and ongoing relationship in which home and school share information and consciously collaborate to enrich students' learning. For the principal, fostering true interaction is a tall order indeed, but there are several approaches principals can encourage among school personnel that increase the quantity and quality of interaction.

Building Better Homework

Homework in secondary school may be a source of contention in families. Parents may be frustrated by adolescents who seem unwilling or unable to say what assignments they have. Parents who work long hours and have limited time to spend with their adolescents may resent the time homework takes away from family life. This may be especially true if the homework assignments require help the parents are unable to give, or if parent and child both perceive the assignments as pointless drudgery.

Homework may be the most frequent opportunity the school has to involve parents in an interaction with the curriculum, but the opportunity is frequently wasted. Principals can do much to help teachers design better homework by providing examples of assignments that show off students' learning and invite parents' active participation.

Epstein and her colleagues (1992) developed a homework program called TIPS (Teachers Involve Parents in Schoolwork), which is designed to promote a collaborative relationship between teacher and parent. The general approach of the recommended TIPS homework activities is for students to explain something they have learned in school to someone at home. Rather than making parents responsible for teaching or correcting lessons, TIPS assignments allow them to join the teacher in validating and reinforcing the students' learning.

Morris and Kaplan (1994) describe a program in which parents and students read the same book and then meet for a "book talk" session with other students and parents who had read the book. Sometimes the sessions were led by a parent and sometimes by school personnel, including administrators, librarians, and teachers. Morris and Kaplan report an enthusiastic response from parents, who were often surprised by the quality of the literary discussion their youngsters could produce.

A structured and systematic program is not the only way to encourage parents' interaction with their adolescent learners. Whenever parents are invited to become partners in learning rather than homework inspectors, the principle of interaction is applied.

As part of an interdisciplinary unit called "When Worlds Collide," I invited my middle level students and their parents to watch a related science fiction movie together. Parents and students both answered questions that centered on key ideas from the unit, such as "When the aliens (which in some cases were from Earth) landed on another planet, did they try to learn how to live on the new planet, or did they try to make it more like their home planet?" Parents often enjoyed introducing their children to classic movies such as *Forbidden Planet*, and students' understanding of the them was often enhanced by hearing a parent's answers to questions.

Parents as Audience

As Cotton and Mann's (1994) findings suggest, parents are most involved when their own children are the focus. Schools might, therefore, look for ways to highlight the accomplishments of students in ways that encourage parents to act as witnesses and participants. Interdisciplinary units planned by teams in my former school often ended with a culminating activity designed to bring in parents as an "active audience" for their child's work and that of other students.

The "When Worlds Collide" unit ended with a fair at which teams of students attempted to "sell" visitors on the advantages of the colony they had designed for another planet. Students created a display for each colony and a brochure advertising its advantages. They also had designated salespersons discussing the adaptations people would have to make to live on the planet. Parents who visited the fair were given a supply of "money" to invest in colonies that seemed potentially profitable or to buy passage to one that seemed like an attractive place to settle. A variety of science, social studies, language arts, science, art, and math skills were on display. What's more, the activity was fun.

As a middle level language arts teacher, I transformed the biography unit in the curriculum into an "I Have a Dream Award" competition. After studying the Reverend Martin Luther King, Jr., and his famous speech, teams of students were given a nomination form and invited to read biographies with an eye toward choosing a figure who exemplified his ideals. Those teams whose nominees became finalists made presentations to a panel of parent judges who listened and asked probing questions about the presentation and the written nomination. This was not only a highly authentic communication activity for students, it was also an invaluable opportunity for parents to interact with students and with the curriculum.

Jacobsen (1998) created a comprehensive chapter on collaboration between parents and schools. She added several ideas for building on parents' interest in their own children to help them interact with the curriculum. She suggested, for instance, that students contribute to newsletters that are sent home or that they write letters describing their learning to which their parents can reply. She also suggested that parents and students can be asked to bring in family photos or brief reminiscences to be included in class books or newsletters about current units.

Principals can play an important role in supporting these efforts. First they can provide important logistical support by helping teachers to schedule facilities, and by working with parent organizations to provide refreshments and publicity. Second, they can draw to teachers' attention parents who have been willing and able to help with big projects. Perhaps most important, principals can stay involved enough in these events that they can provide sincere and knowledgeable recognition to students and teachers. Often a little public appreciation is all students and teachers require to begin a valuable interaction between parents and school.

Parents as Experts

Interaction implies that each party in a relationship has a role to play and a contribution to make. One of the most important opportunities for interaction a secondary teacher may have is the parent conference. I used to inadvertently startle parents at the beginning of conferences by starting out with the question, "What would you like to tell me about your child?" I eventually learned to warn them they would be asked to share with me the crucial knowledge they had about their children, their pattern of school achievement, and their interests and personality traits at home.

I gradually developed a list of questions that included "How does your child's performance so far compare with previous years?" "What subject (if any) does your child talk about at home?" "What methods have previous teachers used successfully?" The answers gave me a much more complete picture of the student as an individual and ensured that information would be given as well as received by all parties during the conference.

Parents can be drawn into the curriculum when they are treated as knowledgeable informants about subjects their children are studying. In my middle school, for example, parents were asked to contribute examples of "real-world math" or "real-world writing" and describe how they used those subjects in managing a home or in their occupations. I started every school year by having students interview their parents for stories that happened before the students' earliest memories. Reflecting on their earliest childhood helped students relive some fond memories and "family folklore." The interviewing also allowed them to reflect on how far they had come toward being an adult.

My colleague who taught social studies often constructed giant time lines on which important family milestones could be situated among "official" events in history. At one of our unit culminating activities students and parents were invited to contribute information about their ancestors to a Heritage Wall that remained in the cafeteria for several days. As part of the same Heritage fair, grandparents were invited to participate in a videotaped interview about their experiences during the Great Depression and World War II.

Two points need to be noted about involving parents in the curriculum more often: Schools must be sensitive to the wide variety of students' homes. Parents were the usual source for the early childhood tales, for instance, but students were told to interview "someone who has known you for a long time and cares about you."

The second point is that adolescents may feel a conflict between the school's desire to draw parents into an interaction with them and their increasing need for independence. Actually, I was surprised how little of this I saw as long as there was some "elbow room" for the student to be with peers. I was also surprised to note that adolescent students' difficulty relating to their parents did not always extend to someone else's parents. In this sense, school became an important vehicle for keeping adolescents connected to appropriate members of the adult community.

REFERENCES

Cotton, E.G., & Mann, G. (1994, November). *Encouraging meaningful parent and family participation: A survey of parent involvement practices in California and Texas.* Paper presented at the 21st Annual Conference of the National Middle School Association, Cincinnati, Ohio.

Epstein, J.L., et al. (1992). *TIPS: Teachers involve parents in schoolwork, language arts, and science/health. Interactive homework in the middle grades: Manual for teachers.* Baltimore: Johns Hopkins University, Center on Families, Communities, Schools, and Children's Learning. (ERIC Document Reproduction Service No. ED 355 032)

Jacobsen, J. (1998). *Content area reading: Integration with the language arts.* Albany, NY: Delmar.

Morris, N.C., & Kaplan, I. (1994). Middle school parents are good partners for reading. *Journal of Reading, 2,* 130–131.

Smith, C. (1996). Context for secondary reading programs. In D. Lapp, J. Flood, & N. Farnan (Eds.), *Content area reading and learning: Instructional strategies* (2nd ed.). Boston: Allyn & Bacon.

Reaching Beyond Yourself: A Middle School Service Learning Program

Martha A. Magner

In the United States, a country that has had a long history of charitable service to those in need, the loss of volunteers is a serious problem in the short term for the agencies and in the long term for the failure to develop a population of citizens with the value of service, responsibility for others, and altruism. *Service learning* is the somewhat modest title given to a program to attain a most ambitious goal: providing students with the opportunity to recognize the needs of their communities and to take responsibility for helping to meet those needs. As the basic structure of the family has changed, so have the demands on each of its members. There are few opportunities and often little time for our young adolescents to experience the rewards that come from providing service to those outside their family constellation. It is not surprising that service organizations report a drastic drop in the numbers of people willing to give them time and energy.

The context for literacy learning includes the community in which students live, and literacy can help them connect with that community in new ways. The middle school environment and philosophy provide an especially favorable opportunity for connecting students with services in their communities. Young adolescents are seeking to define themselves through enhancing their self-esteem. A service learning program that allows community-based organizations to reach out to young adolescents offers a positive opportunity at this critical point in their lives. Experiencing the satisfaction that providing service to another human being can bring carries a message to young adolescents that they are valued and can make a constructive difference. Agencies that are the beneficiaries of these services are munificent in the expression of their admiration and appreciation so that the young adolescent receives confirmation of his or her worth.

The last several years have seen a growing interest in service learning as an opportunity for educational reform. Many educators see it as a strategy for putting learning into context, engaging alienated youth, introducing problem solving into schools, providing opportunities to learn about various careers, and building school/community relations. It is a redefining of service as an activity undertaken for learning and as an activity that can shape or be shaped by the curriculum. Students deal with problems that are not contrived, and they must contribute their energy and knowledge to solve them. Through the experiences, young adolescents can gain a clearer understanding of themselves as partners in meeting community needs. The foundation of true learning in such a program is the planned connection between the service and the learning along with a conscious reflection on the experience.

June 2000 marked the end of 10 years of a service learning program at the A. MacArthur Barr Middle School in Nanuet, New York. The program developed as an attempt to overcome the mismatch between the intellectual and emotional needs of the young adolescent and the typical middle school curriculum as described in the report of the Carnegie Council on Adolescent Development on middle schools. At the A. MacArthur Barr Middle School, the decision was made to develop a program in which the traditional divisive factors of society such as age and ethnicity are bridged through helping others.

The Nanuet program was suggested by the school principal, and after extensive preparation by the initial team, it was implemented with the help of the National Helpers Network in New York City. Then, with the approval of the New York State Department of Education, the program became an integral part of the Home and Careers Curriculum. The stated purposes of this program are

- to offer service to the students' own community,
- to provide students the opportunity to apply skills and knowledge learned in home and careers classes to real-life situations,
- to create conditions by which students feel known and are a part of something, and
- to provide leadership opportunities.

The team designed a program that involved all the eighth-grade students during the quarter in which they would ordinarily be assigned to home and careers classes. Sites were chosen that were as close to the school as possible. They included nursery schools, preschools, elementary schools, a school for severely handicapped children, a nursing home, and a senior citizen's center. The home and careers teacher became the coordinator of the program and worked closely with the director at each site to design the appropriate programs for the individual sites. She also visited sites each day and was in continual contact with the site supervisors throughout each quarter so that problems and triumphs were recognized and training activities remained relevant to the young adolescents' on-site experiences.

One of the major drawbacks to the initiation of this type of program is transportation. The team at Nanuet came up with a creative solution to this thorny problem. Arrangements were made with the school district to transport the students to the sites during the periods when home and careers classes were taught. This involved dividing the students into two groups (as they would have been divided on the school campus) and then arranging for two buses to make two round trips. On the first trip, the buses dropped the first group of students at each site. They returned to the school to pick up the second group, then as the second group was being dropped off the first group was picked up to return to the school. The third trip was to pick up the second group of students and return them to the school. To make this possible, each Service Learning period was scheduled so that it was preceded or followed by an activity or lunch/recess period. This allowed more flexibility in getting the students to the sites and back to school on time. This scheduling procedure provided each student with the opportunity to spend about 1 hour a day for 5 days each week working at the sites.

One of the most important elements of the program is that the students are always interacting with people. Some of that interaction is done through writing (see Activity 1). They are not assigned isolated tasks that would soon become meaningless for the young adolescent. Instead, they are performing a needed service for a fellow human being. At the elementary school the students assist the teacher with whole class activities, one-on-one tutoring, art activities, book making, and media productions.

Activity 1
An Open Letter to the Program Leader

At the beginning of any new educational experience, it is helpful to think about your strengths and weaknesses. It is also helpful for your teachers to learn about how their students view themselves. One way to accomplish this is to have you write a letter that tells the site leaders things they need to know about you, such as

- your outside interests and hobbies
- subjects you like or dislike in school
- how you spend your free time
- what you like or don't like about people
- how you want to be treated by others
- what you perceive to be your strengths and/or weaknesses in dealing with others
- what concerns you have in terms of service learning
- what three or four personal characteristics are likely to help you do your job in service learning
- what three or four characteristics may cause you difficulty in doing your job in service learning
- what two strong characteristics do you hope to develop further in service learning and two not-so-strong areas you hope to improve

At the day-care centers, students help the young children with art activities, read to them, and often oversee hygiene care. The nursery school activities are similar, but, in addition, the students help with circle games, singing, and dancing. At the school for the physically and mentally handicapped, the students assist with exercise, eating, puppet shows, academic work, and socialization. Those assigned to the nursing home help transport the patients, serve lunch, play games, draw sketches of the seniors, and engage them in conversation.

Reflection is an integral part of the service learning experience. Students are encouraged to write about their daily experiences in a journal (see Activity 2). Each week trained teachers work with groups of

---

Activity 2
Suggestions for a Daily Journal

Each student will be required to keep a daily journal of his or her experiences in service learning. Your reflection teacher will be discussing your experiences during your PEP or activity period.

The journal is basically for you. It is a place to try ideas, to make sense of what you are doing and how you are feeling. It's a place to practice writing and do some deep thinking. Set aside a special notebook for this journal; don't use the notebook for anything else. At least once a week, or whenever you have been at the placement site, write a paragraph describing your experiences. You might also want to write about the feelings and ideas that have been triggered by them. The questions that follow suggest some things you might write about, but are certainly not the only things. On any one day you might write on one or two, but by the end of the project you should have written at least once on nearly every one of them.

- What new skill did you learn?
- What did you do in your work that was fun or satisfying?
- Did you get an idea that would improve your work? This program? The world?
- What did you do that helped you get along and work with others?
- What criticisms did you receive and how did you respond to them?
- What compliments were you given and what did they mean to you?
- What happened that made you feel uncomfortable or unhappy?
- What did you do today that made you feel proud? Why?
- What were some of the things you wanted to say today and did not?
- What did you learn from a disappointment or failure?
- What did you discover about other people?
- How did your feelings about any person change as a result of today's activities?

---

about 10 students to direct and encourage them to think about their experiences during the week, to share their journal entries, and to form conclusions about the effect these experiences have had on them and the people with whom they interacted each day. They are encouraged to share both their feelings and concerns with the group and also to keep a journal recounting their many experiences.

It is reflection, along with the human connection, that primarily differentiates service learning from community service. It allows the experience to be far more important in the development of the students than simple community service. By analyzing their experience during reflection, the students come to understand the dynamics that are occurring, and can plan to make the experience more beneficial for themselves and the individuals at the sites. One language activity that helps students achieve this understanding is interviewing one of the professionals at the site (see Activity 3).

At the conclusion of their time in service learning, each student is responsible for a major project depicting his or her feelings and experiences at the site (see Activity 4). The individual student may choose from various forms of presentation including an essay, videos with written

---

Activity 3
Informational Interview

Identify someone at the site you are helping and interview them. It may be the supervisor or director at the site of some other employee. Tell that person that you would like to ask them some questions about their work. You could ask them the following questions:

1. What is the purpose of this organization? Include the service that is provided and to whom.

2. What are some of the different jobs available here?

3. What is the general description of your job?

4. How did you get started in this job?

5. What other jobs have you had? What was your first?

6. What specific skills are needed for this job?

7. What personal qualities are needed for this job?

8. What do you like and dislike about your work?

9. What would you change if you could? (about the job or yourself)

10. How does your work affect your personal life? (family, leisure, stress)

11. Do you think the need for workers in this field will increase or decrease in the next 10 years? Why?

12. What kind of education and training is needed for this kind of work?

Activity 4
Leaving Something Behind: A Product

Preparing a presentation or product helps you pull together what you have learned, and also gives your teachers a concrete tool to use in evaluating individual and group accomplishments and the program as a whole.

- Plan early what kind of product you or the group will make.
- Allow plenty of time for revising, editing, correcting, and practicing.
- Set deadlines.
- Don't save the whole production for the last few weeks; produce parts of it as you go along.

Here are some sample types of final projects:

1. Make a formal presentation of the project to an appropriate audience such as parents, the school board, or another class or group at your school, or bring in a resource person such as your principal or a school board member. The point is to have the chance to tell an outside audience what you have achieved.

2. Produce a lasting document of the project: photo essay, videotape, booklet, or slide presentation. Such a document preserves achievements, and the process by which they were made for others who want to do something similar.

3. Prepare a tip sheet to pass on things you have learned to later participants. For example, middle school students in child-care programs have developed "Tips for Reading Aloud to Young Children."

4. Case Study: Observe one of the people you are helping or an adult coworker closely over a period of time, taking notes while you are at your placement or immediately afterward. Look for specific actions, interactions, or comments that seem particularly important for the individual you are observing. Use concrete details in describing this person's appearance, personality, and behavior in your case study.

5. Communication Problems: Identify and describe one example of a communication problem that was caused by two people not understanding each other's situation. This problem might involve you or it might be between two other people you observe. Describing the problem in detail may help you figure out what caused the problem.

6. A playwriting project leading to a performance for the school or community, perhaps with senior-youth relations as a theme.

7. A storytelling project that could result in telling stories or writing a short storybook.

8. A program of singing or dancing, emphasizing the cultural backgrounds of those involved or the popular culture appropriate to the participants (jointly learning the Lindy and break dancing, for instance, or comparing through films and videotapes the styles of Fred Astaire and Michael Jackson).

explanations, photographic essays with written explanations, audiotapes with a script, a manual for those students who will spend time at the site in the future, a collage of the people and activities at the site with written and oral presentations, case studies of the people at a site, or oral histories from the seniors at the nursing home. These projects and presentations become part of the evaluation process by the teacher, the site supervisor, and the other students.

Each June the eighth-grade students are given the opportunity to talk to the seventh-grade students about their experiences at the various sites. The seventh-grade students are then asked to write the names of their first three site choices on an index card. As the home and careers teacher plans for the coming year every effort is made again to give each student his or her first choice.

The students are fully prepared for their sites during the first week of each quarter. Under the direction of the home and careers teacher they learn about the site and the skills needed at each placement. Therefore, they arrive fully trained and aware of their responsibilities. The receiving organizations see them as energetic and enthusiastic resources and problem solvers ready to work and provide valuable assistance to the staff. This type of placement in challenging situations where they associate with adults enables them to gain experience and knowledge that can serve to strengthen and extend classroom skills. It involves them in active roles, establishes new relationships with adult facilitators, and thus alters their role in both places. They are able to test and explore new skills and career options while participating in activities that yield visible outcomes and a sense of efficacy. In addition, they are provided with leadership opportunities and can become role models for younger students.

At a time when schools are being attacked for not providing their students with the ethical values needed in U.S. society, the service learning program is designed as an instrument to help adolescents develop altruism and responsibility for others. These are values on which civilizations thrive and with which individuals with diverse beliefs concur. They are also values that provide a foundation for developing literacy in a context that is personally, socially, and culturally relevant. The service learning program has set for itself an ambitious goal—providing students with the opportunity to recognize the needs of their communities and to take responsibility for helping to meet those needs.

REFERENCES

Andrus, E. (1996). Service learning: Taking students beyond community service. *Middle School Journal*, *28*(2), 10–18.

Beane, J. (1993). *A middle school curriculum: From rhetoric to reality* (2nd ed.). Columbus, OH: National Middle School Association.

Carnegie Corporation. (1989). *Turning points. Preparing American youth for the 21st century*. New York: Carnegie Corporation.

Fertman, C.I., White, G.P., & White, L.J. (1996). *Service learning in the middle school: Building a culture of service*. Columbus, OH: National Middle School Association.

Shine, J. (1996). Service learning. A promising strategy for connecting students to communities. *Middle School Journal, 28*(2), 3–9.

Using Data to Improve Literacy Learning for High School Students

Michael C. Biance and Judith L. Irvin

When reading the recently released National Education Goals Report (1998), it is easy for educators working with students everyday to become disheartened. When the question is posed, "Has the U.S. increased the percentage of students who meet the National Education Goals Panel's performance standard in reading?", the response is: grade 4–no change; grade 8–no change; grade 12–worse. Initiatives alone, whether implemented at the national, state, or district level, cannot bring about improvement in literacy. They can generate some immediacy, some momentum, and hopefully a supportive infrastructure, but the real improvement happens in schools and with individual students.

In this article, we discuss ways to use the data normally available to educators to improve the literacy learning program in individual schools. We advocate analyzing data by cohort groups, such as incoming ninth-grade students, to understand the impact of a particular instructional program over time. This approach allows educators to view school efforts more systematically and facilitates the identification of trends that may affect decisions made for students and teachers. Disaggregating data (breaking it down into sub-parts) by reading skill and by class period provides teachers with the information they need to help their students.

Using Student Cohorts for Data Analysis

Just as a photograph can capture the image of a person at a specific time given a set of specific circumstances, assessment also describes student performance at a particular time and given particular circumstances. Just as one may think the photograph is not a good portrayal, a particular assessment may not give an accurate or holistic "picture." It is important therefore to get beyond the inadequacy of one data set, and look at all of the data available on students from multiple perspectives, especially over time.

When norm-referenced test scores are released, the press typically compares the current scores to the previous year's scores (generated by a different group of students) and makes a determination of success or failure

From *Voices from the field*, *2*(2), 12–14, Spring/Summer 2000. Reprinted with permission of the National High School Association.

of the school's instructional program. The responses to these published test scores range from celebration to "We had a bad year." All too often, instructional programs are immediately changed (e.g., a new reading program is purchased), staff training may be imposed, and bureaucratic paperwork is required to solve "the problem." Another approach, however, is to analyze the success of a cohort of students over time. Then, when new instructional programs are implemented, decisions can be made that are supported with data. Some useful questions to ask are:

- How has this particular group of students fared as a result of a particular instructional program?
- Is there a shift of students in the lowest quartile (those who were assessed at between 1–25%) to the next quartile during their high school career? Why or why not?
- Are the students in the middle quartiles showing an upward movement? Why or why not?
- Are the students in the highest quartile (76–100) continuing to achieve at that level? Why or why not?
- What strategies are being used with the students in each of the quartiles?

Many states also require a competency test as a condition for graduation. Many of these high stakes tests espouse "higher standards" and report the percentage of students who pass or fail. Questions of the alignment of the competency test with the curriculum and with other tests may help high school educators use these tests to make decisions about the instructional program. Some useful questions to ask are:

- What is the relationship of the students' achievement on these tests to their achievement on the norm-referenced tests?
- What is the alignment of the curriculum and teachers' instructional practices of the reading skills assessed on each test?

A study of state level tests conducted by the Southern Regional Education Board (SREB) led researchers to conclude that "proficiency" on one assessment may or may not be equivalent to "proficiency" on another nationally normed assessment (Musick, 1996). When states have attached high stakes (i.e., a passing score is required for graduation) to a test, these tests generally have lower standards. The SREB study pointed out the disparity between student performance on state tests and National Assessment of Educational Progress (NAEP) standards. Musick (1996) has stated, "For example, many states report that 70 percent and 80 percent of their students meet their own performance standards for student achievement on the state tests in mathematics and reading. Yet, only about

30 percent of the students in these states score at the "proficient" (good enough) level on the National Assessment" (p. 3). Passage rates on state high stakes tests should not necessarily be considered a statement of high academic achievement nationally and must be scrutinized before programmatic decisions are made.

Disaggregating the Data

Using total school scores for school improvement is akin to treating an illness with a general antibiotic. If a broad-brush approach does not work, then a more specific targeted diagnosis may be performed. Disaggregating data provides specific information on the front end of the school improvement process. The establishment of a cohort allows one to analyze a particular group of students in a variety of ways over time. Evaluating program effectiveness over time can be guided by asking relevant questions such as:

- How did males versus females fare?
- How well have the various ethnic groups achieved?
- What has been the impact of students taking particular subjects (e.g., reading)?
- How well have students who have been in particular instructional programs (e.g., Computer Assisted Instruction) achieved on these various assessments?
- How did students in a particular quartile who were in a special program (e.g., At-Risk, Title I) do as compared to their counterparts who were not in that program?
- Was there a correlation between the students instructional program and their demonstration of mastery of specific skills on the test?
- Can a profile of students who either did not pass a state high stakes test or scored in the lower quartiles be developed?

It is only when this type of data is displayed can one begin to discern the areas in need of further investigation. Additionally, after disaggregating the data in these various ways, cohorts can be compared by asking questions such as, Have the last three cohorts (this year's freshmen, sophomores, and juniors who have taken a reading course) shown similar amounts of improvement year to year?

Alignment

The school summary of test scores presented by the media may do nothing more than encourage complacency or demoralize good faith efforts of teachers and administrators. Since norm-referenced tests and state tests have limited numbers of items per skill area, the identified deficiencies must be further assessed. If further testing is needed, it must line up with the items tested on the state tests in order to provide teachers with the information they need to address any deficiencies. The selection of effective programs or interventions therefore must be based upon data indicating identified specific student needs. When instructional programs, interventions, or materials are selected in this way, more assessment data points can be established and used to monitor student progress. This alignment also provides the opportunity for the instructional program to be monitored, evaluated, and fine tuned over time.

Student Placement

Test data reflecting poor student performance often result in blaming students for not learning, teachers for not teaching, and administrators for not providing effective instructional programs. However, the culprit for poor performance is often poor placement of students in courses, which restricts their opportunity to learn what is needed. For example, a high school curriculum specialist was charged with developing a plan to address a perplexing problem: Only 43% of the school's students were passing the communications section of the state high school competency test, which was administered in the eleventh grade but actually required only ninth grade proficiency. After analyzing this target group, the specialist discovered that only 34% of the students had taken a reading course at the high school level. Analyzing the characteristics of cohort groups is often the only way to assess the reason for the low performance of students. Some useful questions to ask are:

- Compared to the norm-referenced test quartile distributions, what courses are cohort students taking?
- Have the students who did not do well on the communications section of the high stakes state test been enrolled in reading classes?
- If students are in English classes, are the skill areas identified as problematic by the assessment data maintained through regular assignments?
- What assessment data and criteria are used for student placement, and is placement giving students the instruction they need?

Making Meaningful Data Available to Teachers

If systemic change is to occur, every component of the system (the school) must be examined (Senge, 1990). For instance, if a recurring problem for a cohort group is using diagrams or reading informational text, these data need to be provided to all teachers. However, the mere communication of deficiencies will not suffice. To be most helpful, teachers must see profiles of their classes by period with the deficiencies noted. Teachers may need in-service or peer coaching about effective intervention or teaching strategies to address these deficiencies.

From a more proactive articulation perspective, the identification of ninth grade cohorts provides the opportunity to "go both ways" with the data. Besides monitoring this group during their high school career, it is possible to trace their progress before ninth grade. The analysis of student gains in reading and specific skills from elementary through middle school provides a longitudinal perspective of both individual student performance and instructional programs. This information can have a dual impact by signaling that improvements may be necessary in curriculum or student services. Furthermore, when data is disaggregated by feeder school, the data provide elementary and middle school principals valuable information on the strengths or weaknesses of their former students who are now in high school. All of this information can be used in K–12 school improvement planning.

Taking Action

Improving literacy learning in the high school will come about only when the problem is approached systematically. As overwhelming as the task might seem, and despite the pressures of increased accountability, the tools to enhance literacy learning do exist. A thoughtfully designed data analysis plan uses cohorts, disaggregates the data to identify trends over time, aligns instructional programs, incorporates strategies and materials to meet specifically identified student needs, assures proper student placement, and involves all teachers. These steps are necessary to make significant gains in test scores. More importantly, taking a strategic approach to the school improvement of literacy learning is what our students deserve.

REFERENCES

Musick, M. (1996). *Setting education standards high enough.* Atlanta, GA: Southern Region Education Board.

National Education Goals Panel. (1998). *1998 National Education Goals Panel report.* Washington, DC: Author.

Senge, P. (1990). *The fifth discipline: The art and practice of the learning organization.* New York: Doubleday.

A Commitment to Reimagining Adolescent Literacy Learning

Shakespeare referred to the future as "the undiscovered country." Educators cannot hope to map that country while standing on the its borderline at the beginning of a new century. It is natural, though, to peer into the distance and try to catch a glimpse of the terrain we and our students will eventually traverse. For their first issue of 2000, the editors of *Reading Research Quarterly* invited prominent literacy theorists and researchers to respond to questions about the future (Readence & Barone, 2000). These questions included the following:

- What will literacy instruction be like in the next millennium?
- How will literacy be defined?
- What will the political climate be in literacy in the future?
- What will classrooms and schools look like in the new millennium?
- What are the expectations for literacy materials/children's literature in the next millennium?

Although these questions are not specific to adolescent literacy, they certainly reflect major concerns that have been expressed by teachers and addressed by the authors of articles in this volume. The answers that were given serve to highlight three important concepts that will at least influence the conversation as educators try to imagine new ways in which adolescents will use, learn, and be influenced by literacy.

Multiple literacies refers to the vast range of symbols, purposes for using symbols, and modes of communication that people are mastering in the new millennium. Moje (2000) points out the connection between student diversity and a more complex view of literacy:

> Because we will be striving to teach for a just and democratic society, we will need to broaden our sense of what it means to be literate, which suggests that in schools of the new millennium we will teach literacies. We will make use of multiple forms of representation as alternative ways for students to make and communicate meaning. As we teach print literacy we will want to draw from the different literacies that students bring to school learning. (p. 129)

Critical literacy refers to ways language users can be more aware of who created the material they are reading and what purposes the author might have been trying to achieve. From a critical literacy perspective, each text provides opportunities to examine both the culture in which it was written and the cultures of those who read it.

Leland, Harste, Ociepka, Lewison, and Vasquez (1999) have developed reading instruction around text sets that involve students in discussing "how systems of meaning and power affect people and the lives they lead" (p. 70). They contend,

> As literate beings, it behooves us not only to know how to decode and make meaning, but also to understand how language works and to what ends, so that we can see ourselves in light of the kind of world we wish to create and the kind of people we wish to become. (p. 71)

This concept differs from the kind of critical thinking that is characterized as "reading beyond the lines."

A critical stance involves much more than "understanding" the meaning of printed text. It embraces the possibility of social action that is inherent in many texts and is conscious of the social differences that are related to literacy. In many respects, it is the opposite of the standards-based performance model that is being advocated today.

Critical media literacy applies the idea of being aware of the social systems involved in creating and interpreting texts to media and popular culture. Teaching a critical stance is not intended to discourage use of popular culture. Carmen Luke (1999) notes that study of popular movies and television shows has long been a required part of Australian language arts instruction. She argues that the pervasive influence of popular media makes it a necessary to guide students to recognize ways they can be manipulated and to consider how they want to use media.

Information literacy is a concept that encompasses both the use of technology and an approach to teaching and learning that says that the process of finding, evaluating, organizing, and sharing information should be the principal focus of content area instruction. The American Association of School Librarians (2000) has issued *Information Literacy: A Position Paper on Information Problem Solving* that begins by noting,

> To be prepared for a future characterized by change, students must learn to think rationally and creatively, solve problems, manage and retrieve information, and communicate effectively. By mastering information problem-solving skills students will be ready for an information-based society and a technological workplace.

Each of the articles in this section is relevant to understanding one or more of these key new concepts. Harold Foster shows that reflecting on the past is an important element of envisioning the future. He draws from the story of the Wizard of Oz to remind us that guiding adolescents to literacy independence requires a balance between broad theoretical understanding and old-fashioned dedication. Foster also reminds us that commitment takes courage: courage to use what we have already learned in the face of opposition, and courage to acknowledge how little we really know.

Marino Alvarez makes the point that technology promises more than substituting electronic texts for print. He shows how the instant access to information made possible by the Internet and World Wide Web allows teachers and students to co-create an "emergent" curriculum that crosses disciplinary barriers and engages students in sharing solutions to meaningful problems with real audiences outside the classroom.

Thomas Bean's research with his two daughters illustrates the difficulties teachers face when they attempt to engage students with traditional textbook reading. In a world where so many kinds of communication are available to adolescents for so many purposes, educators will need to rethink the place of textbook reading that is done primarily for purposes of earning grades.

Cynthia Lewis explores the ways that a popular genre such as horror stories can be a vehicle for helping students examine all the texts they use in their lives. Her account of a critical approach in action provides concrete examples of how a text meaning can differ significantly based on the readers' identification with one or more social groups.

William Kist weaves together the many threads that might make up the fabric of instruction in future classrooms. Although the new concepts and criteria he discusses may at first be daunting, Kist seems optimistic that change will eventually be change for the better, and more students will be engaged in more meaningful tasks.

Several of these articles include the authors' own questions that might guide research at the beginning of a new century. All of them are imbued with a determination to closely watch and listen to the literate lives of adolescents today as a step toward supporting the literacy independence they will need for the future.

REFERENCES

American Association of School Librarians. (2000). *Information literacy: A position paper on information problem solving.* Chicago: American Association of School Librarians, American Library Association.

Leland, C., Harste, J., Ociepka, A., Lewison, M., & Vasquez, V. (1999). Exploring critical literacy: You can hear a pin drop. *Language Arts, 77*(1), 70–73.

Luke, C. (1999). Media and cultural studies in Australia. *Journal of Adolescent & Adult Literacy, 42,* 622–626.

Reflections on the Past, Directions for the Future

Harold M. Foster

'm packing light for the 21st century—three items: a video of *The
Wizard of Oz*, a pen, and an empty journal. Step closer. Look inside
my suitcase and you'll understand why those are the things I choose to
pack.

The Wizard of Oz

I want *The Wizard of Oz* with me. After all, it is one of the few movies that
I can see again and again and still have a good time. It's colorful, the
music is good, it brings back the best memories of childhood, and the story...well, the story.... The story is about a search to complete human
beings. It seems this movie tells us we all need three ingredients to be
whole, and we all know what those three ingredients are. They are as in-
grained in the psyches of Americans as most other life-directing myths
or parables. Even now I can hear the Scarecrow singing, "If I only had a
brain," and the Tin Man echoing, "A heart," and the Lion following,
"Some courage." Yes, I want my often-watched video of *The Wizard of Oz*
to remind me that, like the Scarecrow, Tin Man, and Lion, an English/lan-
guage arts teacher of the new century needs a brain, a heart, and some
(well, maybe more than *some*) courage.

A Brain

A brain will help us remember all the lessons we have learned about language teaching. We learned these lessons from many folks. Forget about
bringing professional texts they each wrote (too heavy for carry-on lug-
gage), and forget about bringing the actual people (some will be traveling
on their own and some, sadly, have already traveled on to other places).
What I can ask my brain to bring is an assimilation of all their lessons.
To do that, I must first decide which people have most influenced my
thinking about language learning. That's a big task, and I'll probably of-

From *Voices from the Middle*, 7(2), 4–9, December 1999. Reprinted with permission of the National
Council of Teachers of English.

fend by leaving off someone's favorite (if that happens, then pack your own bag and put in whomever you choose!), but here's my carry-on list:

Lev Vygotsky taught us that language is social and kids learn language by speaking and listening to others. Also, he taught us that our job as teachers is to provide the scaffolding upon which our students will build their language abilities.

Noam Chomsky gave us a structure for understanding how people learn language holistically. Chomsky's grammar structure proposed that the most important unit of language is the meaning-carrying simple, declarative, active sentence—a unit we are all genetically capable of learning.

Jean Piaget showed us how learning takes place by doing—reading, writing, speaking, listening. Piaget also made it clear to us that we should be patient with our young students who must be allowed to over generalize, work with the whole, make mistakes in order to develop within large stages.

Frank Smith taught us that readers read in groups of words, often predicting the meaning of several specific words in any group, and that those readers who read one painful sounded-out word at a time will forget what the word means when they reach the next word.

Ken Goodman elaborated on this even further by describing how readers predict meaning, sometimes wrongly because of the need to comprehend even when very few words are missed. Goodman showed us how to look at this miscuing as a necessary step in developing as a reader.

James Moffett gave us a language sequence based to a large extent on the stage principles of Piaget. At every stage, from the simplest to the most abstract, language users worked with real reading and writing, not merely contrived classroom exercises.

Nancie Atwell gave us a complete view of writing in a workshop setting, a view so comprehensive and clear that she became the change agent for English/language arts teachers everywhere. Nancie Atwell became the example for so many of us as we worked to develop classrooms where teachers serve as mentors and guides—more like coaches than English teachers.

Donald Graves showed us that we can teach the writing process in the earliest of elementary grades. He made us see that we could turn the youngest of our students into writers. His methods are exemplars of the whole-to-part approach to teaching English/language arts.

Louise Rosenblatt provided for us a redeeming view of literature teaching that just might save reading. Her transactional theory of reading literature gives us the tools to respect our students without denying the differences they bring to our classrooms.

Next, after choosing the people, I've got to decide what the main lesson is that they *all* offered. I think they taught us that language education is about making meaning. Let's do this one again. The main lesson is that people read about subjects and people write about subjects. Simple enough. *But not simple at all.* It took us a long time to learn this lesson, and we needed those brilliant teachers. When I further distill what those people have offered, I find their theories provide the following principles:

- Language is a social activity that requires friendly audiences to learn.
- Language grows from whole to part and meaning is where we begin.
- We all develop in certain ways from concrete thinking to abstract thinking in stages that require interaction.
- Language learning is language doing. (Foster, 1994)

These are important principles. They show us that people can't be told *how* to learn language; instead, they must *do* language. They must write, read, speak, listen, and observe. As I think about this, some particular points about writing and reading literature come to mind.

Writing. Writing requires two skills: fluency first and control second. I cannot become a writer by only learning the control parts of writing—revision and editing. I must first be allowed the freedom to compose, the freedom to play with ideas, the freedom to get them down and see what they are about before I have the discipline of revision and editing imposed upon the writing act. The following are a kind of writer's bill of rights based on what our best teachers have taught us, folks including Donald Murray, Janet Emig, and Donald Graves, along with Nancie Atwell, Lucy Calkins, and Linda Rief.

Student writers are guaranteed the following:

- meaningful topics;
- freedom to write without interference;
- freedom to develop voice and discover meaning;
- the opportunity to address many audiences;
- responses to the writing;
- help in understanding the nature of correctness in writing;
- help with the skills of editing and revision;
- flexible approaches to instruction based on the needs of each writer;
- connections with reading, viewing, and speaking;

- writing places;
- writing time; and
- technology for writing.

Reading/literature. Easily the most important text on teaching literature for the millennium is Louise Rosenblatt's *Literature as Exploration*, written in 1938. Rosenblatt refutes the idea of a single correct "best" meaning to any given text (the position of New Critics). Instead, her reader response position allows readers to formulate multiple correct interpretations of a text. Such a view permits our diverse readers to read and interpret without waiting for the teacher to tell them what the correct reading and correct interpretation is (which I could only do when I had the Teacher's Guide that told me what the correct interpretation was!).

Indeed, Rosenblatt brought back the very core of the literary experience, allowing students to empathize with what they read and permitting students to bring their background to interpret and appreciate a literary work. Rosenblatt's ideas are the ultimate democratic approach to reading:

> A specific reader and a specific text at a specific time and place: change any of these, and there occurs a different circuit, a different event—a different poem. (Rosenblatt, p. 14)

When Rosenblatt talks about "the poem," she is referring to all literary works because she sees all literature as subjective and as multilayered as poetry. In effect, her point is that a work of literature only exists when a reader places meaning on it. Meaning resides in each reader in different ways, based on different life experiences. Thus, *Huckleberry Finn*, for example, may be interpreted differently by people of different ages, different races, different religions, different educational and economic experiences. Who will be correct? They may all be correct and all their interpretations may be provable by careful reading of the text. However, when teachers assert that there is only one correct reading, they have, in effect, eliminated the students from the literary experience. Remember literature, like language, is about making meaning. Literature isn't about learning how to experience literature; literature is about the experience.

Literature shared within the framework of a response-centered classroom allows those discussions that create empathy, understanding, and connections among students to emerge. Rosenblatt gives us an idea of how to allow connections among students to emerge. Rosenblatt gives us an idea of how to allow connections, valid student responses to literature based on student experiences. She gives us the framework for how to keep literature alive in the new, wired, multiple-literacy 21st century. It is our challenge in the millennium to learn how to apply Rosenblatt's reader response theory to a solid and successful pedagogy.

Although there is still much to learn about the teaching of literature, we can take the foundations of reader response and a plethora of reader-based theories with us through that Y2K door. We are no longer encumbered by rigid, teacher-centered rules when we teach literature. We have a good start on how to translate those reader-based theories into practice with things such as reading and writing workshops, literature circles, minilessons, and the writing process. Plus we have also been blessed by an abundance of new literature for our students to read. Before the 1970s, it was Shakespeare and Twain and Frost. Now we can add Paul Zindel, Judy Blume, S.E. Hinton, Cynthia Voigt, Robert Cormier, Laurence Yep, Katherine Paterson, Gary Soto, Chris Crutcher, Christopher Paul Curtis, William Sleator, Naomi Shihab Nye, Paul Janeczko, Gary Paulsen, Walter Dean Myers, Jacqueline Woodson, Sandra Cisneros, and, well, the list goes on.

As I consider instructional practices and authors, I must recognize the impact that media and technology have (and will continue to have) on my students. I've got to consider how I'll teach language learning within the media-driven, technology-based world.

Crossing over. This new world we cross over to every day is a world increasingly influenced by technology. A hard drive is no longer a trip with six kids in the car. Booting up doesn't have a thing to do with putting on your shoes. Surfing doesn't require a board, but it does require the Web, which has nothing to do with spiders but does have something to do with a mouse. Laptops aren't where grandchildren sit, mail doesn't require a stamp, and periods are now called dots. The question isn't "Are you going to use technology?" but rather "What does it mean when you don't?" More important, what does it mean when some schools have access to the information highway and others don't? As Kylene Beers recently asked me, "Who's being forced to sit at the back of the technology bus, and what's it going to take to make sure all students have access to information with the most current technology?"

Not only do we need to teach our students about technology and ensure their access to it, but we also need to teach them media literacy. We are a media-driven society. We love our movies and magazines, television programs and even infomercials for good reasons. They are strong and powerful media on every level, nourishing, entertaining, illuminating, visionary. We will need to study and teach all forms of media, equipping our students to handle the information age of the new millennium; to know not only how to use the technology, but how to interpret the media from TV and movies to the future—integrated multimedia, computer TV, Web sites, movies on demand, banking, shopping, entertainment. These media compete with the written media, which they will never replace. Our goals for the study of these media are to create citizens who use the media as tools, as enrichment for their lives, rather than creating slaves to the illusory and often dangerous images fed to all of us by the media (Foster, 1994). This is our challenge and we will certainly need all of our brains to help us with this one.

A Heart

With all that, you might think my suitcase is full. No way. I've certainly got room for a heart. Can't think about teaching without thinking about kids and can't think about kids without thinking about a heart. Look at kids. All of them. In particular, right now I'm thinking about Brandi, Jason, and Laticia, three kids who, like so many of the kids we've all taught, come from strong families, families who have provided them computers and books and magazines and newspapers. Families who serve as reading role models, families who manage dinners together at least once or twice a week where ideas are discussed and futures are planned. Above all, Brandi and Jason and Laticia have families who model human relationships that contain love and dignity, not all the time, but certainly most of the time. Teachers of Brandi and Jason and Laticia take them to the stars. And these kids need their teachers. The parents who have prepared them for school are not teachers. Those parents depend upon the teachers to teach, inspire, nurture, and to make it possible for these students to reach the goals their families equipped them to reach.

When I think of kids, I also think of Dawn. Dawn lives in a hard-scrabble world with a loving but busy and poor working mother. Dawn, who is filled with promise and the optimism of a courageous young person, met her guide to the future when she walked into her English classroom last year. I watched Dawn in that classroom, saw her read and love difficult texts, and then saw her become a secure and proud writer. I saw her accomplish those things because of a teacher who taught with her heart as well as her head. Dawn has college plans like Brandi. But what does Dawn plan to become? What else but an English teacher?

Finally, I remember Andy. Andy never speaks in class, never looks at anyone, just sits. Dawn and Andy have the same English teacher. But Andy is more difficult, challenged, somewhere far away. This magnificent teacher almost got to him, almost got him to perform unbelievably as King Lear in a class-based performance. Andy stepped back at the last minute, breaking all of our hearts. He was almost willing to become a part of the community of readers in his class, but not quite. The difficult lesson Andy teaches us is that we may not be successful with all of our kids. The kids at the end of the 20th century seem so complicated, so inexplicable. His teacher mourned this failure with Andy more than she celebrated the success with Dawn. Because this teacher taught with her head but inspired with her heart, she touched more than she realized.

Teaching is in the heart, not just the head. We need our hearts to inform our heads. Hearts say, "Don't be stupid, head. Language teaching is teaching ourselves. We are stories, we read stories, we write stories, true stories, made-up stories." Hearts say, "Once we cut the meaning out of English teaching, what's the point? What do we teach?" As Paulo Friere reminds us, teaching the word means teaching the world.

Courage

Like the lion in search of courage, I'm looking for mine right now to be sure it gets packed. I'm suggesting we'll all need much courage in the future as the politicians continue to legislate how reading and writing ought to be taught. I'm a bit peeved at having to pack this courage because I am not the one who has made English teaching into an "either/or" proposition. Instead, folks who want quick fixes have created either/or debates (either phonics or whole language, for example) and have often based their arguments on statistical studies. Nothing wrong with statistics as long as you realize that statistical studies offer one picture and that picture generally can't help us teach our students to

- make sense of texts;
- make meaning out of what they read and see and write;
- make critical judgments in regard to manipulative media;
- read and write effectively for high-level careers; and
- transmit a thoughtful, kind-hearted, literate culture to their future offspring.

These "skills" take more than a quantitative test and a number indicating a so-called reading ability. These take the mind of a skilled English teacher who has the heart to love her students and the courage to do what's right for them. So we need courage to

- resist ever going back to where we were before we learned what we did;

- resist abandoning our books—both our young adult novels and our classics—to those censors who would question material that generates questions in our students;
- resist those who claim English is nothing but a skill-driven subject;
- resist those who want to impose inauthentic test after test;
- resist those who wish to abandon public education altogether; and
- resist those who demand a return to a world that never was.

This will take enormous courage as constructivism, response-centered approaches, workshop classrooms, the reading and writing process, authentic assessment, and student-centered learning come under attack from critics who insist they know better how to teach when often they have never taught at all.

Courage my friends, courage.

The Pen and the Journal

Time to pack the other two items in my carry-on: a pen and a journal. These are tools I will use to begin exploring the future of literacy teaching. I'll probably switch to a laptop relatively soon into the new century, but right now it's a little too heavy to carry on and a little too short on battery power. More important, perhaps we should all begin the future in our own handwriting to remind ourselves that this is personal; this is about us, what we cherish and hold dear—or love of teaching, our love of language, our love of kids.

With my pen and my journal I want to explore questions I wonder about. I hope you'll bring your pen and journal and jot your thoughts about similar questions. Then we'll have to share thoughts, insights, suggestions, worries, successes. In that sharing, I bet we'll discover that our brain, our heart, and our courage often lead the way. Here are questions I'll be wondering and writing about:

- How do we bring all our children into the literacy club?

  —those who do not speak English;

  —those challenged by disabilities;

  —those battered by abuse; and

  —those just puzzling and difficult to reach.

- How do we embrace the successful strategies of the past and still stay open to strategies of the future?
- How do we enhance what we know now about language and learning?

- What do our students teach us about teaching them?
- What, if anything, can be quantified in literacy education?
- How does technology impact written literacy?
- What is the future of reading and writing?
- What does authentic assessment in the year 2000 and beyond look like?
- How do we do this while standing in the shadow of state-mandated minimum competency tests?

These and other questions need to be answered, and soon our blank journal will be filled. Maybe we ought to bring two journals and another pen.

Conclusion

A pen, a journal, and *The Wizard of Oz*. Into the new millennium we go carrying with us all that we have learned, our brains; all that we believe and love, our hearts; and all the strength we have to stay on course, our courage. We carry also our journal full of blank pages, and with our pen we will fill in the ideas and strategies that we learn, renewing as we always do this remarkable, but complex and never completed profession of ours.

May your Y2K problems be minor, and may all of us find the way to teach the children of the 21st century to be literate, kind, and wise.

REFERENCES

Atwell, N. (1987). *In the middle: Writing, reading, and learning with adolescents.* Portsmouth, NH: Heinemann.

Beers, K., & Samuels, B. (1998). *Into focus: Understanding and creating middle school readers.* Norwood, MA: Christopher-Gordon.

Calkins, L. (1994). *The art of teaching writing* (Rev. ed.). Portsmouth, NH: Heinemann.

Chomsky, N. (1975). *Reflections on language.* New York: Pantheon.

Emig, J. (1983). *The web of meaning. Essays on writing, teaching, learning, and thinking.* Upper Montclair, NJ: Heinemann.

Foster, H.M. (1994). *Crossing over: Whole language for secondary English teachers.* Fort Worth, TX: Harcourt Brace.

Friere, P., & Macedo, D. (1987). *Reading the word and the world.* South Hadley, MA: Bergin and Garvey.

Goodman, K. (1977). *Miscue analysis.* Urbana, IL: National Council of Teachers of English.

Graves, D. (1983). *Writing: Teachers and children at work.* Portsmouth, NH: Heinemann.

Moffett, J. (1968). *Teaching the universe of discourse.* Boston: Houghton Mifflin.

Murray, D. (1990). *Expecting the unexpected: Teaching myself—and others—to read and write.* Portsmouth, NH: Heinemann.

Piaget, J. (1959). *Language and thought of the child* (3rd ed.) (M. Gagain, Trans.). London: Routledge & Kegan Paul.

Probst, R. (1988). *Adolescent literature: Response and analysis.* Portsmouth, NH: Heinemann.

Rief, L. (1992). *Seeking diversity: Language arts with adolescents.* Portsmouth, NH: Heinemann.

Rosenblatt, L. (1983). *Literature as exploration* (4th ed.). New York: Modern Language Association.

Smith, F. (1982). *Understanding reading: A psycholinguistic analysis of reading and learning to read.* New York: Holt, Rinehart and Winston.

Vygotsky, L.S. (1978). *Mind and society: The development of higher psychological processes.* Cambridge, MA: Harvard University Press.

Developing Critical and Imaginative Thinking Within Electronic Literacy

Marino C. Alvarez

Many students in the primary grades have made the transition from using the computer as a "mechanized workbook" to using it as a tool with which stories can be written, read, and animated, and to which music can be added as an accompaniment. They are learning how to use compact discs to access information. Examples of students using technology in creative ways while meeting the needs of ethnic and linguistic diversity are available in the literature (e.g., Papert, 1996; Tipton, Bennett, & Bennett, 1997).

As students progress into the middle and high school grades they learn to use and program graphic calculators, write computer programs, create Web pages, publish papers, and access multiple resources from around the world via the World Wide Web. They interact with other students, scientists, authors, university professors, and others via e-mail, and carry on dialogues through chat lines, newsgroups, and discussion groups. Each of these improves their literacy and communication skills as they interact, using various forms of speech, dialogue, symbols, and logic in the process (Alvarez, 1996b).

Paths Toward Meaningful Learning

Recently our son Christopher, age 13, asked for an e-mail account. I told him we did not subscribe to an independent company but used our university account, which he could not access. In less than 2 days he had made inquiries and established his own e-mail address via Netscape. When he became interested in personal Web pages, he did some research and within 3 days had developed his own. He also engages classmates in a chat line devoted to personal dialogues, which include discussions of homework assignments.

Our son is not atypical; he represents a vast number of adolescent students who are learning with technology and are resourceful in finding pathways to satisfy their curiosity about the changing role of technolo-

From the *NASSP Bulletin*, *82*(600), 41–47, October 1998. Reprinted with permission of the National Association of Secondary School Principals.

gy. These students are adapting their views of literacy and accommodating the different types of skills that electronic literacy affords.

For example, e-mail and chat lines require students to engage in communications that are coherent and often spontaneous. This interactivity departs from passively receiving information via the radio or television or from a textbook that presents information in a linear format. When accessing information on the World Wide Web, the conventional reading model changes from linear and sequential to an electronic text that takes the reader/viewer from one place to another through a series of choices. Students need to critically analyze and make cogent decisions when reading this electronic text, interpreting graphics, watching videos, and making connections with audio recordings. They must also be discerning when processing electronic information to determine its accuracy and worth.*

While reading electronic text the reader/viewer is given hyperlinks to other related sources. Linking to these sources demands concentration and the ability to make critical judgments. This involves a high degree of literacy that goes beyond the range of expository discourse appearing in traditional textbooks. Research skills (searching for in-depth knowledge of a specific subject) need to be distinguished from library skills that require searching for information (Risko, Alvarez, & Fairbanks, 1991). To maximize learning with technology the teacher needs to develop lessons and assignments in which students interact with the Internet and World Wide Web in meaningful circumstances. This requires an emergent rather than a fixed curriculum.

An Emergent Curriculum

The demands imposed on administrators and teachers by a fixed curriculum are enormous. Teachers who are required to follow a set curriculum guide, teach a fixed body of knowledge, implement lessons that are textbook bound, and are held accountable to an end-of-the-year standardized test have difficulty with students who want to pursue the paths of inquiry afforded by technology. Too often students and teachers are stifled by imposed and restricted assessments based on past achievements. Once students have the opportunity to show what they can do, they may give a truer indication of what they can accomplish and, therefore, be instrumental in forging new policies for meaningful learning and assessment.

---

* For an excellent article on helping students to make informed use of the Internet, see "Teaching Students to Fish: Proper Use of the Net," by Alan C. November in *High School Magazine*, September 1998.

The key is for teachers and administrators to channel the energies of their students who are involved with electronic interactive environments and make use of their talents and their interest by devising emergent curricula that engage them in meaningful inquiry. In classrooms where teachers think along with their students and are supported for doing so by their administrators, students experience a curriculum where meaning is negotiated and ideas are shared and exposed for testing.

Teachers and Students Thinking About Learning

In an earlier *Bulletin* article I mentioned two projects that use technology to create opportunities for teachers and students to think about learning in ways that evolve into a community of thinkers (Alvarez, 1997). In both projects—the Gallatin High School Interdisciplinary Project and the Explorers of the Universe—students are encouraged to incorporate the curriculum with other subject disciplines (e.g., art, music, literature, social studies, science, mathematics, business education, etc.). Students share their interests, values, and ethnic and cultural beliefs in ways that meld their societal curriculum with the formal school curriculum.

Students in the Explorers of the Universe project participate and learn science in a collaborative format with their teachers and with university educators, community resources, and practicing scientists. The project is based on the concept that meaningful learning is achieved when students can integrate their informal learning experiences with their formal in-school experiences. Lessons include authentic tasks and materials related to students' world knowledge, interest, and experience.

Students follow a framework that presents guidelines, but does not inhibit their imagination in the process of working through their self-directed cases. A CD has been developed for students in Explorers of the Universe that contains guidelines for case development and final reports, along with animations for using concept maps and vee diagrams. A section on the CD permits students to record and send their notes via the Internet to the university educator.

Students in the Explorers of the Universe project are making the transition from paper-and-pencil formats and printed texts to those that require varied software to perform tasks and write papers that take a reader/viewer to multiple sites that include graphic representations, audio, and interactive communications. No longer are students bound to books available in the classroom, school library, or community library and local art museums. They can read books and historical documents via the Web from all over the world; view works of art; visit exotic places; go under the surface of the oceans; and leave the planet on a journey through space.

As they write their papers for publication on the Web students develop hyperlinks within their pages to other related sources. The reader/viewer is taken on a journey that traverses a variety of landscapes and media and requires literacy skills beyond those traditionally used in formal school settings. However, cautions must be observed. The reader/viewer must be selective about choices of information sites and use critical judgment to determine if the information is accurate, relevant, useful, or of interest. This mode of inquiry is a departure from traditional textbook readings where facts are sought and minimal effort is exerted to search other sources beyond the boundaries of the textbook.

Students learn to use tools such as concept maps and interactive vee diagrams to plan, carry out, and implement their research investigations. Their maps are constructed using software designed for this purpose (e.g., Inspiration 5.0) and are shared with peers, teachers, scientists, and university educators through the Internet. Interactive vee diagrams are electronically communicated to scientists and university educators and feedback is given to the students. Electronic communications allow students to write for a given audience.

Writing for an Audience

Electronic literacy environments differ from traditional classroom reading and writing activities. This form of language differs from that used with students in the classroom in both purpose and social surrounding. When students are asked to write papers in a traditional class, they know their audience and the expectations of the teacher. The parameters for the writing assignment are given to them and they follow these guidelines as they gather information and finalize their paper. Each student understands the social climate, relationship to other classmates, and what must be done to satisfy the requirements.

When students write papers that appear on the home page of their school's Web site, however, the format changes; the audience is now faceless and unknown, and both the purpose and the conditions in which this form of an electronic communication is distributed affect the thought processes of the student. Students writing a paper for their teacher and classmates may think differently about the process and the content when asked to write a paper that will appear on the Web. Anyone with Web access can read, critique, and respond to the ideas in the paper; therefore, students place a premium on the paper's accuracy, use of technical and specialized vocabulary, and degree of coherence.

Peer review is an important component of preparing papers for publication on the Web. Peers help to focus the audience and provide the author with critical analyses for editing and preparing a final draft. When student researchers write and publish their papers on the Web, they take on the characteristics of a novelist as they tell a story about the events and objects they are researching. Their stories include thoughts and feelings that affect the learning process. The electronic forum provides a venue for stimulating thinking by inviting conversations between student authors and their readers.

The use of technical vocabulary reflects students' understanding of complex ideas. Rote memorization is reduced to a minimum as students realize meaningful understanding cannot be accomplished by this method, especially when trying to communicate their ideas to others. Under these circumstances ideas emerge as interrelationships rather than isolated facts. Ideas are explored across pieces and sets of information acquired through diversified readings accessed through multiple library directories and interactive communications with authors, scientists, peers, and university educators on the Web.

Authentic Materials and Problem-Oriented Tasks

In classroom environments where students are engaged in active learning using authentic materials in problem-oriented situations a positive attitude is evident in the level of achievement reached and the satisfaction expressed by administrators, teachers, and students. These conditions are further enhanced when the types of engagement present authentic problems in a context that needs to be addressed by letting students show what they can do through a variety of resolutions.

The International Reading Association has a Web site (http://www. reading.org) that contains links to resources for administrators, teachers, students, parents/guardians, and education support personnel. Although these links may change, the reader/viewer is presented with some outlets that may stimulate ideas for individual, family, and collaborative educational pursuits.

Conclusion

Electronic literacy is affecting both the societal and formal school curriculums (Alvarez, 1996a; Reinking, 1998). Adolescents are using computers in the workplace, church, community, local, and college/university libraries, community centers, and their home. The workplace in a global society demands technological changes and proficiency in electronic literacy skills (Mikulecky & Kirkley, 1998). To meet these challenges, reading specialists need to be more visible in middle level and high schools. Reading specialists should have the skills and the opportunity to work with both adolescent students and their teachers in content area disciplines within traditional and electronic literacy environments.

Reading specialists are being hampered in their efforts due to minimal funding for adolescent literacy programs (Alvarez, 1998). Funding under Title 1 compensatory education programs for grades 7, 8, and 9 is only 16%. For grades 10, 11, and 12 the funding is at 5%. The largest funding is allocated for grades 1–6, equaling 69% (U.S. Department of Education, 1994–1995). These funding figures have remained the same for the past 20 years (Davidson & Koppenhaver, 1988). This lack of funding for assisting adolescents having reading problems or difficulty making this transition to electronic literacy environments affects our society.

If we are to meet the challenges of a global society and the needs of a diversified adolescent population, it is vital that an emergent curriculum be our focus: a curriculum that challenges students to engage in meaningful learning activities by offering problem-oriented tasks using authentic materials and affords opportunities for multiple resolutions. This type of curriculum spurs the imagination of passive learners. In the process, teachers take advantage of the knowledge and skills their students bring into the classroom, and make use of their skills by helping them make the transition into realms of electronic literacy.

REFERENCES

Alvarez, M.C. (1996a). A community of thinkers: Literacy environments with interactive technology. In K. Camperell & B.L. Hayes (Eds.), *Literacy: The information highway to success* (Sixteenth yearbook of the American Reading Forum). Logan, UT: Utah State University.

Alvarez, M.C. (1996b). Explorers of the universe—Students using the World Wide Web to improve their reading and writing. In B. Neete (Ed.), *Literacy saves lives.* Winchester, England: United Kingdom Reading Association.

Alvarez, M.C. (1997, November). Thinking and learning with technology: Helping students construct meaning. *NASSP Bulletin.*

Alvarez, M.C. (1998). Adolescent literacy: Are we in contact? In E. Sturtevant, J.A. Dugan, P. Linder, & W. Linek (Eds.), *Literacy and community* (Twentieth yearbook of the College Reading Association). Platteville, WI: College Reading Association.

Davidson, J., & Koppenhaver, D. (1988). *Adolescent literacy: What works and why.* New York: Garland.

Mukulecky, L., & Kirkley, J.R. (1998). Changing workplaces, changing classes: The new role of technology in workplace literacy. In D. Reinking, M.C. McKenna,

L.D. Labbo, & R.D. Kieffer (Eds.), *Handbook of literacy and technology: Transformations in a post-typographic world.* Mahwah, NJ: Erlbaum.

Papert, S. (1996). *The connected family: Bridging the digital generation gap.* Atlanta, GA: Longstreet Press.

Reinking, D. (1998). Introduction: Synthesizing technological transformations of literacy in a post-typographic world. In D. Reinking, M.C. McKenna, L.D. Labbo, & R.D. Kieffer (Eds.), *Handbook of literacy and technology: Transformations in a post-typographic world.* Mahwah, NJ: Erlbaum.

Risko, V.J., Alvarez, M.C., & Fairbanks, M.M. (1991). External factors that influence study. In R.F. Flippo & D.C. Caverly (Eds.), *Teaching reading and study strategies at the college level.* Newark, DE: International Reading Associations.

Tipton, P.E., Bennett, C.K., & Bennett, J.A. (1997, November). Using technology to overcome the challenges of diversity. *NASSP Bulletin, 81*(592), 23–30.

U.S. Department of Education. Compensatory Education Program, 1994–1995. Washington, DC.

Rock 'n' Roll and Horror Stories: Students, Teachers, and Popular Culture

Cynthia Lewis

Recently, my 13-year-old son was stopped in the hallway by a teacher who questioned whether his T-shirt met the school's dress code. He wore a rock T-shirt depicting the dancing figures of women who would not be considered attractive according to media standards. It seems that the T-shirt's message is in the eye of the beholder. As my son explained it to me, the T-shirt is meant to make a statement about the sexist images on most rock paraphernalia. As the teacher saw it, the T-shirt is disrespectful to women. Yet the meaning of a message is influenced by the context of its production as well.

What if the teacher had known that the rock band was an all-female feminist band? Would that change her interpretation of its message and her interaction with my son? As educators, many of us feel it is our duty to police the popular culture of young people in school—a place where, ironically, we continue to consume our own culture. For instance, in addition to their many other functions, the teachers' lounges in the schools where I have worked have served as centers for sports pools, home decorating tips, soap opera updates, and other signs and symbols of popular culture.

The stances teachers take toward popular culture matter. When we exclude and police, or when we look the other way, we set up limiting dichotomies. We tell our students that some texts are worthy of serious analysis—*Romeo and Juliet*, for example—whereas others are not—TV's *The Simpsons*, perhaps, or other media-related texts. Yet, we dispense even this message inconsistently. After all, certain low-culture media texts, those related to sports, for instance, have always been welcomed and analyzed at school, leading to conversations between teachers and particular groups of students who care about or participate in athletics.

These students can take class time to talk with a teacher about the Final Four (U.S. college basketball championships), whereas students

Reprinted from the *Journal of Adolescent & Adult Literacy, 42*, 116–120, October 1998.

whose interest is, say, rock music receive only the scorn of adults who bemoan the violent and sexual content of MTV. Inadvertently, perhaps, we privilege the particular forms of popular culture that young people share with many adults, especially those forms that male adolescents share with men. The rest, we either fear or trivialize.

Horror Fiction in the Classroom

Here, I'd like to suggest other strategies for responding to the popular culture in our students' lives. Just as an informed response to my son's rock T-shirt would require an awareness of how teens consume and how artists and corporations produce the T-shirt, an informed response to popular culture in the classroom requires that we consider how our students use it in light of the economics of its production.

The illustrations I'll use are of 11- and 12-year-old boys as they talk with peers in class about a horror series book, *Bobby's Back* (Pickford, 1993), and its relationship to horror films. *Bobby's Back* is the first in a series of books about a young man who seeks murderous revenge on a group of five people (four of them female) who teased him when he was a child. Let's listen in as the boys (not their real names) relate this book to other horror books and movies they all have seen.

Brian: Jason's better than Freddy. Jason kills more people. One movie he kills like 15 people. The most Freddy ever killed was 5, 6.

James: They run from him and they get like a mile away, and then they turn around and he's right there and he's just walking.

Tyler: Who cares who kills more people?

Brian: Jason doesn't even act real.

Mark: The guy is like running away from Jason and he stops and Jason is right in front of him, and he's only walking.

Brian: They're never even scared.

[James makes the sounds from the theme song for the movie *Friday the Thirteenth*.]

Clearly this conversation is not the sort sanctioned in most classrooms. It is, however, in keeping with the masculinist discourse that dominates outside the classroom—language that values violence much as the boys seem to do (Jason is better because he kills more people). The masculinist tenor of the overall discussion is evident, too, in its violence toward females in several of the sections I do not include here. In those sections the boys talk about a girl being hit in the head with a harpoon gun and a mother, who herself was a killer, getting her head chopped off. The boys talk about these events with very little commentary.

Males in horror fiction are of two general types. Either they are violent, dangerous, and vengeful or they are strong, commanding, and protective. No other versions of masculinity are made available to readers of young adult horror fiction. I'd like to suggest, however, that talk about violence and a concern for those who feel fear in the face of violence give the boys a way of examining and questioning such rigid versions of masculinity. At the same time, such talk provides them with an opportunity to resist and challenge the more feminized climate of this classroom, one in which girls' reading and response practices were the expected behaviors.

The meaning of a popular text is shaped, in part, by who is using it, the context in which it is being used, and the purpose it serves. Another look at the boys' discussion of horror books and films will help us to see how these meanings develop and change as the boys interact and respond playfully to one another's comments.

James: Jason's better. He carries a chainsaw.

Tim: It's really scary.

Mark: Not always. He uses anything he can find.

[The conversation turned to a movie about Freddy.]

Tyler: What happened? How does [Freddy] get killed? How does he get killed?

[The boys discuss other movies about Freddy.]

Brian: They conquer him in a video game, like.

Sam: Isn't there a Jason versus Freddy?

[The boys discuss other movies about Freddy and Jason.]

Brian: *Free Willy* scared me.

[laughter]

Tyler: *Free Willy* versus *Jaws*.

Sam: Care Bears scared me.

Tyler: Oh, *Free Willy* versus *Jaws*. Oh!

Brian: The Smurfs versus Jason.

[Several boys repeat the above, laughing as they speak.]

Brian: The Flintstones could bash his face in.

James: Bam Bam Bam Bam.

Sam: Bambi versus the Smurfs.

Tyler:	*Free Willy* versus *Jaws*.
Sam:	Willy versus Shamu.
James:	Tyler versus Mark.
Brian:	*Free Willy* versus Jaws.
Brian:	Mark versus Tyler.

[James is making *Jaws* noises.]

Sam:	This dummy on the cover versus *Jaws*.
Sam:	We started out talking about *Bobby's Back*. Now we're talking about Bambi versus Spiderman!

As a woman who has been a teacher of one kind or another for all of my adult life my first impulse when I hear students engage in conversations of this sort is to cut them off! However, after reflecting on this literature discussion, I want to make a case for the social work these students are engaged in. First, and this is no small matter, the students who are speaking in this segment (and others in this ½-hour discussion) are *all* academic outsiders within their classroom; a few are social outsiders as well. Here they are animated, engaged, and participatory; a stance that is highly uncharacteristic for them and one they maintain throughout this literary event.

Second, the language used throughout this excerpt is playful, parodic, and performative in ways that allow the students, in Anne Dyson's words, "to play with each other and with powerful societal images" (1997, p. 283). In this case, and earlier in the conversation as well, the boys bring up the issue of fear. Earlier, we heard Brian say admiringly that the characters in the film were never even scared. Here, Tim admits that Jason's chainsaw was scary, and soon after that the parodic exchange begins; an exchange that is almost entirely related to fear.

Perhaps this conversation serves as a way for the boys to abstract themselves from the fears they have being members of a culture where they are supposed to be fearless in the face of monstrous opponents. R.W. Connell in *Gender and Power* describes "hegemonic masculinity" as one that aims to dominate femininity as well as other masculinities through "power, authority, aggression, and technology" (1987, p. 187).

It would be scary, I dare say, to take on those attributes, and the boys deal with this condition through parody and performance. They juxtapose something scary with something that's not (*Free Willy* vs. *Jaws*), then something not scary with themselves (Care Bears scare me!), and finally one of them against another—but in play not aggression. The tone is lively, quick, and innovative. The boys are collaborators in performance and in audience. Indeed, being an audience member is to be a part of the performance itself—so entwined are the two. Within the context of this particular classroom, this was a subversive event employing language in opposition to the social discourse of the classroom, yet allowable within it. The boundaries in the classroom culture were permeable enough to allow for this transgression, this sharing of local knowledge among certain members of the classroom culture.

Social Uses of Popular Culture

This discussion occurred among students who were sharing their responses to books they had chosen for "free choice" reading, in a classroom that would be considered student centered. It seems especially important to examine how popular culture is used in just such classrooms because it is in these contexts that students feel empowered to bring into the classroom cultural symbols and materials of the sort that teachers and other adults would rather not legitimize. An assumption underlying the notion of "free choice" is that when students choose their own texts and topics, they are expressing their individual voices and identities. However, given a chance to choose what they want to read, write, and talk about, students often choose subjects that expose group identities—that is, the everyday materials of their lives that constitute "popular" culture.

Indeed, the popular culture of young people is not about individual voices and identities. At the local level, in classrooms and communities, popular culture is related to social and cultural group identities, allegiances, and exclusions. At the global level, popular culture is even more removed from the individual expressions of voice and identity since it is produced largely through multinational corporations and disseminated across a wide range of audiences and geographies. Therein lies one of the many contradictions of popular culture. While its expression can be oppositional and resistant (in that youth subcultures often oppose authoritative cultural norms), it is also co-opted by and reproduced through the very authoritative structures it opposes.

It's an interesting irony, I think, that what we call "free choice" in terms of students choosing the books they want to read is clearly not free of the need for social connection at the local level and the influence of dominant culture at the global level. The substantial investment adolescents place in these symbolic materials is overshadowed by the economic investment corporations make in targeting youth as consumers of popular culture.

One common response that teachers have to popular culture—to worry over its effects on students who are seen as passive consumers—is mistaken given that readers actively revise texts as they read rather than passively consume them (Moss, 1989). While I am arguing that the boys whose conversations I have just shared are doing just that, I don't want to overestimate the control that young people have over the messages promoted by popular culture. The boys' desire for aggression and fearlessness is promoted by popular culture through corporate interests (McRobbie, 1984).

Some theorists argue that popular culture is solely an instrument of capitalism, while others argue that it emerges from marginalized groups (youth, for instance) as the expression of their need to revise social inequities and subvert social norms (Swiss, Sloop, & Herman, 1998). Still others argue for the difficult task of finding a space between these extremes, one that recognizes that while subcultures can be sites of resistance, they are also sustained, and sometimes created, by those who stand to reap economic benefits. So, while the boys we listened in on clearly were engaged in the social work of appropriating popular culture for their own important uses, a steady diet of such conversations would not help them to understand its constitutive process.

I'd like to suggest that school ought to be a place where young people can talk about and use popular culture, at times without teacher input, so that they may challenge authoritative norms. In any case, we have little choice but to try to understand what our students do with popular culture and what it does for them. The 12-year-old female students in one classroom I have in mind chose to read series books by R.L. Stine or Christopher Pike whenever they had a chance to choose a book. In these books, females are often placed in precarious situations, and although they might be involved in extricating themselves from these situations, the male characters ultimately save the day.

The girls talked about these books during free moments at school and often outside of school. One student told me that her friend didn't read these books and was therefore left out of many conversations. The books carried a certain status that resulted in important allegiances and bonds among the girls. When I asked one student, Mackenzie (not her real name), why the girls read Stine and Pike whereas the boys in her class did not, her explanation surprised me:

> Most of the main characters are girls. Like, the girls are the ones that have the problems and they are the ones with the boyfriends that kill them and things like that. So it's basically...it puts boys in a bad position to read about guys killing girls.

From my perspective as a feminist teacher, I was not able to imagine any ways in which "guys killing girls" could be empowering to girls and dis-empowering to boys. Yet, something about these books allowed Mackenzie to feel in control of male violence and in touch with female perceptions of that violence.

Often, it seems, the contradictory nature of much popular culture is related to its appeal. Males killing females would not seem to place girls in control, yet Mackenzie used what many of us would see as an anti-female story line to command authority, both in terms of how she was willing to read this text and in terms of how she would interpret the boys' tendency to dismiss these series books. Although males often denigrate females for reading and enjoying series and romance books (and this classroom was no exception), she was able to interrupt this commonplace trivialization of female activity by pointing out that boys don't want to read such books because they don't want to see themselves in a negative light.

I'm suggesting here that the social and political uses of popular culture must be examined, ways in which its use creates allegiances, marking the boundaries of who's in and who's out, and enabling those with less power to make their own tactical use of those who hold more (de Certeau, 1984).

Asking Critical Questions

At times, however, our roles as teachers should include teaching students to probe and resist popular cultural texts in the same way that we ought to teach students to interact with canonized texts (Lewis, in press). Instead of persuading students to revere all that has been deemed "great literature" and forsake the movies, books, and television shows they love, we need to engage students in conversations about the uses they have for a range of texts in their lives. And we adults have to be willing to examine our own consumptions as well. Why do we enjoy watching a soap now and then, listening to our generation's rock music, or entering a sports pool? How do we use these activities? What purposes do they serve?

But to get beyond this inquiry into how and why we consume popular culture, we might also ask students to examine how particular forms of popular culture work on audiences as they do, who is responsible for producing and disseminating popular cultural texts, and whose interests are served by the production and consumption of these texts. For example, while I was encouraged by Mackenzie's response to R.L. Stine because it pointed to ways in which she revised the storyline to protect her own interests, I was not as hopeful about another part of our conversation in which she told me that reading about girls in dangerous situations taught her to be careful. "I read a book where a girl was walking down the street and a guy was chasing her, and so now I'm walking down the street, you know, looking, making sure no one's chasing me."

Had this comment been part of a classroom discussion, I would consider it ripe for what Anne Simpson calls "critical questions" (1996), questions that probe textual ideology by examining such issues as how texts position readers to respond in particular ways and who benefits from such preferred readings. I'd be interested in pursuing these questions in response to Mackenzie's perspective on having learned an important lesson—to be careful—from one of R.L. Stine's books. Who benefits from this lesson? Not Mackenzie, who has learned, in this case, to feel powerless in the face of male violence. How is it that this popular text works to shape Mackenzie as a reader who feels she must protect herself from males as an ordinary part of her day?

As adults and teachers, we may well be put off by images of youth in relation to popular culture. We tend to view young people either as menacing producers of violence and sex, or dupes of advertisers who sell violence and sex. It's no wonder, then, that many educators either prohibit uses of popular culture in their classrooms or resign themselves to its presence and look the other way. Some years ago, a primary teacher I visited tried to enforce a "No Ninja Turtles" rule for writers' workshop, which led to a proliferation of Ninja Rhinoceros stories the likes of which she never could have imagined. If we choose not to examine the social and political uses of popular culture and not to bring the serious analysis of its forms into the classroom, these expressions of group identities may simply go underground, leading to the disassociation of that which figures most prominently in the everyday lives of our students.

REFERENCES

Connell, R.W. (1987). *Gender and power*. Stanford, CA: Stanford University Press.
de Certeau, M. (1984). *The practice of everyday life*. Berkeley, CA: University of California Press.
Dyson, A.H. (1997). Rewriting for, and by, the children: The social and ideological fate of a media miss in an urban classroom. *Written Communication, 14*, 275–311.
Lewis, C. (in press). The quality of the question: Probing culture in literature discussion groups. In C. Edelsky (Ed.), *Making justice our project: Critical whole language teachers talk about their work*. Urbana, IL: National Council of Teachers of English.
McRobbie, A. (1984). Dance and social fantasy. In A. McRobbie & M. Nava (Eds.), *Gender and generation* (pp. 130–161). London: Macmillan.

Moss, G. (1989). *Un/Popular fictions*. London: Virago Press.

Pickford, T. (1993). *Bobby's back*. New York: Bantam.

Simpson, A. (1996). Critical questions: Whose questions? *The Reading Teacher, 50,* 118–126.

Swiss, T., Sloop, J., & Herman, A. (1998). *Mapping the beat: Popular music and contemporary theory*. Malden, MA: Blackwell Press.

Intergenerational Conversations and Two Adolescents' Multiple Literacies: Implications for Redefining Content Area Literacy

Thomas W. Bean, Shannon K. Bean, and Kristen F. Bean

I t's Tuesday night after dinner, and Shannon, my 16-year-old daughter, hunches over a plastic model of Flyer, the plane that the Wright Brothers flew successfully in 1903 at Kitty Hawk. She's building this intricate aircraft as part of a project exploring various inventions from the Industrial Revolution. Her social studies teacher regularly uses art, music, and a host of other options to engage students in a deeper understanding of events depicted in their textbook, *World History: Patterns of Civilization* (Beers, 1991).

Kristen, my 12-year-old daughter, is in our converted garage that serves as an office writing a science report about protists on our aging home computer. Kristen regularly uses writing to chronicle her experiences and think about them. She writes stories, essays, and notes to friends, and uses writing as a way of organizing her world.

Through intergenerational conversations with my coauthors Shannon and Kristen, I began to see that we have defined content area literacy too narrowly. This narrow view of what it means to be literate leads to a crisis mentality and simplistic solutions to very difficult challenges facing adolescents today.

In this article, we first consider how literacy experts and society usually define what it means to be a literate reader and writer. We then explore a concept about literacy I call *functionality* through the voices and views of Shannon and Kristen. I decided to use the term *functionality* after reading weekly tallies of Shannon's and Kristen's use of time across school reading and voluntary reading, talking on the phone, playing video games, watching and talking about movies with friends, and engaging in other forms of discourse in various school and community settings. We talked about these various forms of discourse to gain an idea of what

Reprinted from the *Journal of Adolescent & Adult Literacy, 42*, 438–448, March 1999.

functions each activity served in their lives. Qualitative research on adolescents' literacy practices in social contexts outside school is just beginning to inform our thinking about how to transform literacy practices in classrooms (Luke, 1994).

As this is an interpretive analysis of our conversations about Shannon and Kristen's multiple literacies, we want to shed some light on our respective experiences, biases, and values (Creswell, 1994; LeCompte & Preissle, 1993). It is through this sociocultural lens that we explored Shannon and Kristen's multiple literacies.

Shannon and Kristen are upper middle class white adolescents. They have been raised in a nuclear family with both parents working in education-related careers. They are both enrolled in honors classes and view school as a means of getting ahead in life as well as a place where strong social bonds are made with friends. They typically earn A's and B's in their content area classes. They have an array of hobbies and interests requiring significant amounts of time, financial support, and dedication.

Our home sits on a little over an acre of land in the foothills on the outskirts of Las Vegas, Nevada, USA. A dirt and gravel road fronts our Spanish-style house, and large expanses of open desert still remain in this equestrian neighborhood. Most of the homes are custom built and range from older homes like ours, built in the 1970s, to more contemporary houses built to accommodate the recent population boom in Las Vegas.

Large, planned subdivisions are nearby, and new schools continue to be built at a rapid pace. Shannon and Kristen both attend new schools in attractive suburban neighborhoods. The student population on the northwest side of Las Vegas is predominantly white with some Hispanic, African American, and Asian Pacific students enrolled. While many religious affiliations are represented, a significant Mormon population resides in the area. Many of Shannon's and Kristen's friends are Mormon, and both girls have attended Mormon summer camps, dances, and other church-related events.

Shannon spends many hours outside school training her western pleasure quarter horse, Drop the Top, and competing in shows in the southwest. Kristen prefers performing arts like her school's chorus, as well as training and showing her cocker spaniel, Benny. Shannon and Kristen spent their early years in rural Hawaii attending schools with Native Hawaiian children and immersing themselves in island culture. They are sensitive to racial stereotyping and have friendships with students from a variety of racial groups and socioeconomic classes. Their mom is a preschool teacher and former Girl Scout leader in the Keaukaha Hawaiian community.

As a qualitative literacy researcher, I also want to share my experiences, biases, and values. I was raised in an upper middle class home in Honolulu. I graduated from Punahou School and the University of Hawaii with a major in English. Growing up in the ethnically and culturally rich milieu of Honolulu and, later, the Big Island of Hawaii, shapes some of my outlook on ethnicity and culture. Following graduate school at Arizona State University, I have spent the past 22 years in academe. The past 5 years have been devoted to researching high school students' responses to multicultural literature. I view adolescence as a difficult period in our society and one where little funding is available to researchers interested in expanding our knowledge of adolescents' multiple literacies across various racial, gender, and socioeconomic categories.

I serve on the International Reading Association's Adolescent Literacy Commission. The Commission is currently raising awareness of adolescents' literacy challenges through various forums including conference presentations and planned town meetings. The present study is designed to add to our knowledge base in this area and follows a tradition of sociocultural thinking prominent in the work of American, European, Australian, and other researchers in critical literacy.

Sociocultural Theory and Literacy

Sociocultural theorists view literacy as social practice rather than simply a cognitive process (Gee, 1990; Lankshear, 1997). As a social practice, literacy has ideological dimensions (Street, 1995). For example, out-of-school literacy practices may be viewed by some as inferior to in-school literacy practices (Street, 1995). There is a need to better understand how adolescents view the functions of in-school and out-of-school literacy.

Sociocultural factors including gender, race, class, and home life influence how literacy is practiced and the role it plays in achievement and identity development in adolescence. For example, some research on white, adolescent, middle class girls' reading of popular romance novels shows the novels mirrored the girls' interest in a culture of consumption and beauty (Christian-Smith, 1991). When teachers attempted to replace romance novels in independent reading assignments with what they viewed as quality young adult literature, the girls resisted by bringing their favored romance novels into school. They were astute critics of the novels, recognizing the disparity between idealized fictional boyfriends and their own less glamorous and imperfect lives. Christian-Smith argued that classrooms should develop a curriculum of critique where students compare and contrast a romance novel's version of social relations versus students' real life experiences.

Cherland (1994) notes that adolescent girls learn gender roles through reading and discussing romance novels with their peers. Unfortunately, without an opportunity to critique this work, the novels perpetuate a society where girls are likely to read more than boys and emotional responses to books remain the province of girls. Gee and Crawford (1998) note, "All the other identities students bring to the classroom are relevant to whether and how they affiliate with school" (p. 225).

These sociocultural views of literacy suggest we need to transform literacy practices in schools through a curriculum of critique, broadening the literary canon, and recognizing the role of multiple literacies in adolescents' lives (New London Group, 1996). As a result of our combined thinking about what it means to be literate moving into the future, we point to ways content area teachers can tap students' broad, rather than narrow, sense of functionality in the school and classroom setting. We want to caution the reader that this work represents the combined views of one literacy professor and two white, upper middle class teenage girls. Taken in that context, we hope our views stimulate conversations about adolescent literacy that move beyond traditional definitions and rapidly aging curriculum frameworks. We start by considering traditional definitions of literacy.

Traditional Definitions of Literacy

The editors of the International Reading Association's *The Literacy Dictionary* (Harris & Hodges, 1995) tackled the difficult task of defining literacy. They justifiably devoted a long section to arguing against a single definition of literacy, finally offering five definitions. The first of those five defines literacy as "the ability to read" (p. 140). Definitions of adolescent literacy generally acknowledge the greater demands of secondary text reading.

Secondary and content area literacy is typically defined with reference to the school and subject area classroom context. For example, "content area literacy is defined as the level of reading and writing skill necessary to read, comprehend, and react to appropriate instructional materials in a given subject area" (Readence, Bean, & Baldwin, 1998, p. 4). Similarly, Vacca and Vacca (1996) state that content literacy is "the ability to use reading and writing to learn subject matter in a given discipline" (p. 8).

We want to argue that our current definitions of literacy in the content areas and our instructional efforts need to be expanded. In order to do so, we want to share Shannon's and Kristen's efforts to examine their own uses of literacy from the standpoint of functionality. We first define what we mean by this term.

Functionality

The Webster's dictionary in *Compton's Interactive Encyclopedia* (1994) definition of the word *function* includes "to serve a certain purpose." Functionality, then, suggests that activities we engage in serve some valued purpose in our lives. These may range from efforts to forge a social identity as an adolescent to accomplishing an academic or athletic goal. Functionality also implies that adolescents have a sense of purpose and agency in their actions (Moore, 1996). They make choices between a host of available activities and use their time accordingly.

In order to get a better idea of how Shannon and Kristen allocated their time, I asked them to keep a weekly tally of activities over 2 weeks during the spring 1998 school term. I tried to keep this one-page form as easy to work with as possible, knowing their overloaded backpacks didn't need additional weight. Table 1 displays the tally sheet. We then used this as a basis for talking about the functionality of each activity and any other aspects of literacy that were stimulated by this conversation. We audiotaped these after-dinner conversations. In addition, I jotted down reflective notes and key quotes from our conversations. Shannon and Kristen then read and edited the material I wrote in draft form, making suggestions for improvement.

Shannon's View of Functionality

Shannon, in 10th grade, charted her use of time over 2 weeks. Table 2 shows how she allocated her time during this period. The rank order of activities in Week 1 showed that phone use was first, television and video second, computer use third, novel reading fourth, text reading fifth, and magazine reading sixth. During the second week, phone use was again first, computer and video tied for second, and magazine and text reading tied for third. Novel reading did not occur this week. During this second week, a male classmate committed suicide. Much of Shannon's phone use that week was devoted to consoling friends and talking with other classmates who had moved out of state about the funeral. Shannon has a real interest in the field of psychology and helping others, and the phone is a valued link to her network of friends.

When we conversed about her tally of activities the first evening after dinner, I began by asking Shannon what sort of function each of the various discourse activities served for her. We audiotaped our conversation on an

Table 1
Self-observation tally

Name _____

Grade _____

School _____

Dates tallied _____ to _____

Directions: Use the following eight-item code to tally each category for 7 days (Monday through Sunday).

Time:	1–5 minutes	5–15 minutes	15–30 minutes	30–45 minutes	1 hour	2 hours	3 hours	4–5 hours
Code:	1	2	3	4	5	6	7	8

	Text reading	Novel reading	Magazine reading	Computer use	Phone use	TV, movies, video/video games
Mon						
Tues						
Wed						
Thurs						
Fri						
Sat						
Sun						

Table 2 Shannon's self-observation tally						
	Text	Novel	Magazine	Computer	Phone	TV/video
Week 1	1 hour	2 hours	30 minutes	4 hours	22 hours	14 hours
Week 2	1 hour	0	1 hour	9 hours	14 hours	9 hours

unobtrusive microcassette recorder. I then transcribed our words. The following excepts serve to illustrate Shannon's view of functionality in literacy activities.

Me: What sort of functions does text reading serve for you?

S: Those are just things we read in class. Like in class the teacher will bring out a book. Most of my teachers don't use a textbook very often. They mostly lecture. So I don't use a textbook much.

Me: What about novel reading?

S: Those are mostly novels we have to read for school. In English.

Me: So the novels you read on a weekly basis would be mostly school related?

S: Yeah. Because we're required to do so much for school. You know we really don't get to choose much so it's basically all I do.

Me: There's no self-selection?

S: No.

Me: Do you read any books that are multicultural novels?

S: I know we're doing some new play called *Billy Bob* or something.

Me: Not *Billy Budd?*

S: *Billy Budd.*

Me: *Billy Budd* is by Melville. (They had just finished reading and watching the video version of Herman Melville's *Moby Dick*, 1961.)

Shannon viewed text reading and novel reading in school as vehicles for homework and a means to get a good grade. In contrast, magazine reading served more personal functions. She consistently read magazines including *Horse Illustrated, Teen,* and *Seventeen.* She read this material "just for fun...to learn stuff. I read stuff I'm interested in...related to my life I guess."

Computers served a more utilitarian function in Shannon's world. She used them to "type out homework. It makes things look neater. Also because computers are being used a lot more often and I'm trying to get used to using one. I'm getting better at typing."

Shannon offered her most affective response in our conversation to my question about functions of phone use.

S: The phone? It lets me express my feelings. Learn about myself. It's comforting to talk to your friends...find out what's going on in the world. I don't know. Help people out.

Movies, video, and video games held a similar value in her world.

S: It's relaxing. It's something to go out and do with your friends. Fun. It's enjoyable. Sometimes it's actually educational, surprisingly.

Me: What if you turned this whole thing on its head and in school you did movies, magazines, and phone? You didn't do this other stuff (texts, etc.)? We said we're revolutionizing the curriculum!

S: I would enjoy school a whole lot more. I mean some of the teachers try to make it more interesting and involve it more in your life. Some of them just don't do it.

Shannon has a very positive opinion of those teachers who meet her criteria for engagement in learning. The model of the Wright Brothers' plane mentioned in the vignette at the beginning of this article is one of the many creative ways her social studies teacher connects the curriculum and selective text readings in *World History: Patterns of Civilization* (Beers, 1991) to elements of student choice, individual agency, and multiple routes to meaning. Shannon also has a clear sense of the dual roles writing serves her in school and with her friends.

S: We write essays in world history. And, um, sometimes it helps you to understand things better—to understand what you are learning. To get a better grip on things. And get a good grade. You know, sometimes they are not always fun or interesting. Half the time they are pretty boring.

Me: What about all the other writing you do?

S: I write notes to my friends. Christine, people that are far away. Um, that's pretty much all the writing I do offhand—it's mostly just for notes. Almost every day. My notes aren't that long but I write every day.

Me: How do those get from one person to another?

S: In the halls if you see somebody you give it to them. Once in a while I'll write Lisa and when I see her on the weekend I'll give it to her. Half the time I've already told her everything in it. But sometimes it helps you to get your feelings out if you write a note. It helps you discover who you are.

When I asked Shannon if she thought adolescents did more or less reading than previous generations, she said, "maybe less but we have other things like teen phone lines and computer online services. We can get information faster now than reading a book."

Asked what she would want to bring if she was shipwrecked on a deserted island, Shannon would ditch everything else in order to bring a phone with her. In addition, other technology-based devices like video games, VCRs, and computers would be missed, but not as much as a phone. In a print-rich culture, Shannon's preferred mode of communication is oral language, although she does supplement this with notes to friends. Her use of discourse is extensive but reading plays mainly a utilitarian function in school—to get good grades.

Outside the school setting, reading magazines that connect to her equestrian interest and teen life occupy what little time she has for free reading. Writing serves the dual functions of producing papers for school and communicating with friends. Writing also serves the function of catharsis when crises confront Shannon and she needs to work through a problem. Shannon's younger sister also shared her views of literacy.

Kristen's View of Functionality

Kristen, in sixth grade, also charted her time over 2 weeks. Table 3 shows how she allotted her time during this period. The rank order of activities in Week 1 showed that television, video games, and movies were first; novel reading second; phone use third; magazine reading fourth; text reading fifth; and that no computer use occurred this particular week. During the second week television, video games, and movies ranked first;

Table 3
Kristen's self-observation tally

	Text	Novel	Magazine	Computer	Phone	TV/video
Week 1	30 minutes	3 hours	80 minutes	0	95 minutes	8 hours
Week 2	10 minutes	3 hours	35 minutes	30 minutes	3 hours	21 hours

phone use and novel reading tied for second; magazine reading was third; computer use fourth; and text reading fifth.

When we conversed about her tally of activities the first evening after dinner, I began by asking Kristen what sort of function each of the various discourse activities served for her. We taped our conversation, and the following excerpts from the transcription illustrate Kristen's view of functionality in literacy activities.

Me: Tell me a little bit about your textbook reading.

K: I don't do much. All I really do is like, we just started our English book. Mostly I do stuff in my science book. We just answer questions and do stuff like that.

Kristen said that the main function of text reading was "to learn about science." She had much more to say about novel reading.

K: We have to read 10 minutes in our second-period class and in our reading class and in our science class at the beginning. And then I have to read at night for 20 minutes if I do my homework.

Me: Is this SSR?

K: Yes.

Me: Do you pick what you want to read for SSR?

K: Um, yeah, but we're not allowed to read comics.

Me: At home for the 20 minutes?

K: Sometimes we have to read the book that we're reading and sometimes we can read anything we want.

Me: What are some titles of things that you read?

K: *The Face on the Milk Carton* (Cooney, 1990) we read for class in Reading. I just started another book.

Kristen viewed novel reading as a means to learn how to read and spell. She was much more expansive when we talked about magazine reading.

K: I have my *Teen* magazine. I get that every month. Sometimes I get stuff from the grocery store like little magazines and stuff. Other people bring magazines and I read them.

Me: Any other magazines that you read?

K: *Teen Machine*. It has like all stars and stuff. Like Leonardo DiCaprio. The teen one is about teens and stuff—stories to learn about stuff. *Teen Machine* is to learn about your favorite stars.

Me: You decide to read these, right?

K: Yeah.

Kristen talked about using the computer to look up information on the CD-ROM encyclopedia for science and about keeping a journal. She used the software program *The Amazing Writing Machine* to create her journal. She also mentioned going online and viewed the computer's function as one that promotes fun and learning.

Me: It looks like you had a lot of phone use.

K: I talk to my friends.

Me: You have a digital address book too. Do you know how to set that up?

K: Mumhm.

Me: What function does the phone serve?

K: To talk on the phone with your friends.... I don't know.... If you need something you can know it by calling people. Like if it's an emergency or something like that.... Or if you forget your homework.

Kristen had very clear television preferences and logged significant time keeping up with her shows.

K: I watch *Dawson's Creek* and I watch that every Tuesday. And sometimes it's on other nights. It's about a bunch of teens and the reason, I was reading in a magazine, the reason I like it so much is because you're kind of like in their

	place sometimes so like you need to know what happens for next time.
Me:	You mean kind of like a soap opera?
K:	Yeah. Every Tuesday they have a different one and it goes on and on.
Me:	You have other shows you watch too.
K:	Oh yeah. *Saved by the Bell* every day. And I watch *Figure It Out* every night at 5:00. These people go on there and do cool stuff and you have to guess what they did.
Me:	Like a quiz show?
K:	Yeah. And I want to be on there.

Kristen also talked about playing video games. She viewed these activities as entertainment and as a way to relax. She said, "It calms you down."

Writing was important to Kristen and served a variety of functions.

K:	I write stories and I write a journal every day.
Me:	What kind of stuff do you put in your school journal?
K:	The teacher asks us questions. If you were in blah blah blah situation, what would you do? In English.
Me:	What about note writing?
K:	Just a little. I just write to my friends. You are not allowed to talk in school so you write notes. Except if the teacher catches you.
Me:	Do you ever write if you feel bad about something?
K:	Yeah, and then I throw it away.

When I asked Kristen if she thought she did more reading or less reading than previous generations, she said "I think I'm doing more. We do more work than you guys did, I know that." I asked her why she felt this way and she replied, "because we have more technology and they can do more things with it 'cause we're lucky, so they just make the stuff and we get to do it."

Shipwrecked on a deserted island, Kristen would ditch all else and bring a television set and a phone. Failing that option, a laptop computer with an online connection would be next on her list. Kristen's world is one connected to imaginative and visual representations. Television, computers, and other technological devices like video games are inseparable from reading once she is away from school.

Buckingham's (1993) research on children's uses of television viewing shows it is more than a passive escape. Rather, television serves social functions as young viewers interpret and discuss characters in shows like *Dawson's Creek*. Television characters are treated in a similar fashion to characters in a novel. Children are astute viewers, and Buckingham's intensive interviews with children show they are able to discern the differences between their worlds and those depicted on television. Television viewing and discussion offers another forum for defining one's cultural identity. Buckingham suggests we engage students in talk contrasting television worlds and day-to-day life in terms of gender issues, stereotyping, special effects, and a host of other possible topics. Thus, television offers a vehicle for intertextual connections with print and critical thinking that is not fully exploited in our present curriculum.

In school, reading functions as a means to answer questions and work on spelling for Shannon and Kristen. Outside school, reading and writing connect directly to imagining life as a performing artist, acting in plays, singing, and creating new worlds.

Shannon's and Kristen's views of in-school literacy reveal a traditional, cognitive emphasis, while their perceptions of out-of-school multiple literacies involving technology show a more sociocultural view. Their definitions and those of other adolescents argue for an expanded view of literacy in the content areas.

An Expanded Definition of Content Literacy

The concept of functionality suggests that adolescents allocate varying levels of energy and interest to literacy activities serving particular functions in their lives. For example, Shannon and Kristen use contemporary technology very naturally to maintain social networks that support their emerging identities. They also complete school tasks to earn grades but a strong affective element is missing from this activity. On rare occasions, they find that school assignments, like building the Wright Brothers' model plane, capture their interest and enthusiasm.

Our text-driven definitions of literacy belie the multiple literacies in adolescents' lives. Adolescents "read" the signs of their school, peer, and home cultures astutely (Nielsen, 1998). "By reading and writing the texts of their lives, they are reading and writing themselves" (Nielsen, 1998, p. 4). These out-of-school literacy activities help adolescents explore their emerging identities vicariously across print and nonprint formats.

In her case study of five academically successful 12- and 13-year-old girls, Finders (1997) viewed literacy as a social dimension affording or denying adolescents the cultural capital to advance class identity and power. She viewed signing yearbooks, note writing, trading teenzines, and cooperatively completing homework as a kind of "literate under-life." This literate underlife provided the freedom, independence, and sense of agency that was missing in the highly constricted world of school, where talk was discouraged. The social roles established outside the classroom directly influenced power relationships within the classroom (Finders, 1997). Thus, the function of social roles in adolescents' literacy development is crucial but often ignored in definitions of content literacy and in curriculum design.

Adolescent boys also find their sense of agency and voice diminished as they move into the middle grades. Worthy's (1998) compelling account of her sixth-grade son and friend's growing disinterest in reading was directly related to few opportunities to talk about books in school. Instead, a preponderance of teacher-selected and teacher-directed assignments reduced their enthusiasm for reading.

A number of prominent literacy scholars have called for a broader, more contemporary view of what it means to be literate going into the next decade. For example, the New London Group (1996), made up of sociocultural theorists, states, "Literacy pedagogy has traditionally meant teaching and learning to read and write in page-bound official, standard forms of the national language" (p. 61). Yet we now use a multitude of new text forms including visual and audio multimedia technology. Teachers should tap students' natural interest in these new forms of discourse in order to help students code shift across various modes of representation

Similarly, Heath (1991) argues that schools overrely on print to the exclusion of oral language communication. Shannon, Kristen, and their peers use oral language as a means of socially crafting their identities and problem solving in a high technology culture. "We need to know more about alternative ways of learning and of using language in order to add these ways to those already valued in the classroom" (Heath, 1991, p. 21). Semiotics offers some clues about how we might reconceptualize literacy in content area classrooms.

Reconceptualizing Literacy in Content Classrooms

The field of semiotics explores sign systems (Berghoff, 1998; Kress & van Leeuwen, 1996). Social semiotics suggests that the past dominance of verbal, written language is a cultural norm that is changing as we increasingly become accustomed to computer-generated images and icons to communicate (Kress & van Leeuwen, 1996). Sign systems include art, music, drama, mathematics, print, and oral language. A sign "can be anything that stands for something to someone" (Berghoff, 1998, p. 520). Young children at the preschool stage naturally use multiple sign systems to interpret their worlds. As they advance into content area learning, adolescents may be discouraged from tapping this rich intertextual source. Our narrow focus on linguistic and logical skills diminishes the contribution multiple sign systems can make in adolescents' literacy learning.

Multiple sign systems allow students to "think beyond the confines of language" (Berghoff, p. 521). Indeed, the nature of texts is currently being transformed by electronic representations that include visual images, sound and video clips, links to other texts, and even the opportunity for readers to transform a text with their own ideas (Berghoff, 1998; Kress, & van Leeuwen, 1996). Outside the narrow confines of school, adolescents routinely explore multiple sign systems through film, video games, phone conversations, hip-hop, rap, and styles of dress, as well as notes that are written, intricately folded, and passed surreptitiously to their peers. The functions of these activities hold value for adolescents that can contribute to content learning if teachers expand their sometimes narrow view of literacy.

When there is a sharp divide between the culture of the school and the students who are the stakeholders in a school, students may choose to reject the official curriculum (Kaser & Short, 1998). For example, when traditional texts, postreading literal questions, and little discussion are the norm in a content classroom, this signals to adolescents that the function of learning is to get a grade. Kaser and Short (1998) contrast the polar opposite messages students confront daily as they move from school culture to peer and home settings.

> The goal of schools in our modern global society is to create productive citizens who have marketable skills. The goal of education in traditional oral societies is for children to learn how to become human beings—to figure out who they are and where they fit in the broader scheme of things. (p. 192)

Is it possible to unify these disparate cultures through a different curriculum design in content classrooms? Yes. Indeed, many content area teachers successfully bridge school, peer, and home cultures in the lessons they design. Shannon's social studies teacher does this by offering students choices in how they come to understand periods in history by expressing their learning through mosaics, models, and rap songs. These count for a percentage of the grade in history and are evaluated on the time and effort students put into creating their particular project.

For example, Shannon and five other students collaborated to write, perform, and make a rap audiotape on the "exploration of the western hemisphere." The following is one of 20 verses they wrote and performed:

> Pizzaro another conquistador bold
>
> Came to Peru searching for gold
>
> Indians of Peru already there
>
> Called the Incas but Pizzaro didn't care
>
> He ripped them off every chance he got
>
> Stole gold and silver from the new world's pot.

Much like Shannon's social studies teacher, Kristen's science teacher engages students in writing science reports that connect to their interests outside school. For example, Kristen was asked to write a report on any animal and explain why she selected it. Kristen wrote about dogs. The following excerpt from her four-page paper shows the intertextual links between Kristen's intense personal interest in dogs and the academic tasks of researching and writing about them in science.

> My favorite dog, the cocker spaniel, comes from the European wolf. There's also the Indian wolf, the Chinese wolf, and the North American wolf. I have two cocker spaniels and I have had a cocker spaniel and poodle mix for all my life. I have learned a lot about them. To have a normal dog is a lot of responsibility like grooming and bathing. But to have a show cocker spaniel it is much more responsibility. Every day you have to groom them with two types of combs, a slicker and a metal comb.

Kristen usually writes a rough draft of her work on lined paper, moving to the computer to develop another rough draft to be printed and polished. She sees direct, intertextual links between her home and community life and that of her sixth-grade science classroom. Although there is only one computer in this class serving over 30 students, they gather in groups to access information on the Internet for their various research papers and lab projects.

The functions of literacy now encompass a wide array of sign systems and call for a citizenry able to effectively use oral language, phones, pagers, cell phones, computers, electronic mail, the Internet, art, music, drama, film, video games, and digital aids of all kinds. In this complex world, being literate no longer means learning to read and write. Students also need sociotechnical literacy (Bruce, 1997).

Contemporary adolescents are accustomed to fast text presentations. They act on electronic text by constructing, transmitting, and modifying discourse via computers, video games, voice mail, and computer-based simulation games (Lankshear & Knobel, 1997). School-based texts and didactic teaching appear slow compared to the fast-paced digital world adolescents know (Lankshear & Knobel, 1997). The computer is now a seamless part of thinking, composing, and problem solving. Our printed texts, devoid of moving images and sound, pale in comparison to digitized text. Our conception of literacy in classrooms and our uses of literacy need to change from an autonomous, cognitive-based learning to read print model to one that encompasses socially interactive technologies.

Bruce (1997) argues that rather than adopting a stance in opposition to new technologies older generations fear might replace traditional reading and writing, we should embrace this transformation and its creative, humanizing possibilities. Our concept of literacy is in constant reconstruction as it has been throughout history (Bruce, 1997). In Shannon's and Kristen's functional view of literacy, artistic, technological, and traditional print representations merge in a mosaic of meaning that they tap naturally in and out of school. Fortunately, some of their teachers capitalize on this larger view of literacy and its many functions to create lessons and projects that tap the full range of their talents and potential.

Content teachers must move away from a dependence on didactic, text-bound modes of teaching that place adolescents in passive roles. Recent research that includes adolescents' voices and views shows the sharp divide that exists between their lives outside school and inside school (Alvermann, Hinchman, Moore, Phelps, & Waff, 1998). Until we bridge this gap by tapping the multiple literacies in adolescents' lives, we will continue to see adolescents develop a disinterested cognitive view of in-school literacy functions and a more enthusiastic sociocultural view of out-of-school discourse functions.

REFERENCES

Alvermann, D.E., Hinchman, K.A., Moore, D.W., Phelps, S.F., & Waff, D.R. (Eds.). (1998). *Reconceptualizing the literacies in adolescents' lives* (pp. 3–26). Mahwah, NJ: Erlbaum.

Alvermann, D.E., & Moore, D.W. (1991). Secondary school reading. In R. Barr, M.L. Kamil, P.B. Mosenthal, & P.D. Pearson (Eds.), *Handbook of reading research: Volume II* (pp. 951–983). White Plains, NY: Longman.

The amazing writing machine [Computer software]. (1996) Novato, CA: Broderbund Software.

Beers, B.F. (1991). *World history: Patterns of civilization*. Englewood Cliffs, NJ: Prentice Hall.

Berghoff, B. (1998). Multiple sign systems and reading. *The Reading Teacher, 51*, 520–523.

Bruce, B.C. (1997). Literacy technologies: What stance should we take? *Journal of Literacy Research, 29,* 289–309.

Buckingham, D. (1993). *Children talking television: The making of television literacy.* London: Falmer Press.

Cherland, M.R. (1994). *Private practices: Girls reading fiction and constructing identity.* London: Taylor & Francis.

Christian-Smith, L.K. (1991). Readers, texts, and contexts: Adolescent romance fiction in schools. In M.W. Apple & L.K. Christian-Smith (Eds.), *The politics of the textbook* (pp. 191–212). New York: Routledge.

Compton's interactive encyclopedia [CD-ROM]. (1994). Carlsbad, CA: Compton's New Media.

Cooney, C.B. (1990). *The face on the milk carton.* New York: Bantam Doubleday.

Creswell, J.W. (1994). *Research design: Qualitative & quantitative approaches.* Thousand Oaks, CA: Sage.

Finders, M.J. (1997). *Just girls: Hidden literacies and life in junior high.* New York: Teachers College Press.

Gee, J.P. (1990). *Social linguistics and literacies: Ideology in discourse.* London: Falmer Press.

Gee, J.P., & Crawford, V.M. (1998). Two kinds of teenagers: Language, identity, and social class. In D.E. Alvermann, K.A. Hinchman, D.W. Moore, S.F. Phelps, & D.R. Waff (Eds.), *Reconceptualizing the literacies in adolescents' lives* (pp. 225–245). Mahwah, NJ: Erlbaum.

Harris, T.C., & Hodges, R.E. (1995). *The literacy dictionary: The vocabulary of reading and writing.* Newark, DE: International Reading Association.

Heath, S.B. (1991). The sense of being literate: Historical and cross-cultural features. In R. Barr, M.L. Kamil, P.B. Mosenthal, & P.D. Pearson (Eds.), *Handbook of reading research: Volume II* (pp. 3–25). White Plains, NY: Longman.

Horse illustrated. Irvine, CA: Fancy Publications.

Kaser, S., & Short, K.G. (1998). Exploring culture through children's connections. *Language Arts, 75,* 185–192.

Kress, G., & van Leeuwen, T. (1996). *Reading images: The grammar of visual design.* London: Routledge.

Lankshear, C. (1997). *Changing literacies.* Buckingham, England: Open University Press.

Lankshear, C., & Knobel, M. (1997). Literacies, texts, and difference in the electronic age. In C. Lankshear (Ed.), *Changing literacies* (pp. 133–163). Buckingham, England: Open University Press.

LeCompte, M.D., & Preissle, J. (1993). *Ethnography and qualitative design in educational research* (2nd ed.). San Diego, CA: Academic Press.

Luke, A. (1994). Introduction. In M.R. Cherland (Ed.), *Private practices: Girls reading fiction and constructing identity* (p. xiv). London: Taylor & Francis.

Melville, H. (1961). *Moby Dick.* New York: Penguin.

Moore, D.W. (1996). Contexts for literacy in secondary schools. In D.J. Leu, C.K. Kinzer, & K.A. Hinchman (Eds.), *Literacies for the 21st century: Research and practice* (45th yearbook of the National Reading Conference, pp. 15–46). Chicago: National Reading Conference.

New London Group. (1996). A pedagogy of multiliteracies: Designing social futures. *Harvard Educational Review, 66*, 60–92.

Nielsen, L. (1998). Playing for real: Performative texts and adolescent identities. In D.E. Alvermann, K.A. Hinchman, D.W. Moore, S.F. Phelps, & D.R. Waff (Eds.), *Reconceptualizing the literacies in adolescents' lives* (pp. 3–26). Mahwah, NJ: Erlbaum.

Readence, J.E., Bean, T.W., & Baldwin, R.S. (1998). *Content area literacy: An integrated approach* (6th ed.). Dubuque, IA: Kendall/Hunt.

Seventeen. New York: Burgess.

Street, B. (1995). *Social literacies: Critical approaches to literacy in development, ethnography, and education.* London: Longman.

Teen. Boulder, CO: Petersen.

Vacca, R.T., & Vacca, J.L. (1996). *Content area reading* (5th ed.). New York: HarperCollins.

Worthy, J. (1998). "On every page someone gets killed!" Book conversations you don't hear in school. *Journal of Adolescent & Adult Literacy, 41*, 508–517.

Beginning to Create the New Literacy Classroom: What Does the New Literacy Look Like?

William Kist

was 17 years old before I realized the power of film as a communicative medium. One evening during my senior year in high school, a group of about 20 of us went to the local cinema to see Woody Allen's *Manhattan.* Toward the end of the film, the Woody Allen character has a serendipitous moment. He is talking into a tape recorder, recording ideas for a short story he is writing. He begins to muse about what makes life worthwhile—Groucho Marx, Willie Mays, and Louie Armstrong's recording of "Potatohead Blues" (Allen & Brickman, 1982). And then he suddenly stops. He adds, "Tracy's face." We cut to the next scene, and he's running through the streets of Manhattan, with Gershwin music ("Strike up the Band") accompanying him on the soundtrack. We track along with him as he runs for blocks. He is running to catch up with Tracy before she can leave town.

I remember having my own serendipitous thought at this moment—"Woody Allen is communicating with me through the writing and directing of this film." He was communicating with me first by imagining this character and then by capturing him on film, to the accompaniment of this music and this camera movement. Before that, I had thought of film primarily as an entertainment medium, something made on a Hollywood assembly line. Now I saw that it could be a personal statement from one person. And it had its own force—I realized that I could not adequately put into words the message that Allen was communicating by having his character fly down the street underscored by Gershwin. His communication to me could possibly be "translated" into words—something like "love is worth holding onto no matter what"—but these words couldn't begin to evoke the same understandings I received from the statement he had communicated via the filming of this character running through the streets.

Reprinted from the *Journal of Adolescent & Adult Literacy, 43,* 710–718, May 2000.

I began to watch films differently, fascinated with the fluency and power of the combinations of all of the embedded "communications" in a film. I began to think about the story and the direction and all of the technical elements that communicate with an audience. The medium of film became a meaning-making device, one that I had not previously used or even considered using. Eventually, I bought a 16mm film camera and shot my own film. I believe, in making films, I was able to "say" things and even to think things that I couldn't do using the medium of print.

It is significant to me now, as a professional educator, that my pivotal Manhattan learning experience took place outside of school. Even when I became a teacher, I showed films mainly to support and enrich a printed text.

Over the last 3 years, my journey as a literacy scholar and teacher has led me to a reexamination of what "literacy" has meant in the past and what it can mean in the future. I believe (along with many others) that we must now begin to think in terms of a new "literacy," one that opens all of our classrooms to multiple forms of expression such as film.

Throughout my research, however, I have been frustrated by the lack of description of what a new literacy might look like in practice. If we are to embrace a new definition of literacy, and go forward with restructuring our schools in this manner, we must begin to have some notion of how these classrooms would take shape. This article is an attempt to sketch out a depiction of such a classroom.

Based on a review of the work of scholars in this area, I am bringing forth five characteristics of a pedagogy for a new literacy. These five characteristics can serve as a starting point for teachers who are interested in attempting to create classrooms that embrace a new literacy. I hope also that these five characteristics can serve as a beginning for forming guiding principles to create policies and practices that will lead to new literacy classrooms.

A Rationale for Creating a New Literacy Classroom

Ample rationale has been provided for new literacy classrooms. The case has been made that young people need this new literacy because of the onslaught of new communication tools (Buckingham, 1993; Buckingham & Sefton-Green, 1994; Eisner, 1994, 1997; Kress, 1997; Luke & Elkins, 1998; New London Group, 1996). This is a time when the forms and outlets of expression available to people are multiplying very quickly. Our children now have more ways of learning about the world and more ways of expressing themselves through technology, the use of which continues to grow exponentially (Negroponte, 1995). This technology is increasingly multimodal (New London Group, 1996), encompassing forms not only of print but of combinations of graphic art, music, mathematics, drama, cinema, and others.

The International Reading Association/National Council of Teachers of English *Standards for the English Language Arts* (1996) also speak to the need for students to achieve literacy in both print and nonprint texts. Eisner (1997, 1994) has even suggested a new definition of literacy, encompassing more than just one symbol system. His is the definition of the "new" literacy that I will be using in this article:

> In order to be read, a poem, an equation, a painting, a dance, a novel, or a contract each requires a distinctive form of literacy, when literacy means, as I intend it to mean, a way of conveying meaning through and recovering meaning from the form of representation in which it appears. (Eisner, 1997, p. 353)

A classroom that teaches for a new literacy would be one that honors all forms of representation. Such a classroom would be truly representationally diverse and would create a climate that acknowledges "cognitive pluralism" (John-Steiner, 1997). John-Steiner's (1997) concept of cognitive pluralism is one where "there is a diversity of representational codes or languages of the mind" (p. xvi). In such a classroom, students would be free to "read" and "write" in a variety of these "languages of the mind." This freedom to read and write in various forms must be explicitly declared and modeled by the teacher (Greeno & Hall, 1997; Tishman & Perkins, 1997).

Students would also be free to interact (as apprentices) with teachers and their peers. John-Steiner (1997) in her study of artists, mathematicians, and physicists, found that a balance in childhood between individual and social activities was perceived by the participants as being key to their development as thinkers. "Vital relationships across generations and between peers are documented.... When these collaborations are successful, novices develop fluency, and learn how experienced artists and scientists think" (John-Steiner, 1997, p. xxiii).

Classrooms of cognitive pluralism would benefit students not only cognitively but affectively as well. The line of research focusing on the "engaged" reader (Guthrie, 1996) suggests that engaging classrooms allow for some student choice over work that is to be done. The work of Csikszentmihalyi (1990, 1991, 1993) has demonstrated that artists even reach a kind of "flow" (highly engaged) state when they are working in their media of choice.

Beyond the cognitive and affective benefits, a case for a new literacy has also been made based on the fact that the new communication tools are not politically neutral (Bruce & Hogan, 1998; Gee, 1996; New London Group, 1996) and that all voices in our classrooms need to be allowed to be heard, no matter the medium being used (Delpit, 1995; Willinsky, 1990).

What would such a new literacy classroom look like? As mentioned, this article attempts to depict one, using five characteristics as a starting point. The five suggested characteristics of new literacy classrooms are that they feature ongoing, continuous usage of multiple forms of representation; explicit discussions of symbol usage currently and throughout history; ongoing metadialogues in an atmosphere of cognitive pluralism; a balance of individualized and collaborative activities; and evidence of active, engaged students. In each following section, I will give a brief overview of specific characteristics and examples of how each may be demonstrated in a new literacy classroom.

Ongoing, Continuous Usage of Multiple Forms of Representation

Currently, schools are not able to keep up with the rich symbol world that young people encounter outside of school (Eisner, 1997; Kress, 1997). A new literacy classroom would attempt to close that gap in instruction. In such a classroom there would be ongoing, continuous usage of multiple forms of representation. This would mean that students would read and write using a variety of media on a daily basis. Using alternate forms of communication would not be a component of a one-time "unit." All media, including technologically driven media, would be evidenced in student reading and in student production or writing, and this would occur in all subject areas. The media would become merged with daily practice (Bruce & Hogan, 1998).

The new literacy classroom would resemble a studio. The new literacy school would actually consist of many studios under one roof. There would be studios for writing; for shooting films and videos; for drawing, making sculpture, and shaping metals and other materials; for dancing; and for acting and directing. There would also be science and math studios (perhaps still called laboratories). There would be studios for growing and studying living things. Each teacher would have studio space of his or her own, making his or her own meaningful work in multimedia, serving to model for students.

The school would not only have multiple venues for expression, it would have multiple venues for "receiving" expression: areas for reading; places to view works of art and theater, dance, and film; spaces for experiencing exhibits of science and math. The literacy teacher in such a school would become a coach of human expression. As such, the literacy educator would become a kind of teacher of teachers and a metaguide of thinking and communication—both of the giving and of the receiving.

Students would be reading and writing in multiple media, and their work would ultimately be evaluated in a multimodal way (New London Group, 1996). As the New London Group (1996) states, "all meaning-making is multimodal" (p. 81) with many media including linguistic, visual, and aural "grammars" simultaneously. Hence, student work would need to be evaluated taking into account each mode of meaning embedded in the work as well as the relationship between the modes. A student-designed Web page, for example, would be evaluated on its print content, its graphic design content, its sound content, and the interplay between each of these forms of communication.

Explicit Discussions of Symbol Usage, Past and Present

A new literacy classroom would develop students' "critical literacy" (Gee, 1997) including explicit ongoing discussions of symbol usage, past and present. Students would become critical readers and writers of texts, enabled "to detect and handle the inherently ideological dimension of literacy, and the role of literacy in enactments and productions of power" (Lankshear, Gee, Knobel, & Searle, 1997, p. 46).

The new literacy teacher would frequently discuss the nature of the symbols that some semioticians say are all around us, both in human and nonhuman forms (Deely, 1990; Merrell, 1995). Students would come to know that the process of symbol making and symbol receiving (semiosis) is apparently with humans from birth, that the earliest gestural, iconic representations of an infant and the crude scribblings of a toddler are indications of a basic human need for semiosis (Danesi, 1993).

The subtext of the usage of these symbols would also be a crucial part of the new literacy curriculum. It would be pointed out to students that along with the similarities, there are great differences in the way cultures and even individuals represent the visible world (Gombrich, 1960). The history of symbol making would be covered, including the development over the centuries of new forms of communication. Students in the new literacy classroom would learn that, as new forms of communication have developed, external situations have determined to what extent they have been allowed to develop and be used, due to complex political, economic, and cultural forces (Harris, 1989; Manguel, 1996).

A project for students could be to research stories of fear that have often accompanied the development of new forms of communication. Students could focus on Plato's views that the medium of writing (print) would ruin human memory (Ong, 1982). A contrast could be drawn between Plato's feelings about print and the ancient clerics' views about the largely oral spread of early Christianity (Resnick, 1991). The resulting focus on catechism in church settings, Resnick argued, has worked its way into schools, with the catechism format being an influence on the early primers that continues to influence the format of instruction hundreds of years later. Students could also either read or view the film of *The Name of the Rose* in which Eco (1980) describes a Franciscan abbey that allowed access to print only to a privileged few. Students could also investigate and report on fears that have surrounded the birth of such forms of communication as radio, comic books, television, and the Internet (Buckingham, 1991).

Within content area classrooms, prereading, during-reading, and postreading activities could allow students to explore how a text "constructs reality textually and positions readers" (Lankshear et al., 1997, p. 53). Some examples of questions that may be asked about a text include the following: Why is this topic being written about? How is this topic being written about? What other ways of writing about the topic are there? What version of events/reality is foregrounded here? Whose version is this? From whose perspective is it constructed? What other (possible) versions are excluded? Whose/what interests are served by this representation? (pp. 51, 54). In the example provided by Lankshear et al., the school media specialist plays an important role in this process by gathering multiple versions of reality about a subject presented in multiple forms of representation.

Students Engaged in Ongoing Metadialogues in an Atmosphere of Cognitive Pluralism

New literacy classrooms would feature students engaged in ongoing metadialogues as they think through problems and create products in an atmosphere recognizing cognitive pluralism (John-Steiner, 1997)—for reasons due to human cognition but also for reasons due to principles of democracy. As Eisner (1997) has suggested, by allowing young people access to only certain forms of representations, we are providing access only to certain (chosen) forms of experience and understanding (p. 353). One's choice of medium of expression may affect what one thinks, and even what one is able to think (Dewey, 1934/1980; Eisner, 1994; John-Steiner, 1997; Tishman & Perkins, 1997). Students have the right to be taught the "grammars" of a variety of semiotic systems so that they have an extensive reservoir of systems to draw upon when thinking and communicating (The New London Group, 1996).

In a new literacy classroom, the form of representation that one chooses would be thought of not only in terms of the medium but also in terms of the final product. John-Steiner's (1997) study of artists and scientists found that these thinkers made a variety of drawings and writings along the way as they created a variety of projects. She describes four general types of thinking based on their experiences: visual thinking, verbal thinking, the languages of emotion (including music and choreography), and scientific thinking. "Through these varied languages of thought, the meanings of...experiences are stored and organized" (John-Steiner, 1997, p. 8).

Greeno and Hall (1997) have argued that students need to be just as proficient in using such forms of representation as tables, graphs, and equations as they are in using such forms as painting, sculpture, and literature; they need to be able to "practice representation" in many forms. Greeno and Hall found forms such as tables and graphs to be used by people "to aid understanding when they are reflecting on an activity or working on a problem.... These representations help them keep track of ideas and inferences they have made and also serve to organize their continuing work" (pp. 364–365). Choice of representational form (both in process and as product), therefore, becomes extremely significant for the person wishing to read or express something—this choice affects the content of thought itself. The new literacy classroom would include much in the way of "practice representation."

As an example of this practice representation, in confronting a math or science problem, a teacher might briefly focus on each of the many symbol systems available for use, modeling how symbols are used by scientists (and artists) and interpreted by audiences in each medium, and letting students know that all forms of representation are equally valued. The teacher might then model for students how he or she would use a certain form such as a graph or model to work through a problem.

Students would be taught, however, that there are certain "Design conventions—Available Designs—that take the form of discourses, styles, genres, dialects and voices, to name a few key variables" (New London Group, 1996, p. 75). Students would be made aware that the context of a situation brings with it a "structured set of conventions associated with semiotic activity" (New London Group, 1996, p. 75). The New London Group suggests exercises such as asking students to pretend they are certain professionals, ones who have competing interests. Gee (1997) suggests having students think how their different identities are shaped as they come into different discourse situations.

In the new literacy classroom, students would be utilizing multiple forms of representation in the context of real work. Brown, Collins, and Duguid (1989) suggests that an appropriate educational structure would be "cognitive apprenticeships," in which teachers would "embed learning in activity and make deliberate use of the social and physical context" (p. 32). Students would be the cognitive apprentices to the teachers who would be engaged in real work themselves. As teachers worked through problems or challenges, they would model (even stating out loud as kind of a verbal stream of consciousness) their thinking processes, including the forms of representation they were using. As students worked in their studios and their laboratories, they would be able to draw upon the modeling they had seen, yet they would be free to use the complete spectrum of forms of representation that are available to them.

A Balance of Individual and Collaborative Activities

In her study of the young lives of creative individuals, John-Steiner (1997) notes that many described a collection of early experiences that struck a balance between solitary experiences and collaborative experiences. A new literacy classroom would maintain such a balance.

Educators have long been drawn to the need for individualization of instruction despite the demands of educating large numbers of young people. Gardner (1983, 1993, 1995) has argued persuasively for a theory of multiple intelligences. Most recently, he has argued against a rigid interpretation of his theory, instead emphasizing the viewing of each child as unique, with a unique blend of intelligences (Gardner, 1995). It would seem that this unique blend of intelligences that we each have would include a bent for seeing the world and expressing ourselves in individualized ways.

Recently, writers with autism have given us a glimpse into their unique forms of thinking, sometimes describing "thinking in pictures" (Grandin, 1995; Williams, 1992). The thinking and communication experiences of those with autism may be relevant to the need to individualize instruction and allow for diversity of expression for all children. Temple Grandin (1995), who is autistic, wrote the following:

> I think in pictures. Words are like a second language to me. I translate both spoken and written words into full-color movies, complete with sound, which run like a VCR tape in my head. When somebody speaks to me, his words are instantly translated into pictures. (p. 19)

One way that individualization would come about in a new literacy classroom would be through allowing for student choice of medium. Such a classroom would allow children to have some individual choices, to let them think through problems and projects, modeling after the teacher, in any media they choose. The teacher would play a key role here, modeling his or her own individualized thinking processes in working through a problem or developing a project.

In addition to featuring much individualized activity, the new literacy classroom would include time for social interaction. John-Steiner (1997) found the external surroundings of creative individuals and their influences during their childhood to have been quite significant in their development as creators and thinkers; this time served as "apprenticeships" with their parents, mentors, and teachers. Our choices of sign systems to use are heavily influenced by those who are around us at an early age and the incipient culture and history (Cole & Scribner, 1978; Vygotsky, 1934/1986). The new literacy classroom would include many collaborative activities as well as completely individualized ones.

In a new literacy classroom, there would be a continual going back and forth between solitary work and collaborative work. The new literacy teacher might use a contract system in which certain assignments could be completed alone and certain assignments could be completed collaboratively. Although students would be allowed choices, certain assignments could be created to lend themselves to collaboration and certain ones to more individualized work. Making a video, for example, in most cases, requires more than one person to do the work. Writing a poem may not. The balance between individualized and collaborative activities would be a key component of a new literacy classroom.

Evidence of Engaged Students

A classroom in which each student's individuality of representation is respected would be motivating to students (and to teachers) and enhance engagement. Such a classroom would contain students who are often highly involved in their work. Almost a century ago, Dewey (1913/1975) describes the unity of effort that resulted from individualization of instruction. "But this effort never degenerates into drudgery, or mere strain of dead lift, because interest abides—the self is concerned throughout. Our first conclusion is that interest means a unified activity" (Dewey, 1913/1975, pp. 14–15). Elements of individualization and self-selection can be motivating to children's work within the medium of print (Gambrell, 1996; Hunt, 1970/1996; Turner & Paris, 1995; Worthy, 1996). It would seem that extending this individualization and self-selection to include the form of representation that is being read or written would build student motivation to learn even more and that motivation would lead to engagement. Motivation is one of the components of the concept of the engaged reader (Gambrell, 1996; Guthrie, 1996). In a new literacy classroom, students would be fully able to experience the "honored voice," defined by Oldfather (1993) as "a deep responsiveness of the classroom culture to students' expression: written, oral, and artistic" (Oldfather, 1993, p. 672).

In a new literacy classroom, students might even sometimes be in a state of "flow." A line of research that seems closely aligned with the concept of engagement is Mihalyi Csikszentmihalyi's concept of flow, or the psychology of peak experiences (Csikszentmihalyi, 1990, 1991, 1993). Csikszentmihalyi studied the optimal experiences of a cross-section of artists, athletes, and craftspeople, and found similarities in their descriptions of their peak experiences—similarities that cut across particular activities. After peak experiences, people described being totally engrossed and involved with the task at hand. The process of what was being done was enthralling.

While certainly not every moment in the new literacy classroom would be flow-inducing, in the new literacy classroom we would often find students who are deeply engrossed in their active work. Outside of school, students may already be experiencing this flow state through their involvement with multiple forms of expression, via uses of technology. Students may have gotten used to sometimes being in a state of flow, and teachers will have no choice but to follow. The ability to have some choice regarding form of representation (to both read and write) could have an impact on students' levels of engagement or flow states. A classroom in which each student's individuality of representation is respected would also be one in which students would be motivated to learn.

Diversified Expression in the Classroom

If classrooms and schools were redesigned along the lines of the characteristics just described, there would be many resulting pedagogical and sociocultural consequences. If classrooms embraced a broadened definition of "literacy," I believe literacy educators would become leaders of overall school reform and redesign. Our classrooms and schools would look much different with literacy educators who teach for a new literacy. The pedagogy of a new literacy classroom would consist of "immersion in meaningful practices within a community of learners who are capable of playing multiple and different roles based on their backgrounds and experiences" (New London Group, 1996, p. 85). Students would be allowed time to work on projects of their own in a kind of ongoing multimedia readers'/writers' workshop. All of this work would be kept in an electronic portfolio over the course of all of the student's years in school. Over years of schooling, each student's work would reflect an immersion in reading and writing in many forms.

Classrooms would become interdisciplinary in nature as students examine symbols and what they tell about various content information (Lankshear et al., 1997; Lusted, 1991). In a school that embraces a broadened definition of literacy, students would become expert users of symbols, no matter what content they are studying. The lessons of the "English classroom" would become embedded in the practices of students as they work on projects that are interdisciplinary. The arts and technology would not be seen as "add ons" but as embedded features of daily life (Bruce & Hogan, 1998). Indeed the classroom would be similar to the resource-rich, interdisciplinary environment that students currently live in outside of the school day (Eisner, 1997; Kress, 1997).

There are sociocultural consequences of such a pedagogy as well. In such a classroom, no one form of representation would be prized above another. Knowledge of forms of representation and different discourses would be made explicit for students enabling them to make effective use of them (Buckingham, 1990; Delpit, 1995; Gee, 1996). The new literacy classroom would provide examples of all of the available forms so that students could make politically informed decisions when reading or writing (Delpit, 1995). The symbol systems of this type of classroom would not just give lip service to the concept of freedom and pluralism (Warren, 1996).

It could be argued that providing access to multiple forms of representation could become a civil rights issue. In a classroom that embraces multiple forms of representation, students' individual choices of symbol systems would not be discriminated against or controlled. Celebrating language diversity, in all its forms, would become a part of the curriculum (Delpit, 1995). A new literacy classroom would enable students to become aware of the menu of symbol systems available for use in various situations. The discussion of these available systems would be brought out in the open. This new literacy may even narrow the culture gap between teachers and students (Lusted, 1991), as students and teachers meaningfully share common experiences with many media. Ultimately, allowing for more diversified forms of expression in schools may not be a choice that educators get to make. Students, parents, and teachers may soon demand this freedom either via charter schools or home schooling. More and more students will want to experience in the classroom the same feeling of situatedness and involvement that they are able to achieve outside of school. These multiple forms of literacy are habit-forming. Flow is addicting. I believe students will want the right to have their Manhattan experiences at school.

REFERENCES

Allen, A., & Brickman, M. (1982). Manhattan. In *Four films of Woody Allen* (pp. 179–186). New York: Random House.

Brown, J.S., Collins, A., & Duguid, P. (1989). Situated cognition and the culture of learning. *Educational Researcher*, 32–42.

Bruce, B.C., & Hogan, M.P. (1998). The disappearance of technology: Toward an ecological model of literacy. In D. Reinking, M. McKenna, L. Labbo, & R. Kieffer (Eds.), *Handbook of literacy and technology: Transformations in a post-typographic world* (pp. 269–281). Hillsdale, NJ: Erlbaum.

Buckingham, D. (1990). Making it explicit: Towards a theory of media learning. In D. Buckingham, (Ed.), *Watching media learning: Making sense of media education* (pp. 215–225). London: Falmer Press.

Buckingham, D. (1991). Teaching about the media. In D. Lusted (Ed.), *The media studies book* (pp. 12–35). London: Routledge.

Buckingham, D. (1993). *Reading audiences: Young people and the media.* Manchester, England: Manchester University Press.

Buckingham, D., & Sefton-Green, J. (1994). *Cultural studies goes to school: Reading and teaching popular media.* London: Taylor & Francis.

Cole, M., & Scribner, S. (1978). Introduction. In L.S. Vygotsky, *Mind in society* (M. Cole, V. John-Steiner, S. Scribner, E. Souberman, Eds. & Trans.), pp. 1–14. Cambridge, MA: Harvard University Press.

Csikszentmihalyi, M. (1990). *Flow: The psychology of optimal experience.* New York: HarperCollins.

Csikszentmihalyi, M. (1991). Literacy and intrinsic motivation. In S.R. Graubard (Ed.), *Literacy: An overview by fourteen experts* (pp. 115–140). New York: Hill & Wang.

Csikszentmihalyi, M. (1993). *The evolving self: A psychology for the third millennium.* New York: HarperCollins.

Danesi, M. (1993). *Messages and meanings: An introduction to semiotics.* Toronto: Canadian Scholars' Press.

Deely, J. (1990). *Basics of semiotics.* Bloomington, IN: Indiana University Press.

Delpit, L. (1995). *Other people's children: Cultural conflict in the classroom.* New York: The New Press.

Dewey, J. (1913/1975). *Interest and effort in education*. Carbondale, IL: Southern Illinois University Press.

Dewey, J. (1934/1980). *Art as experience*. New York: Perigee Books.

Eco, U. (1980). *The name of the rose*. New York: Harcourt Brace.

Eisner, E. (1994). *Cognition and curriculum reconsidered* (2nd ed.). New York: Teachers College Press.

Eisner, E. (1997). Cognition and representation: A way to pursue the American dream? *Phi Delta Kappan, 78*, 349–353.

Gambrell, L.B. (1996). Creating classroom cultures that foster reading motivation. *The Reading Teacher, 50*, 14–25.

Gardner, H. (1983). *Frames of mind: The theory of multiple intelligences*. New York: Basic Books.

Gardner, H. (1993). *Multiple intelligences: The theory into practice*. New York: Basic Books.

Gardner, H. (1995). Reflections on multiple intelligences. *Phi Delta Kappan, 76*, 200–209.

Gee, J.P. (1996). *Social linguistics and literacies: Ideology in discourses*. (2nd ed.). London: Falmer Press.

Gee, J.P. (1997). Foreword: A discourse approach to language and literacy. In C. Lankshear, J.P. Gee, M. Knobel, & C. Searle (Eds.), *Changing literacies*, (pp. xiii–xix). Cambridge, England: Open University Press.

Gombrich, E.H. (1960). *Art and illusion: A study in the psychology of pictorial representation*. Princeton, NJ: Princeton University Press.

Grandin, T. (1995). *Thinking in pictures: And other reports from my life with autism*. New York: Random House.

Greeno, J.G., & Hall, R.P. (1997). Practicing representation: Learning with and about representational forms. *Phi Delta Kappan, 78*, 361–367.

Guthrie, J.T. (1996). Educational contexts for engagement in literacy. *The Reading Teacher, 49*, 432–445.

Harris, W.V. (1989). *Ancient literacy*. Cambridge, MA: Harvard University Press.

Hunt, L.C., Jr. (1970/1996). The effect of self-selection, interest, and motivation upon independent, instructional, and frustrational levels. *The Reading Teacher, 50*, 278–282.

International Reading Association & National Council of Teachers of English. (1996). *Standards for the English language arts*. Newark, DE & Urbana, IL: Authors.

John-Steiner, V. (1997). *Notebooks of the mind: Explorations of thinking* (Rev. ed.). New York: Oxford University Press.

Kress, G. (1997). *Before writing: Rethinking the paths to literacy*. London: Routledge.

Lankshear, C., Gee, J.P., Knobel, M., & Searle, C. (1997). *Changing literacies*. Cambridge, England: Open University Press.

Luke, A., & Elkins, J. (1998). Reinventing literacy in "new times." *Journal of Adolescent & Adult Literacy, 42*, 4–7.

Lusted, D. (Ed.). (1991). *The media studies book: A guide for teachers*. London: Routledge.

Manguel, A. (1996). *A history of reading*. New York: Viking.

Merrell, F. (1995). *Peirce's semiotics now: A primer.* Toronto: Canadian Scholars' Press.

Negroponte, N. (1995). *Being digital.* New York: Knopf.

New London Group. (1996). A pedagogy of multiliteracies: Designing social futures. *Harvard Education Review, 66*(1), 60–92.

Oldfather, P. (1993). What students say about motivating experiences in a whole language classroom. *The Reading Teacher, 46,* 672–681.

Ong, W.J. (1982). *Orality and literacy: The technologizing of the word.* London: Routledge.

Resnick, D.P. (1991). Historical perspectives on literacy and schooling. In S.R. Graubard (Ed.), *Literacy: An overview by fourteen experts* (pp. 15–32). New York: Hill & Wang.

Tishman, S., & Perkins, D. (1997). The language of thinking. *Phi Delta Kappan, 78,* 368–374.

Turner, J., & Paris, S.G. (1995). How literacy tasks influence children's motivation for literacy. *The Reading Teacher, 48,* 662–673.

Vygotsky, L.S. (1934/1986). *Thought and language.* Cambridge, MA: The MIT Press.

Warren, D. (1996). Practice makes perfect: Civic education by precept and example. In J.N. Burstyn (Ed.), *Educating tomorrow's valuable citizen* (pp. 119–135). Albany, NY: State University of New York Press.

Williams, D. (1992). *Nobody nowhere: The extraordinary autobiography of an autistic.* New York: Avon Books.

Willinsky, J. (1990). *The new literacy: Redefining reading and writing in the schools.* New York: Routledge.

Worthy, J. (1996). A matter of interest: Literature that hooks reluctant readers and keeps them reading. *The Reading Teacher, 50,* 204–212.

Subject Index

Page references followed by *f* indicate figures.

A

B

C

COLLABORATIVE EDUCATION: benefits of, 153–157; establishing partnerships in, 146–148; examples of, 149–152; goals of, 148; instructional framework for, 147; knowledge-based approach in, 147; new forms of, 233–234; nonteaching staff in, 157–159; parents in, 160–164; process of, 146–147; reading specialists in, 145–159; student involvement in, 157–159

COME A STRANGER (VOIGHT), 56

COMMISSION ON ADOLESCENT LITERACY (IRA), 4–5

COMPUTERS. *See* technology

CONSCIENTIZATION, 37

CONTENT AREA LITERACY, 210–211; expanded definition of, 219

CONTROL: need for, 12

CONVERSATIONS: about books, 14

CRITICAL LITERACY, 179, 230

CRITICAL MEDIA LITERACY, 179

CRITICAL QUESTIONS: about popular culture, 204–205

CROSSING OVER: WHOLE LANGUAGE FOR SECONDARY ENGLISH TEACHERS (FOSTER), 109

CURRICULUM: emergent, 192–193

D

DATA ANALYSIS, 173–177; student cohorts for, 173–174

DEALING WITH DRAGONS (WREADE), 54

DECONSTRUCTIONISM, 231

THE DIARY OF ANNE FRANK, 56

DIRECTED READING/THINKING ACTIVITY (D-R-T-A), 75

DISABILITY: vs. variability, 8

DIVERSITY: appreciation of, 236–237

DOUBLE-ENTRY JOURNALS, 97–98

DRAGON SONG (MCCAFFREY), 51

DROP EVERYTHING AND READ (DEAR), 64

E

EITHER-OR DEBATES, 187

ELECTRONIC LITERACY, 192–196

ELECTRONIC LITERARY MAGAZINE, 88–90

ELECTRONIC PORTFOLIO, 88–90

ELECTRONIC TEXT, 192

ELEMENTARY STUDENTS: reading to, 23, 30–31, 33

ELLA ENCHANTED (LEVINE), 50

E-MAIL, 90–94, 92*f,* 191–192

EMERGENT CURRICULUM, 192–193

Emig, Janet, 183
enablement, 15–17
engagement, 12–15, 234–235
English as a second language instruction. *See* language minority students
evaluation: for student selection, 24
Explorers of the Universe program, 193–194

F

Failure to Connect (Healy), 85
flow, 235
foreign language speakers. *See* language minority students
free-choice reading: for middle school students, 64, 65–66; popular culture and, 202–204
functionality, 207, 211–220; adolescent's view of, 211–215; definition of, 211; middle schooler's view of, 215–219
funding: for literacy programs, 196

G

Gallatin High School Interdisciplinary Project, 193
GATSCCORE, 31
Gender and Power (McConnell), 201
gender issues, 9; academic studies of, 45–47; discussion of, 46–47, 54–57; novels dealing with, 47–57; in popular culture, 200–204, 210
girls: academic and social problems of, 45–46, 47; book selection for, 47–57; identity issues for, 9, 46–47; minority, 56. *See also* gender issues
Girls in the Middle: Working to Succeed in School (AAUW), 46
Goodman, Ken, 182
grading, 32
grand conversations, 14
Graves, Donald, 182, 183
Great Books for Girls (Odean), 47

H

Hang a Thousand Tress with Ribbons (Rinaldi), 109
homework, 31; parental involvement and, 161–162
horror fiction, 199–202
Hostile Hallways, 45
How to Catch a Shark (Graves), 84–85
hyperlinks, 192, 194

I

INCIDENTS IN THE LIFE OF A SLAVE GIRL (JACOBS), 108

INDIVIDUALIZED INSTRUCTION, 16, 22, 25–26, 233–235; for middle school students, 66–69

INFORMATION LITERACY, 179

INSTRUCTIONAL MATERIALS. *See* literacy materials

INSTRUCTIONAL METHODS, 15–17, 78; technology and, 82–95

INTERDISCIPLINARY TEACHING, 116–117, 134, 236–237

INTERNATIONAL READING ASSOCIATION (IRA): Commission on Adolescent Literacy, 4–5, 117; position statement on adolescent literacy, 2–4, 8, 117; Web site, 195

INTERNET, 86–89, 191–196

INTERTEXTUAL LINKS, 222

INTERVENTION MODEL FOR AT-RISK STUDENTS, 20–33; components of, 21–24; evaluation of, 32–33; grading in, 32; homework in, 31; one-on-one tutoring in, 22–23, 26–28; sample schedule for, 27*f;* student recruitment and assessment for, 24–25; tailor-made assignments in, 22, 25–26, 27*f;* whole group activities in, 28–31

ISLAND OF THE BLUE DOLPHINS (O'DELL), 48

IZZY, WILLY-NILLY (VOIGHT), 53–54

J

JODY, MARILYN, 90

JOURNALS: double-entry, 97–98; for middle school service learning project, 168, 168*f;* for young adult books, 106–107

JULIE OF THE WOLVES (GEORGE), 48

K

KAUFMAN TEST OF EDUCATIONAL ACHIEVEMENT, 24

KEEPING SECRETS: THE GIRLHOOD DIARIES OF SEVEN WOMEN WRITERS (LYONS), 108

K-W-L (KNOW–WANT TO KNOW–LEARNED) STRATEGY, 29, 30*f,* 147

L

LANGUAGE MINORITY STUDENTS, 40–43; diversity of, 40; English proficiency of, 40–41; instruction in native language for, 41–42; program planning for, 42–43

LEARNER-CENTERED PSYCHOLOGICAL PRINCIPLES (APA), 74, 75–76

LEARNING: content vs. process in, 158

LEARNING DISABILITY: vs. variability, 8

LETTERS FROM A SLAVE GIRL (LYONS), 103–105

POETRY: African American, 107–108
THE POISON PLACE (LYONS), 108
POLITICAL ISSUES, 36–38
POPULAR CULTURE: classroom uses of, 199–202; critical appraisal of, 204–205, 209–210; gender issues and, 200–204, 210; social uses of, 202–204, 219
PORTFOLIOS: active, 100*f*, 101; electronic, 88–90; passive, 96–98; passive-to-active, 98–99, 99*f*; showcase, 97
POWERPOINT PRESENTATIONS, 85–86, 87*f*, 88*f*
PRACTICE, 12, 15
PRACTICE REPRESENTATION, 232–233
PRE-READING PLAN (PREP), 75
PRINCIPALS: as parent-teacher liaisons, 163
PRIOR KNOWLEDGE: application of, 75
PROBLEMATIC SITUATIONS, 75–76

R

RACE. *See* minority students
RADICAL RED (DUFFY), 48
READABILITY FORMULAS, 13
READER RESPONSE THEORY, 184–185
READING: declining rates of, 72, 218; diminished prestige of, 10; free-choice, 64, 65–66, 202–204; as "uncool," 127–128, 131
READING ALOUD: to elementary students, 23, 30–31, 33
READING DISABILITY: vs. variability, 8
READING MATERIALS. *See* literacy materials
READING ROLE MODELS, 121–122, 133
READING SPECIALIST: in collaborative education, 145–159. *See also* collaborative education
RECOGNITION: opportunities for, 23, 31, 134
REPRESENTATIONAL FORMS, 232–233
REVIVING OPHELIA: SAVING THE SELVES OF ADOLESCENT GIRLS (PIPHER), 45
RIEF, LINDA, 183
ROLE MODELS: for reading, 121–122, 133; in school culture, 127
ROMANCE NOVELS, 209
ROSENBLATT, LOUISE, 182, 184
ROTE LEARNING, 14
RUN FOR YOUR LIFE (LEVY), 50–51, 58

S

SACCARDI, MARIANNE, 90
SCHOOL CULTURE: definition of, 126; elements of, 126–128; literacy council

and, 141–142; middle school, 130–132

SCHOOLGIRLS: YOUNG WOMEN, SELF-ESTEEM AND THE CONFIDENCE GAP (ORENSTEIN), 45

THE SECRET OF GUMBO GROVE (TATE), 53, 58

SELF-REGULATION, 77

SEMIOTICS, 220–221, 230–233, 235

SERIES BOOKS, 199–202, 209. *See also* popular culture

SERVICE LEARNING PROGRAM: middle school, 165–171, 167*f*–170*f*

SHABANU: DAUGHTER OF THE WIND (STAPLES), 53

SHOWCASE PORTFOLIOS, 97

SIGN SYSTEMS, 220–221, 230–233, 235

SILENT READING, 22, 64, 122

SINGLE-SEX COOPERATIVE GROUP: for gender issue discussion, 54–55

SMALL-GROUP INSTRUCTION, 16

SMITH, FRANK, 182

"THE SNIPER" (O'FLAHERTY), 29

SOCIOECONOMIC ISSUES, 36–38

SOUTHERN REGIONAL EDUCATION BOARD (SREB) STUDY, 174

SPECIAL EDUCATION, 149, 155

SPELLING WORDS: from young adult books, 107

SPINELLI, JERRY, 14

STAFF DEVELOPMENT, 134

STANDARDIZED TESTS: analysis of/results of, 173–177; literacy council and, 142–143; minorities and, 36–38; practice materials for, 105–106

STORYTELLING, 133

STRATEGY INSTRUCTION, 15–17

SUSTAINED SILENT READING (SSR), 22, 64, 122

SYMBOL MAKING/RECEIVING, 220–221, 230–233, 235

T

TAILOR-MADE LESSONS, 16, 22, 25–26

"A TALK TO TEACHERS" (BALDWIN), 35–36

TEACHERS: collegial support for, 17; as literacy models, 12

TEACHING. *See* literacy instruction

TECHNOLOGY: electronic literary magazine, 88–90; electronic portfolio, 88–90; e-mail, 90–94, 92*f;* emergent curriculum and, 192–193; Explorers of the Universe program and, 193–194; impact of, 82–94, 185–186, 220–223, 227–228; Internet, 86–89; online discussions, 90–94, 92*f,* 93*f;* student enthusiasm for, 191–192, 215, 217, 218; word processing, 83–86

TELEVISION: social functions of, 219